LATIN AMERICAN WRITERS

IN ENGLISH TRANSLATION

BIBLIOGRAPHIC SERIES
No. 30

LATIN AMERICAN WRITERS

IN ENGLISH TRANSLATION

A Classified Bibliography

Compiled by

Willis Knapp Jones

Miami University

PAN AMERICAN UNION + WASHINGTON, D. C. + 1944
Republished by Blaine Ethridge--Books, Detroit, 1972

Library of Congress Catalog Card Number 70-165657
International Standard Book Number 0-87917-006-9

INTRODUCTION

Until a person starts hunting, he has no idea of the abundance of Latin American writing which has been turned into English. If one regards the early Conquistadores as dwellers in the New World -- and certainly many of them were forced by Indian arrows or swords of jealous Spaniards to make it their permanent home -- the number is still greater.

This bibliography is intended to list all Latin American writing from the time of Columbus and Cortes to the present that has been translated into English. The entries have accumulated for a number of years and are now put into form with the assistance of Margaret Booth, of Miami University. In attempting to make it complete, the compiler used his sabbatical leave to search through the New York Public Library (where he acknowledges the great help of F. Ivor D. Avellino, of the American History Room), the Hispanic Foundation of the Library of Congress, and the Columbus Memorial Library of the Pan American Union (Where everyone was lavish with assistance).

Care has been taken to insure accuracy and completeness, but one pair of eyes can not track down all the translations ever made. The compiler did not handle all the titles entered. He did look at most of them available at the Library of Congress; many are also to be found in the Pan American Union. Some entries, however, were taken from other lists, e.g.:

Biaggi and Sanchez y Escribano, English Translations from the Spanish, 1932-38 (Stonington, Conn., Publishing Co., 1939).

Fletcher and Lyman, Guide to Spanish and Spanish American Literature in Translation (Los Angeles Junior College, 1936).

Granier, Latin American Belles Lettres in English Translation (Library of Congress, 1942) (with comments on works listed).

Office of the Coordinator of Inter-American Affairs, English Translations of Latin American Fiction, Drama, and Poetry (1942).

James and Aguilera, Latin American Literature References in English (Pan American Union, 1941).

Dates proved the most uncertain and difficult to obtain. Some writers were apparently born on several occasions. Others, like cowards, died many times. As a working principle, the Library of Congress chronology served as standard, with an * added to show the existence of another date. Unfortunately, the removal from Washington of the Union Catalog, a war safety measure, prevented consultation of it for the dates of some of the writers, especially recent poets.

Great use was made, too, of the New York Public Library cards and of the dating in Grismer's invaluable Reference Index to 12,000 Spanish American Authors (H. W. Wilson, 1939 [Republished by Blaine Ethridge--Books, 1971]).

Brazilian authors provided another stumbling block, with the uncertainty about their family names. Frequently two anthologies, published by the same firm (and sometimes by the same editor) indexed one writer under two names, as for instance Fagundes Varella, who appears sometimes under F and sometimes under V.

Since many who will consult this bibliography will not be acquainted with the Spanish alphabet, authors are listed by English alphabetization.

As will be seen, poetry provided the greatest number of entries. From the time of Bryant and the Editor of the North American Review who, in 1849, filled 32 pages of his magazine with translations of Latin American poetry, inter-American cultural exchange has been most arduously cultivated in poetry.

The list of translated fiction is surprisingly large. After all, it takes longer to translate a story than a poem, and requires more space to print it, yet publishers have been glad to provide the space.

Drama offers the leanest fare. Here the problem is to find an outlet in print. I know of a number of translations of Latin American drama wandering today in search of a publisher, among them three long plays by Florencio Sanchez (who for some reason has not yet appeared in English dress), and an amusing Argentine comedy produced at the University of Wisconsin. Time, and a demand for Latin American dramas in English, will some day bring them into print.

A large number of Englished Latin American essays on a variety of subjects have appeared in magazines and books, and the interest in distant places explains the quantity of Spanish voyages and tales of exploration available in English.

The past year has seen the appearance of two excellent anthologies of translations, one of prose and one of poetry. Their sales will pave the way for other volumes.

Because of lack of space, no attempt has been made to evaluate authors or translations. For those who want a guide through the labyrinth of Latin American literature, two are suggested:

Hespelt, E. H. (and others), History of Spanish American Literature (Crofts, 1941) (in outline form).

Torres-Rioseco, A., Epic of Latin American Literature (Oxford Univ. Press, 1942), supplanting the old reliable by Alfred Coester.

While offering this bibliography in the hope that it will increase our knowledge of our Southern Neighbors, the compiler knows that it is not complete. Only with corrections and additions sent by those who consult it will it ever approach an eventually complete listing of material available for those who want to know how the Latin Americans think, and yet who can not read the works in their original form.

Willis Knapp Jones

[Prepared 1942]

FOREWORD

The Columbus Memorial Library of the Pan American Union welcomes the opportunity to place before the American public this bibliography of Latin American literature, prepared entirely by Dr. Jones.

During the past ten years, interest in the United States in the intellectual production of Latin Americans in Spanish, French, and Portuguese has greatly increased.

This bibliography will serve as an excellent source for those desirous of learning something about history and travel, fiction, essays, and poetry emanating from Latin American authors, and, we hope, will give encouragement to further study of a rich literature, many examples of which are now available.

As a pioneer in the study of comparative literature, Dr. Jones here offers the benefit of his long experience in preparing what we believe to be the most exhaustive compilation so far made on the subject.

Charles E. Babcock
Librarian

CONTENTS

INTRODUCTION ll

FOREWORD IV

History and Travel

Colonial 1
Argentine Republic 9
Brazil 10
Chile 10
Colombia 10
Costa Rica 11
Mexico 11
Peru 12
South America 13
Uruguay 13
Venezuela 13

Essays
(Historical places and people, customs, criticism, etc.)

Argentine Republic 14
Bolivia 15
Brazil 16
Chile 16
Colombia 17
Costa Rica 18
Cuba 18
Dominican Republic 19
Ecuador 19
El Salvador 19
Guatemala 20
Honduras 20
Mexico 20
Panama 24
Paraguay 24
Peru 24
Puerto Rico 25
Uruguay 25
Venezuela 26

Poetry

Argentine Republic 27
Bolivia 31

Brazil 32
Chile 35
Colombia 42
Costa Rica 45
Dominican Republic 53
Ecuador 55
El Salvador 57
Guatemala 57
Haiti 57
Honduras 59
Martinique 59
Mexico 59
Nicaragua 78
Panama 80
Paraguay 82
Peru 82
Puerto Rico 86
Uruguay 88
Venezuela 90
Anonymous 93

Drama

Argentine Republic 94
Brazil 94
Bolivia 94
Chile 95
Cuba 95
Mexico 95
New Mexico 96
Peru 96
Philippines 97
Uruguay 97

Fiction
(Short stories and novels)

Argentine Republic 98
Bolivia 100
Brazil 101
Chile 103
Colombia 106
Costa Rica 107
Cuba 108
Dominican Republic 108

Fiction (Continued)

Ecuador 108
El Salvador 109
Guatemala 110
Martinique 110
Mexico 110
Nicaragua 115
Panama 115

Paraguay 117
Peru 117
Philippines 118
Venezuela 119
Anonymous 120

Addenda

Essays 121
Poetry 122

KEY TO ABBREVIATIONS USED FOR BOOKS MENTIONED 123
LIST OF MAGAZINES MENTIONED 127

INDEX 131

(* indicates date may be questionable)

Acosta, José de, 1540-1600.
   Historia natural y moral de las Indias. Salamanca, 1588. [In Latin]
   —————— —————— Sevilla, 1590.
   —————— —————— First tr.: London, 1604.
   —————— —————— Tr. by Markham for Hakluyt society. London, 1880.
                     (Works of Hakluyt society, series I, nos. 60-61. 2 v.
                     Written after trip to Perú and Bolivia).

Acuña, Christóval de (b. 1597)
   Nuevo descubrimiento del gran río de las Amazonas. Madrid, 1641.
   Voyages and discoveries in South America. London, 1698.
   —————— —————— Reprinted by Hakluyt society, 1859. (Earliest
                     published account of Amazon river).

Alarcón, Fernando, 16th cent.
   "Relatione della navigatione et scoperta che fece il capitano Fernando
   Alarcone..." in Ramusio-Navigationi et Viaggi. 1556.
   —————— —————— Tr. by Hakluyt, in Principal navigations. 1600.
   v. III, pp. 425-439.

Alvarado, Pedro de, 1495?-1541.
   Conquest of Granada in 1524; tr. by S. J. Mackey. New York, Cortes
   society, 1924. 146 p. (With facsimile of Spanish document).

Alvares Cabral, Pedro, 1467-1520.
   Voyage of Pedro Alvares Cabral to Brazil and India; tr. by W. B.
   Greenlee for Hakluyt society. London, 1938. (Works of Hakluyt society,
   series II, no. 81).

Andagoya, Pascual de, d. 1548.
   From Navarrete's Colección de los viajes y descubrimientos... desde
   fines del siglo XV, vol. III, No. 7, p. 393.
   Narrative of the proceedings of Pedrarias Dávila in the provinces of
   Tierra Firme or Castilla del Oro, and of the discovery of the South
   Sea and the coasts of Peru and Nicaragua... Tr. and ed. by Clements
   R. Markham. London, printed for the Hakluyt society, 1865. (Works
   issued by the Hakluyt society. No. XXXIV)

Benavides, Alonso de, fl. 1630. (reached Mexico 1598).
   Memorial que Fr. Juan de Santander de la orden de San Francisco...
   presenta a la majestad católica del rey don Felipe Cuarto. Madrid, 1630.
   —————— —————— Tr. by Mrs. E. E. Ayers in Land of sunshine,
   XIII-XIV. 1900-01.
   —————— —————— Reprinted with notes and illustrations. Chicago,
   1916. (About Indian conversions).

Cabeza de Vaca, Alvar Núñez see Núñez Cabeza de Vaca, Alvar.

Caravajal, Gaspar de, 1504-1584.
   The discovery of the Amazon according to the account of Fray Gaspar de
   Caravajal and other documents; tr. by B. T. Lee. New York, American
   geographical society, 1934. 467 p.

Casas, Bartolomé de las, bp. of Chiapa, 1474-1566.
Brevíssima relación de la destrucción de las Indias. Sevilla, 1552.
_____ Tr. in The Spanish colony, a brief chronicle of
the acts and gestes of the Spaniards in the West
Indies, called the new world, for the space of XL
years... London, 1583.
Tr. in The Tears of the Indians. London, 1656.
_____ Tr. in An account of the first voyages and dis-
coveries made by the Spaniards in America. London,
Darby, 1699.
_____ Fray Bartolomé de las Casas, by McNutt. Putnam,
1909; also, Glendale, California, Clark Company.
Contains translations of Brevíssima relación.

Castañeda de Nágera, Pedro de, 16th cent.
The journey of Francisco Vázquez de Coronado; tr. by George Parker
Winship, with notes and introduction by Frederick W. Hodge. San
Francisco, 1933. (Covering period 1540-1542).

Céliz, Francisco, 18th cent.
Diary of the Alarcon expedition into Texas 1718-1719; tr. by Fritz
Leo Hoffman, from manuscript dated Feb. 10, 1719. Albuquerque,
Quivira society, 1935.

Clavigero, Francisco Javier, 1731-1787.
The history of (lower) California; tr. by S. E. Lake and A. A. Gray.
Starford university press, 1937. 413 p. Tr. from Storia della
California. Cesena, Italy, 1780-81.
The history of Mexico, collected from Spanish and Mexican historians,
from Manuscripts and ancient paintings of the Indians. To which are
added critical dissertations on the land, the animals, and inhabitants.
2d. ed. Tr. by Charles Cullen. London, 1807. 2 v. with maps and plates.

Columbus, Christopher, 1446?-1506.
The log of Christopher Columbus' first voyage to America in the year 1492,
as copied out in brief by Bartholomew Las Casas. New York, W. R. Scott,
1938. 84 p. (A juvenile with sketches, etc.).

The Conquest of Peru as recorded by a member of the Pizarro expedition;
tr. from the Seville edition of 1534 with notes by Joseph H. Sinclair.
New York, 1929.

Cortés, Hernando, 1485-1547.
Five letters of relation to the Emperor Charles V.; tr. by Francis A.
MacNutt. Putnam, 1908; Glendale, California, Clark Co., 1941.
_____ Tr. by J. B. Morris. London, Routledge, 1928; New
York, McBride, 1929.
"Second letter of Cortés"; tr. by J. B. Morris. (In Mexican life,
vol. VIII, March-August, 1932).
"Third letter of Cortés"; idem. Sept., 1932-Jan., 1933.
"Fourth letter of Cortés"; idem. Feb-Mar., 1933.
"Fifth letter of Cortés"; idem. April-July, 1933.
_____ Tr. by P. de Gayangos. London, Hakluyt society,
1868. (Works of Hakluyt society, series I, No. 40).

Cortés, Hernando, 1485-1547 (continued).
    The despatches of Hernando Cortés, conqueror of Mexico, addressed
    to the Emperor Charles V... with an introduction and notes by G.
    Folsom. New York, Wiley and Putnam, 1843. 431 p. incl. illus.,
    map. (Contains his 2nd, 3rd, and 4th letters).
    Cortés's account of the city of Mexico. From his second letter to
    the emperor Charles V. Boston, Directors of the Old South work, 1896.
    Excerpts in The discovery and conquest of Mexico, 1517-1521, tr. by
    A. P. Maudslay; London, Routledge; New York, Harper, 1928.

Díaz del Castillo, Bernal, 1492-1581?
    The true history of the conquest of Mexico... tr. by Maurice Keatinge.
    London, J. Dean, 1800; Salem, Mass. Cushing, 1903.
    _____ _____ With introduction by Arthur D. H. Smith. New York,
                   McBride, 1927, 1938.
    _____ _____ (In Hakluyt society. Works, series II, nos. 23 and
                    30, London, 1908-12).
    Discovery and conquest; tr. by A. P. Maudslay (from exact copy of the
                    original by Genaro García) London, Harrap, N. Y.,
                    Harper, 1928.
    _____ _____ Retold in Conquistador, by Archie MacLeish, Boston,
                    Houghton, Mifflin, 1932.
    _____ _____ Retold for children in Cortéz and the conquest of
                    Mexico, New York, Scott, 1942.
    The memoirs of the conquistador Bernal Díaz del Castillo... containing
                    a true account of the discovery and conquest of
                    Mexico and New Spain; tr. from the original Spanish
                    by John Ingram Lockhart. London, J. Hatchard,
                    1844. 2 v.
    _____ _____ Abridged in The Mastering of Mexico, by Kate
                    Stephens. Macmillan, 1916.

The discovery and conquest of Terra Florida, by Don Ferdinando de Soto...
    ritten by a gentleman of Elvas... and tr. out of Portuguese, by
    Richard Hakluyt. Reprinted from the ed. of 1611. London, 1851. (Works
    issued by Hakluyt society, series I, No. IX)
    _____ _____ De Soto, gentleman of Elvas. True relation. Florida
                    historical society, 1932. Contains tr. from
                    Portuguese by R. Hakluyt.

Dodd, Walter Fairleigh, 1880 - ed.
    Modern constitutions. Chicago, University of Chicago press, 1909.
    (One or more constitutions from each Latin American nation translated).

Enríquez de Guzmán, Alonso, b. 1500.
    Life and acts of Alonso Enríquez de Guzmán; tr. by C. R. Markham.
    London, Hakluyt society, 1862. (Works of Hakluyt society, series I,
    No. 29. (From Mss 1535-1538 in Madrid).

Espejo, Antonio de, 16th cent.
    "El viaje que hizo Antonio de Espejo en el año de ochenta y tres",
    included in Historia de las cosas mas notables, ritos y costumbres
    del gran reyno de la China by Juan González de Mendoza. Madrid,
    1586. Tr. by Richard Hakluyt for Principal navigations, vol. III.

Espejo, Antonio de, 16th cent. (Continued)
New Mexico, otherwise, the voiage of Antony of Espeio who in the yeare 1583 discovered a lande of 15 provinces. London, Thomas Cadman, 1587. Reprinted by F. W. Hodge, 1928.
Account of the journey to the provinces and settlements of New Mexico 1583; tr. by H. E. Bolton, in Spanish exploration in the Southwest. New York, 1916.
—————— —————— tr. by G. P. Hammond and Agapito Rey. Los Angeles, 1929.

Fernández de Quirós, Pedro, 1565-1615.
Voyages of Fernández de Quirós, 1595-1606; tr. by C. R. Markham. London, 1904. (Works of Hakluyt society, series II, Nos. 14-15. 2 v.) Tr. of Historia del descubrimiento de las regiones austriales. Madrid, J. Zarogoza, 1876. 3 v.

Florida exploration.
Spanish approach to Pensacola 1689-1693. Tr. by Irving A. Leonard, Albuquerque, Quivira society, 1939. (21 documents from the Admiral Pez memorial of June 2, 1689 to Reports by Governor Torres y Ayala, Fray Rodrigo de la Barreda and Conde de Galve of May 12, 1694.)

Gallegos Lamerto, Hernán, fl. 1567.
Relación etc., tr. by G. P. Hammond and Agapito Rey, in New Mexico historical review, 1927, vol. II, p. 239-334. (About the Chamuscado-Rodríguez expedition).

Garcilaso de la Vega, el Inca, 1503-1536.
History of conquest of Florida; tr. from the French of Pierre Richilet from original Spanish. From Shipp, Bernard, History of Fernando de Soto and Florida. Philadelphia, 1881.

Gondavo, Pedro de Magalhães, 16th cent.
Histories of Brazil by Pedro de Magalhães; tr. by J. B. Stetson, Jr., with facsimile of 1576 Portuguese original. New York, Cortes society, 1922. 2 v.

González de Mendoza, Juan, 1545-1614.
Historie of the greatand mightie kingdome of China; tr. by R. Parke. London, I. Wolfe, 1588. Tr. of Historia de las cosas más notables, ritos y costumbres del gran reyno de la China. Rome, Grassi, 1585.
—————— —————— Reprinted for the Hakluyt society. London, 1852. 2 v. (Contains also an account of the Espejo exploration in New Mexico. See Espejo, Antonio de).

Herrera y Tordesillas, Antonio de, 1559-1625.
General history of the vast continent and islands of America; tr. by, John Stevens. London, Batley, 1725-26. (covers four decades, 1492-1531, written by official historian) Tr. from: Historia general de los hechos de los castellanos en las islas i tierra firme del mar oceano... Madrid, Imprenta real, 1600.

Herzon, B. G., ed.
Cortez and the conquest of Mexico in 1521. New York, W. R. Scott, 1942. 164 p. Illustrated with 16th century Indian drawings.

"The ill-fated expedition of Miranda, the Venezuelan liberator", in Pan
American magazine, vol. 37, 1924, p. 418-423. From National library
bulletin of Caracas. (About the 1806 expedition from New York and
quoting in Spanish and English the questioning of Lieut. J. H. Sherman,
one of the captives).

International bureau of American republics, Washington, D. C.
American constitutions; tr. by José Ignacio Rodríguez, Washington,
Government printing office, 1906-09.

Juan y Santacilia, Jorge, 1713-1773 see: Ulloa, Antonio de,
A voyage to South America.

Las Casas, Bartolomé de see Casas, Bartolomé de las.

López de Gómara, Francisco, 1510-1560.
Conquest of the West Indies (1578). Tr. by H. I. Priestley. New York,
Scholars facsimiles, 1940. (Exploits of Hernando Cortés).

Magalhães de GOndavo, Pedro de, seé, Gandavo, Pedro de Magalhães.

Magalhães, Fernao de, d. 1521.
Early Spanish voyages to the Strait of Magellan; tr. by C. R. Markham.
London, Hakluyt society, 1911. (Works of Hakluyt society, series II,
no. 28). (Containing reports of survivors).

Markham, Sir Clements Robert, 1830-1916, ed.
Expeditions into the valley of the Amazons, 1539-1540, 1639. Tr. and ed.,
with notes, by Clements R. Markham. London, Hakluyt society, 1859.
(Works issued by Hakluyt society, No. XXIV) Contents: Expedition of
Gonzalo Pizarro to the land of Cinnamon, A. D. 1539-42, tr. from the
2nd. pt. of Garcilasso Inca de la Vega's "Royal commentaries of Peru".
The voyage of Francisco de Orellana down the river of the Amazons,
A. D. 1540-1, tr. from the sixth decade of A. de Herrera's "General
history of the western Indies". New discovery of the great river
of the Amazons, by Father Christoval de Acuña, A. D. 1639, tr. from the
Spanish edition of 1641. List of the principal tribes in the valley
of the Amazons.

Mezieres, Athanase de.
Mezieres and the Lousiana-Texas frontier 1768-1780; tr. and ed. by
Herbert E. Bolton. Glendale, California. (Documents published for
the first time, from the original Spanish and French manuscripts,
chiefly in archives of Mexico and Spain).

Montesinos, Fernando, d. 1652.
Memorias antiguas historiales del Peru. Madrid, Jiminez, 1882.
_____ Tr. by P. A. Means. London, Hakluyt society, 1920.
(Works of Hakluyt society, series II, No. 48)
(Valuable for preservation of part of lost volume of
Padre Blas Valera).

Montoya, Juan de, fl. 1602.
New Mexico in 1602; tr. by G. P. Hammond and Agapito Rey. Albuquerque,
Quivira society, 1938. (First published accounts of expeditions by

Montoya, Juan de, fl. 1602. (Continued)
    Castaño, Oñate and Saldívar). Tr. from: Relación del descubrimiento del
    Nuevo Mexico. Rome, Bartholame Bonfadino, 1602.

Morfi, Juan Agustín, d. 1783.
    History of Texas (1673-1779). Tr. by Carlos Eduardo Castañeda. Albuquer-
    que, Quivira society, 1935. Tr. from: Historia de Texas.

Narrative of some things of New Spain and of the great city of Temestitan,
    Mexico, written by the anonymous conqueror, a companion of Hernán Cortes;
    tr. and annotated by Marshall H. Saville. New York, Cortes society, 1917.
    (Documents and narratives concerning the discovery and conquest of
    Latin America, No. 1).

Niza, Marcos de, 1510-1570.
    Relación, etc., in: Pacheco y Cárdenas, Colección de documentos inéditos.
    de América, III, pp. 325-351.
    —————— —————— Tr. by P. M. Baldwin. In New Mexico historical review,
                         I (1926) pp. 193-223.
    "Discovery of the seven cities of Cíbola", tr. by P. M. Baldwin. (In
    Publications of the Historical society of New Mexico, no. I, Nov., 1926).

Núñez Cabeza de Vaca, Alvar, 16th cent.
    Relación y comentarios. Valladolid, 1555.
    —————— —————— Tr. by Buckingham Smith. Washington, 1851.
    —————— —————— in: The conquest of the River Plate; tr. by Luis L. Do-
                       mínguez for Hakluyt society. London, 1891. (Works of
                       Hakluyt society, series I, no. 81).
    Interlinear to Cabeza de Vaca; tr. by Haniel C. Long. Santa Fe, Writers
    editions, 1936. 37 p. (Covering the period 1528-1536)
    Journey and route of the first European to cross the continent of North
    America, 1534-1536; tr. by C. Hallenbeck. Glendale, California, A. H.
    Clark, 1940. 362 p. (from Valladolid, 1555 edition).
    De Vaca's journey to New Mexico. 1535-1563; tr. by Buckingham Smith.
    Boston, Directors of Old South work, 1896. (Includes chapters 30 and
    36 of Relaciones).
    The Journey of Alvar Núñez Cabeza de Vaca and his companions from Florida
    to the Pacific, 1528-1536; tr. from his own narrative by Fanny Bandelier
    Smith ... New York, Barnes, 1905. 231 p.
    —————— —————— Allerton, 1922.
    The narrative of Alvar Núñez Cabeza de Vaca; tr. by Fanny Bandelier
    Smith. Washington, 1851.
    —————— —————— Reprinted. Albany, Murphy, 1871.
    —————— —————— Reprinted. San Francisco, Grabhorn press, 1929.
    First part of his Relaciones also tr. by F. W Hodge, in, Spanish
    explorers of the southern United States. pp. 19-52. Scribners, 1907.

Obregón, Baltasar, b. 1544.
    Obregón's history of 16th century explorations in western America, entitl
    Chronicle, commentary, or relation of the ancient and modern discoveries
    in New Spain and New Mexico, Mexico, 1584. Tr. and ed. by George P.
    Hammond and Agapito Rey. Los Angeles, Wetzel pub. co., 1928.

Perea, Estevan de, 16th cent.
Verdadera relación de la grandiosa conversión que ha avido en el nuevo
mundo. Sevilla, Estupiñan, 1632; Segunda relación, etc. 1633.
————— ————— Tr. by C. F. Lummis in Land of sunshine, vol. XIV, 1901.
————— ————— Tr. by L. B. Bloom in New Mexico historical review,
vol. VIII, July, 1933.

Pérez de Luxán, Diego.
Expedition into New Mexico made by Antonio de Espejo, 1582-1583; tr. from
document in Archivo general de Indias by G. P. Hammond and Agapito Rey.
Los Angeles, Quivira society, 1929.

Pérez de Villagra, Gaspar, 1555-1620.
History of New Mexico; tr. by Gilberto Espinosa. Los Angeles, Quivira
society, 1933. Tr. from Historia de la Nueva Mexico. Alcalá, 1610.
(Written in verse).

Preciado, Francisco, 16th cent.
"Probable Spanish author from which Francisco Ulloa took 'Relatione dello
Scoprimento che ... va a far l'armata dell illustrissimo Fernando Cortese
Marchesse di Valli', in Ramusio, Navigationi et Viaggi (1556)".
————— ————— Tr. by Hakluyt in Principal navigations (1600)
V. III, pp. 397-424.

Relaciones, etc.
For 177 authors of descriptions of voyages, discoveries, missionary work,
etc. see Wagner, H. R. The Spanish South West 1542-1794. Albuquerque,
Quivira society, 1937. 2 v. (Contains facsimile title pages, translations, notes, etc.).

Rodríguez, Agustín, 16th cent., and Sánchez Chamuscado, Francisco, d. 1582.
"The Rodríguez expedition to New Mexico, 1581-1582"; tr. by G. P. Hammond
and Agapito Rey. (In New Mexico historical review, v. II, 1927,
pp. 239-268 and 334-362).

Sánchez Chamuscado, Francisco, d. 1582. SEE reference to Rodríguez, Agustín.

Sarmiento de Gamboa, Pedro, 1532-1608.
History of the Incas; tr. by Clements Markham. Cambridge, Hakluyt
society, 1907. (From Mss in Göttingen univ.)
Narrative of the Voyages of Sarmiento to the Straits of Magellan.
London, Hakluyt society, 1895. (Works of Hakluyt society, series I, No. 91).
Tr. from Viage al Estrecho de Magallanes, 1579-1580. Madrid, 1769.

Schimidel, Ulrich, 1510?-1579? (Also spelled Schmidt).
Conquest of River Plate; tr. by Luis L. Domínguez. London, Hakluyt society,
1891. (Works of Hakluyt society, series I, No. 81). (Author accompanied
the Pedro de Mendoza expedition into River Plate, 1534-1554) Also in
Purchas, Pilgrims.

Simón, Pedro, b. 1574.
Expedition of Pedro de Ursúa and Lope de Aguirre in search of El Dorado
and Omagua, 1560-1561; tr. by Wm. Bollaert. London, Hakluyt society,
1861. (Works of Hakluyt society, ser. I, No. 28). Tr. of: Noticias
históricales de las conquistas de Tierra Firme. Cuenca, 1627.

Soto, Hernando de, 1500-1542.
    True relation of the hardships suffered by Governor Fernando de
    Soto... during the discovery of the province of Florida; tr. by
    J. A. Robertson. Deland, Florida state historical society, 1932-33.
    2 v. Tr. of: Relaçam verdadeira.
    Narratives of the career of Hernando de Soto in the conquest of
    Florida, as told by a Knight of Elvas; tr. by B uckingham Smith.
    New York, Barnes, 1904. 2 v. ; London, Nutt, 1905. New York, Allerton,
    1922.
    _____ _____ Tr. by Hakluyt society, London, 1609, and
    reprinted by Hakluyt society. London, 1851. (Works of Hakluyt
    society, series I, No. 9).
    Letters of Hernando de Soto and Memoirs of Hernando de Escalante
    Fontaneda; tr. by Buckingham Smith. Washington, privately printed,
    1854.
    Letters written to the Secular Cabildo of Santiago de Cuba; tr. in
    Florida historical quarterly, V. XVI, 1938, p. 174-178.

Staden, Hans, 16th cent. (Also spelled Stade)
    The captivity of Hans Stade of Hesse, 1547-1555; tr. by A. Tootal.
    London, Hakluyt society, 1874. (Works of Hakluyt society, series I,
    No. 51). From first edition in German. Marpurg, 1557.
    Hans Staden; the true history of his captivity; tr. by Malcolm Letts.
    London, Routledge, 1928. (Broadway travellers' series). Also New
    York, Argonaut series, 1929.

Taraval, Sigismundo, 1700-1763.
    The Indian uprisings in lower California; tr. by Marguerite Eyer
    Wilbur from manuscript in Newberry Library, Chicago.

    ----------- --------- Los Angeles, Quivira society, 1931
Ulloa, Antonio de, 1716-1795.
    A voyage to South America; tr. by John Adams. London and Dublin,
    1758. A tr. of: Relación histórica del viage a la América Meridional...
    Madrid, 1748.
    _____ _____ London, Davis and Reymers, 1760-72.
    _____ _____ 4th and 5th ed. London, J. Stockdale, 1806,
                           1807. The account of the scientific work of
                           the expedition, written by Jorge Juan y Santacilia,
                           was published separately. Madrid, 1748.

Vázquez de Coronado, Francisco, 1510-1552.
    Narratives of the Coronado expedition of 1540-1542; tr. by G. P.
    Hammond and Agapito Rey. Albuquerque, University of New Mexico
    press, 1940. A tr. of: Relatione che mando Francisco Vázquez di
    Coronado, in Ramusio, Navigationi. 1556.
    _____ _____ Tr. by Hakluyt in Principal navigations. 1600.
    V. III, pp. 373-380.

Venegas, Miguel, 1680-1764?
    Juan María de Salvatierra of the Company of Jesus; missionary in the
    province of New Spain, and apostolic conqueror of the Californias;
    tr. and ed. by Marguerite Eyer Wilbur. Cleveland, A. H. Clark, 1929.
    Tr. of: El apostol Mariano en la vida del V. P. Juan María de
    Salvatierra, Mexico, 1754.

Venegas, Miguel, 1680-1764? (Continued)
Noticias de California. Madrid, Fernández, 1757. Revised by Padre
Andrés Marcos Burriel, under title, a natural and civil history of
California. London, Rivington and Fletcher, 1759.

Vespucci, Américo, 1451-1512.
The letters of Américo Vespucci; tr. by C. R. Markham. London, Hakluyt
society, 1894. (Works of Hakluyt society, series I, no. 19), Tr. of:
Vita e lettere d'Americo Vespucci. Florence, 1745.

Zárate, Agustin de, b. 1514.
The strange and delectable history of the discouerie and conquest of the
provinces of Peru ... Tr. by Thomas Nicholas. London, R. Ihones, 1581.
Tr. of: Historia del descubrimiento y conquista del Perú, con cosas natu-
rales que señaladamente allí se hallan, y los sucesos que ha avido.
Antwerp, 1555.
_____ Reprinted London, Penguin Press, 1933.
_____ in Kerr, R., A general history and collection of Voyages,
Edinburgh, 1812. Tr. from 1742 French edition.

ARGENTINE REPUBLIC

Alvarez Suárez, Agustín Enrique, 1857-1914.
South America; tr. by G. E. Archilla. New York, 1938. Tr. of: Sud América.
Buenos Aires, 1894. (A W. P. A. project, mimeographed, in 2 vols.)

González Arrili, Bernardo, 1892 -
The life of General San Martín; tr. by Margaret S. de Lavenas. Buenos
Aires, J. Perrotti, 1940. (Publicaciones del Instituto cultural argentino-
norteamericano).

Levene, Ricardo, 1885 -
History of Argentina; tr. by Wm. Spence Robertson. Univ. of North Carolina
press, 1937. (Inter-American historical series) Tr. of: Lecciones de
la historia Argentina. Buenos Aires, Lajouane, 1919.

Mitre, Bartolomé, pres. Argentine Republic, 1821-1906.
The emancipation of South America, being a condensed translation by
William Pilling. London, Chapman & Hall, 1893. Tr. of: historia de San
Martín. 1888.
Excerpt "San Martín", in Inter-American, v. V, 1922, p. 201.
Excerpt from Santos Vega, in Inter-American, v. V, 1921, p. 74-75.

Rojas, Ricardo, 1882-
The Saint of the sword: San Martín; tr. by Hershel Brickell. Doubleday,
Doran, announced for 1942. Tr. of: El Santo de la Espada, 1933.

Seeber, Francisco, 1841-
Great Argentina, tr. by Seeber, from his original volume in Spanish.
Buenos Aires, Peusser, 1904.

BRAZIL

Calogeras, João, 1870-1934.
    History of Brazil; tr. by Percy A. Martín. University of North Carolina
    press, 1939. Tr. of: Formação historica do Brasil.

Costa, Luiz Edmundo da, 1878.
    Rio in the time of the viceroys; tr. by Dorothea H. Momsen. New York,
    Stechert, 1936.

CHILE

Conchalí, Inocencia - see - Riquelme, Daniel, 1857-1912.

Galdames, Luis, 1881-1941.
    A history of Chile; tr. by I. J. Cox. University of North Carolina press,
    1941. A tr. of: Estudio de la historia de Chile, 1906-1907.

Molina, Juan Ignacio, d. 1829.
    The geographical, natural and civil history of Chili. With notes from
    the Spanish and French versions, and an appendix containing copious extract
    from the Araucana of Don Alonso de Ercilla. Tr. from the original
    Italian by an American gentleman, R. Alsop. Middletown, Conn., I. Riley,
    1808. 2 v. Tr. of: Compendio de la historia, jeográfica, natural i civil
    del reino de Chile. Bologna, 1776 and Madrid, Sancha, 1778-95.

Ovalle, Alonso de, 1601-1651.
    An historical relation of Chile, by Alonso de Ovalle, a native of
    St. Jago de Chile; tr. by a member of the Royal society. London, 1703.
    Tr. of: Histórica relación del reyno de Chile, y de las missiones, y
    ministerios que exercita en el la Compañía de Iesvs. Rome, F. Cauallo,
    1646.
    ———— ———— First 6 books condensed in The Complete geographer,
    by A. and J. Churchill. London, 1709, V.III, pp.
    1-138.
    ———— ———— In Pinkerton, J. General collection of the best and
    most interesting voyages and travels. vol. 14.
    London, 1808-14.

COLOMBIA

Arciniegas, Germán, 1900 -
    Knight of El Dorado; tr. by Mildred Adams. Viking press, 1942. Tr. of:
    Jiménez de Quesada. 1939.
    Los Alemanes en la conquista de América. Translation announced by
    Macmillan for 1943.

Henao, Jesús María, 1870 - and Arrubla, Gerardo, 1873-
    History of Colombia; tr. by J. F. Rippy. University of North Carolina
    press, 1937. (Inter-American historical series). Tr. of: Historia de
    Colombia. Bogotá, Escuela salesiana, 1911-12.

COSTA RICA

Fernández Guardia, Ricardo, 1867 —
  History of discovery and conquest of Costa Rica; tr. by A. W. Van Dyke.
  New York, Crowell, 1913.

MEXICO

Blasio, José Luis, 1842-1923.
  Maximilian, emperor of Mexico; memoirs of his private secretary; tr. by
  R. H. Murray. New Haven, Yale University press, 1934. Tr. of: Maximiliano
  íntimo. Paris, Bouret, 1905.
  —————— —————— Excerpts in Mexican life, v.X, September 1934,
                        p. 11, and v. XIII, May 1937, p. 34.

Font, Pedro, d. 1781.
  Font's Complete diary; a chronicle of the founding of San Francisco; tr. .
  by H. E. Bolton. Berkeley, University of California press, 1933.
  —————— —————— Tr. by F. J. Teggart. Berkeley, 1913. (With
  English and Spanish on opposite pages) (Written by Chaplain of expedition
  of Juan Bautista de Ansa - 1775-6).

Landa, Diego de, 1524-1579.
  "Landa's Relación de cosas de Yucatán" ed. and tr. by Alfred M. Tozzer,
  in Peabody museum of American archaeology and ethnology, vol. 18-19, No. I.
  Cambridge, Harvard University, 1941. (Based on C. P. Bowditch, tr. and
  corrected by E. B. Adams).
  Yucatán before and after the conquest; tr. by W. Gates. Baltimore, Maya
  society, 1937.

Lombardo Toledano, Vicente, 1894 —
  The fifth column in Mexico. New York, Council for American democracy,
  1942. 30 p.

Morga, Antonio de, 1559-1636.
  History of the Philippines from their discovery by Magellan in 1521 to
  the beginning of the XVII century; tr. and ed. by E. H. Blair and J. A.
  Robertson. Cleveland, 1907. Tr. of: Sucesos de las islas filipinas.
  Mexico, 1609.
  The Philippine islands... at the close of the XVI century; tr. by
  H. E. J. Stanley. London, Hakluyt society, 1868.

Sahagún, Bernardino, 1500?-1590.
  History of ancient Mexico; tr. by Fanny Bandelier. Nashville, Tenn., 1932.
  Tr. of: Historia de la conquista de Mexico. [Reprinted, Blaine Ethridge, 1971.]
  The Song of Qetzalcóatl; tr. from the Aztec by J. H. Cornyn. Mexico, 1928.
  —————— —————— Yellow Springs, Ohio, Antioch college press, 1930.
                        Excerpts in Pan American magazine, vol. 49, 1930,
  p. 124-131.

Sigüenza y Góngora, Carlos de, 1645-1700.
    Mercurio volante; tr. by I. A. Leonard. Los Angeles, Quivira society,
    1932. Tr. of: Mercurio volante con la noticia de la recuperación de
    las provincias del Nvevo Mexico consegvida por D. Diego de Vargas,
    Zapata, y Luxan Ponze de León. .. Mexico, En la Imprenta de Antuerpia
    de los herederos de la viuda de Bernardo Calderón, año de 1693.

PERU

Almagro, Diego de, 1475-1538.
    Pizarro in Peru, in: Universal anthology, v. XI, p. 318.

Cieza de León, Pedro de, 1518-1560.
    The seventeen years of travel of Peter de Cieza through the mighty
    kingdom of Peru; tr. by Captain John Stevens. London, 1709. Tr. of:
    Primera parte de la chrónica del Perú. Sevilla, 1553; Antwerp, 1554.
    Included in collection of Translations of Captain Stevens. London,
    1711.
    Travels of Peter Cieza de León; tr. by Clements R. Markham, London,
    1864. (Hakluyt series I, v.. 33; series I, v. 68, 1883.)
    The wars of Quito; tr. by C. R. Markham, London, 1913. (Hakluyt series
    II, v. 28). (Includes 53 chapters and other Inca documents about the
    murder of Inca Manco).
    The war of Chupas; tr. by C. R. Markham. London, 1917. (Hakluyt series
    II, v. 42).
    The war of Las Salinas; tr. by C. R. Markham, London, 1923, (Hakluyt
    series II, v. 54).

Garcilaso de la Vega, el Inca, 1503-1536.
    The royal commentaries of Peru; tr. by Sir Paul Ricault. London, Rycaut
    and M. Flesher, 1688. Tr. of: Primera parte de los Commentarios rea-
    les. Lisboa, 1609; Segunda parte. Córdova, 1616.
    Excerpt about Pizarro's journey, reprinted in Expeditions into the
    valley of the Amazons. London, Hakluyt society, 1850.
    Tr. by Clements R. Markham, London, Hakluyt society, 1869-71. 2 v.
    History of the conquest of Florida; tr. from French version of Spanish
    original, in Shipp, Bernard. History of De Soto and Florida. Phila-
    delphia, 1881.

Molina, Cristóbal de, of Cuzco, 16th cent.
    War of the castes: Indian uprisings in Chiapas, 1867-70; tr. by Ernest
    Noyes and Dolores Morgadanes from Spanish Mss. in the Rulane Library.
    Tulane university press, 1934.

Peru discoveries.
    Reports, tr. by C. R. Markham in Hakluyt society, series I, No. 47.
    London, 1872. Contains reports by Francisco de Xeres (secretary of
    Pizarro) about Pizarro's journey, 1524-1533.
    Miguel de Ostete, about expedition to Pachacamac, 1533.
    Pedro Sancho, about distribution of ransom money of Atahualpa.
    Hernando Pizarro, a report to Santo Domingo about Atahualpa.

Pizarro, Pedro, 16th. cent.
    History of the discovery and conquest of Peru; tr. by P. A. Means.
    New York, Cortes society, 1921. 2 v. Tr. of: Relación del des-
    cubrimiento y conquista... del Perú. 1571.

Sancho, Pedro, 16th. cent. (Secretary to Pizarro)
    An account of the conquest of Peru; tr. by P. A. Means, from Gar-
    cía Icazbalceta's translation of Ramusio's Italian version of the
    missing Spanish journal of Pizarro's secretary.   New York, Cor-
    tes society, 1917.   2 v.

SOUTH AMERICA

Bolló, L. Cincinato.
    South America, past and present; tr. by N. Baros.   New York,
    1919.   218 p.

URUGUAY

Fernández Artucio, Hugo.
    The Nazi underground in South America.   Farrar & Rinehart, 1942.

VENEZUELA

Bolívar, Simón, 1783-1830.
    An address of Bolívar at Congress of Angostura, etc.; tr. by Fran-
    cisco Javier Yanes.   Washington, D. C., B. S. Adams press, 1919.

García Naranjo, Nemesis, 1883-
    Venezuela and its ruler; tr. by C. W. Esteva.   New York, Carranza,
    1927.   Tr. of: Venezuela y su gobernante. New York, Carranza,
    1927.

López Contreras, Eleázar, 1883-
    Synopsis of the Military life of Sucre; tr. by Kate Brown Shroeter.
    New York, H. R. Elliot Co., 1942.   Tr. of Sinopsis de la vida
    militar de Sucre, 1930.

Nogales, Rafael, 1879-
    Four years beneath the crescent; tr. by Muna Lee.   Scribners,
    1926.   416 p.

ESSAYS
(Historical Places and People, Customs, Criticism, etc.)

The Book of Chilam Balam of Chumayel; tr. by Ralph L. Roys.
Washington, Carnegie institution of Washington, 1933. (Publication no. 438.) A translation by Ralph L. Roys from the original
M_ya text. Written by last and greatest Maya prophets in first
half of 16th century.

Codex Peresianus.
The Codex Pérez, an ancient Mayan hieroglyphic book; a photogra-
phic facsimile reproduced from the original in the Bibliothéque
nationale, Paris, by Theodore A. Willard.   Glendale, Calif., The
Arthur H. Clark co., 1933.   Reproduction of the Codex, discussion
of the other two books: Dresden codex; Codex Tro (Troana) and
sequel Codex Corresianus. The only ones left after destruction
by Diego de Landa, second Bishop of Yucatán, 1549-1579.

Codex Peresianus.
Mayan Codex Peresianus or Mexicanus (also called no. II Codex Pérez)

ARGENTINE REPUBLIC

Alberdi, Juan Bautista, 1810-1884.
Life and industrial labors of William Wheelwright in South America.
Boston, Williams, 1877.   Tr. of: Vida y trabajos, industriales de
William Wheelwright en la America del Sud. Paris, Garnier, 1876.
The crime of war; tr. by C. J. MacConnell.   London, Dent, 1913.
Tr. of: El crimen de la guerra.   1866.

Alvarez, José Sixto, 1858-1903.
"At dusk" in Pan American bulletin, v.   68, pp. 190. Tr. of:
Un viaje al país de los Matreros.   Buenos Aires, 1920.

Costa Alvárez, A., 1870-
The language and literature of Chile, in: Inter-América, v.   VIII,
1925, pp. 241-248.

Eichelbaum, Samuel, 1894-
The oldest daily of South America (El Mercurio, Chile) in: Inter-
America, v.   II, 1918, pp.77-78.

Ingenieros, José, 1877-1925.
A. Alvarez. His Social ethics, in: Inter-America,   V, 1922,
pp. 269-284.   Tr. of: La evolución de las ideas argentinas.
Buenos Aires, Rosso, 1920.

Lorente, Mariano Joaquín, 1883-
"J. S. Alvarez" tr. in: Inter-America, v.   IV, 1921, p.216.
(Memoirs of "Fray Mocho")

Maeztu, Ramiro de.
From La Prensa, Buenos Aires, Jan. 24, 1926: How to make the Yankee
harmless, in: Living age, Mar. 27, 1926, p.673-676.
"Rodó and the United States", in: Inter-América, v.   IX, 1926, pp.
460-464.

Mota, Arturo de la.
"Agustín Alvarez", in Inter-America, v. . I, 1918, p. 342-349.

Mouchet, Enrique, 1886 - Falcos, Alberto, 1894, and Veyga, Francisco de.
"J. Ingenieros", in Inter-America, v. IX, 1926, pp. 371-391.

Noé, Julio, 1893 -
"Sarmiento, the traveller", in Inter-America, v. IV, 1921, pp. 137-143.

Orpen Dudgeon, Patrick.
"Lo universal en la poesía popular europea: J. M. Synge y F. García Lorca";
tr. by Lloyd Mallan in Fantasy, No. 25, 1941 and No. 26, 1942. (Lecture
given November 1938)

Otero, J. Pacífico, 1874-1937.
"Sarmiento" in Inter-America, v. I, 1918, pp. 308-315.

Rohde, Jorge Max, 1893 -
"Angel de Estrada"; tr. in Inter-America, v. VII, 1924, p. 512-524.

Rojas, Ricardo, 1882-
The invisible Christ; tr. by Webster Browning. New York, Abingdon press,
1931. Tr. of: El Cristo invisible. Buenos Aires, Facultad, 1927.
"Reflections upon Argentine literature", in Inter-America, v. II, 1919,
p. 227-240.
"Bartolomé Mitre": his intellectual personality", in Inter-America, v. V,
1921. p. 181-196.

Samperio, Manuel J.
"An author who has appealed to thousands (Hugo Wast)" in Inter-America,
v. VIII, 1925, p. 535-538.

Ugarte, Manuel, 1878-
The destiny of a continent; tr. by Catherine A. Philips, introduction by
J. Fred Rippy. Knopf, 1925. Tr. of: El destino de un continente. 1923.
Latin American women writers of today, in Mexican life, v. VI, October,
1930, p. 21.

Vedia y Mitre, Mariano de, 1880 -
"The centenary of José Mármol", in Inter-America, v. I, 1918, pp. 131-134.

Wilde, Eduardo, 1844-1913.
"Outward bound", in Inter-America, v. III, 1921.

BOLIVIA

Moreno, Gabriel René, see René-Moreno, Gabriel

René-Moreno, Gabriel, 1838-1914.
Sucre in colonial days, in Pan American bulletin, v. 68, p. 191. Tr.
of: Ultimos días coloniales. Santiago, Chile, 1896.

Rojas, Casto, 1880 –
    Historia financiera de Bolivia. Excerpts in "From communism to slavery",
    in Pan American magazine, v. 31, 1920, pp. 193-195.

BRAZIL

Bilac, Olavo, 1865-1918.
    "An International city", in Pan American bulletin, v. 68, p. 193. Tr.
    of: Una defensa nacional. Rio de Janeiro, 1917.
    "In the middle of the road"; tr. by L. E. Elliott, in Pan American
    magazine, v. 28, 1919, p. 160. Tr. of: Nel mezzo del camen.
    Caçador de Emeraldas. Excerpts, tr. by L. E. Elliott, in Pan American
    magazine, v. 24, 1916. Part 4. tr. by Elliott, idem v. 27, 1918,
    p. 150-3. (About the emerald hunter, Fernão Dias, of 1676).

Carvalho, Elysio.
    "The iron deposits of Brazil and their economic utilization", in Pan
    American magazine, v. 27, 1918, pp. 235-240.

Carvalho, J. R. de Sá.
    Brazilian El Dorado; ed. by C. R. Enock. Toronto, Ryerson press, 1938.

Carvalho, Ronald de, 1893-1935.
    "The Brazilian novel", in Inter-America, v. VI, 1923, pp. 214-221.

Gahisto, Manuel, 1878-
    "Manuel Gálvez and the novel in Argentina" – in Inter-America, v. IV, 192
    p. 168-170. Tr. of: Figures Sud-américaines. Paris, Messein, 1933.

Lima, Jorge de, 1895-
    The short story (in Brazil) – in Inter-America, v. VI, 1923, pp. 303-311

Machado de Assis, Joaquim Maria, 1839-1908.
    "Life"; tr. by Isaac Goldberg, in Stratford journal, v. V, 1919, pp.
    119-29; also, in Goldberg. Brazilian tales.

Ramos, Arthur, 1903 –
    The negro in Brazil; tr. by Richard Pattee. Washington, Associated
    publishers, 1939. Tr. of: O negro brasileiro. 1934.

Santos, Joaquim da Silveira.
    "Tiradentes, hero and saint", in Inter-America, v. V, 1922, pp. 170-178.

CHILE

Barros Borgoño, Luis, 1858 –
    "Don José Toribio Medina , in Inter-America, v. VII, 1924, p. 359-376.
    The problem of the Pacific and the new policies of Bolivia; tr. by J. W.
    Davis. Baltimore, Sun rress, 1924. Tr. of: La cuestión del Pacífico y
    las nuevas orientaciones de Bolivia. Santiago, Imprenta artes y
    letras, 1922.

Donoso, Armando, 1877 —
"Rodó", in Inter-America, v. I, 1917, p. 23-30.
"An evocation of the spirit of Ariel" - idem.

Edwards, Agustín, 1878 —
My native land; tr. by the author and H. Gordon Ross. London, Benn, 1931.
Tr. of Mi tierra. Valparaíso, Universo, 1928.
The dawn, being the history of the birth and consolidation of the republic
of Chile; tr. by the author. London, Benn, 1931. Tr. of: El alba, 1818-
1841. Valparaíso, Universo, 1931.
People of old. London, Benn, 1929.

Opazo Maturana, Gustavo.
"Doña Inés de Suárez (1507-1580)" tr. by George Garvin, in Andean monthly,
v. IV, Feb.-March, 1941, p. 56-58.

Palma, Martín, 1821-1884.
Mysteries of the confessional. London, 1888. Tr. of: Los misterios del
confocionario. 1874.

Pérez Rosales, Vicente, 1807-1886.
"Santiago a Century ago", in Pan American magazine, v. 29, 1919, p. 71-77.
Tr. of: Recuerdos del pasado (Santiago 1870). Translation of Chapter I.

Pinochet Lebrún, Tancredo, 1879—
The gulf of misunderstanding; tr. by C. M. Brenner, W. Sachs, and C. Evers.
Boni and Liveright, 1920. Tr. of: El divorcio de las Américas (Series of
articles in Norte Americano, New York, 1919).

Riquelme, Daniel, 1857-1912. ("Inocencia Conchalí")
"Santiago de la nueva extremadura" (Description of the founding of the
city), in Andean monthly, v. IV, February-March, 1941). p. 120-128.

Torres-Rioseco, Arturo, 1897 —
"The colonial novel"; tr. by Angel Flores in Fantasy, no. 26, 1942, p.45-51.

Zañartu Bustos, Sady, 1893 —
"Calle Agustinas", in Andean monthly, v. IV, February-March, 1941.
p. 115-119. Tr. of: Santiago: Calles viejas.

Zapiola, José, 1802-1885.
"Santiago in 1820", in Andean monthly, v. IV, February-March, 1941,
p. 78-81. Tr. of: Recuerdos de 30 años, 1810-1840. Ercilla, 1932.

COLOMBIA

Gómez Restrepo, Antonio, 1869 —
"Colombian literary notes", in Inter-American, v. V, 1922. p. 388-394.

Isaacs, Jorge, 1837-1895.
"Three letters of J. Isaacs", in Inter-America, v. VI, 1923, p. 160.

Ospina Rodríguez, Mariano, 1805-1885, and Ospina, Tulio, 1857-1922.
"The Israelites and their detractors", in Pan American magazine, v. 40

Ospina Rodríguez, Mariano, 1805-1885, and Ospina, Tulio, 1857-1922. (Cont.)
   May 1927, p. 37.

Reyes, Rafael, 1851 -
   The two Americas: tr. by Leopold Grahame. New York, Stokes, 1941. Tr.
   of: Las dos Américas. New York, Stokes, 1914.

Sanín Cano, Baldomero, 1861 -
   "Spanish American revolutions", in Living age, January 17, 1925.

Suárez, Marco Fidel, 1855-1927.
   "Julio Arboleda", in Inter-America, v. I, 1918, p. 206-210.

COSTA RICA

González, Luis Felipe, 1882 -
   "The intellectual evolution of Costa Rica", in Inter-America , v. VI,
   1923, p. 250-263, 267-268.

González Zeledón, Manuel, 1865 -
   "The two musicians", from La Propia. San José, 1921. In Pan American
   bulletin, v. 68, p. 190.

CUBA

Argilagos, R. G., 1853-1895.
   "Grains of gold", in Inter-America, v. II, 1918, p. 22-29.
   "Thoughts selected from the Works of José Martí", idem.

Bernal, Emilia (1884/1885? -   )
   "Los poetas martires", from Cuestiones cubanas. Madrid, Hernández y G.l
   Sáez, 1928. "G. de la Concepción Valdés: his life and work" - in
   Inter-America, v. VIII, 1924, p. 123-125.

Cabrera, Raimundo ("Ricardo Buenamar") 1852-1923.
   Cuba and the Cubans; tr. by Laura Guiteras and E. Levy. Philadelphia,
   Levy type co., 1896. Tr. of: Cuba y sus jueces.

Chacón y Calvo, José María, 1893 -
   "Manuel de la Cruz", in Inter-America, v. IX, 1925, p. 3-20.

Córdova, Federico de, 1878 -
   "Juan Montalvo", in Inter-America, v. VI, 1922, p. 49-65.

Lamar Schweyer, Alberto, 1902 -
   "Ingenieros: his contribution to American thought", in Inter-America,
   v. IX, 1926, p. 294-296.

Maestre y Arredondo, R., 1908 -
   "Darío", in Inter-America, v. VIII, 1925, p. 291-307.

Martí, José, 1853-1895.
    "Indians of America", in Pan American bull. v. 68, p. 190, tr. of
    "Las Ruinas Indias", in Flor y Lava, Paris.

Martínez Márquez, G.
    "As in dreams", in Inter-America, v. IX, 1926, p. 448-452.

Runken, Juan Enrique ("Joaquín de Zurriaga")
    "Don Quixote in America"; tr. by Underwood, in West Ind. rev. v.IV,
    February 1938, p. 17-18.

Sierra, Antonio M.
    "A. Nervo's mysticism", in Inter-American, v. VI, 1923, p. 236-239.

Varona, Enrique José, 1849-1933.
    "Poems in prose", in Inter-America, v. VI, 1923, p. 212-213.
    Cuba vs. Spain. New York, Ruben's press, 1895. Tr. of: Cuba contra
    España. New York, Figueroa, 1895.

DOMINICAN REPUBLIC

Henríquez Ureña, Pedro, 1890-
    Discontent and promise, in Pan American bull., v. 68, p. 190,
    tr. of: Seis ensayos en busca de nuestra expresión. Buenos
    Aires, 1928.

ECUADOR

Arroyo, César Emilio, 1890 -
    Olmedo, in Inter-America, v. I, 1918, p. 147-156. From the speech,
    "El poeta de la independencia americana, Don José Joaquín de Olmedo",
    reprinted in Retablo, figuras, evocaciones, escenas, Madrid, Bib-
    lioteca Ariel, 1921.

Montalvo, Juan, 1832-1889.
    "On Pichincha", in Pan American bull., v. 68, p. 190. From Los
    héroes de la emancipación de la raza hispanoamericana. Simón
    Bolívar, in Siete Tratados. Besanzon, Joaquin, 1880.

EL SALVADOR

Ambrogi, Arturo, 1878-
    "The shade of the wild fig tree, in Pan American bull., v. 68, p. 190,
    tr. of: El libro trópico. San Salvador, Imprenta nacional, 1915.

GUATEMALA

Falla, Salvador, 1845-1935.
"Central America and her problems a century ago", in Pan American magazine
v. 37, 1924, p. 439-446. From: El foro de Guatemala.

Gómez Carrillo, Enrique, 1873-1927.
Among the ruins; tr. by Florence Simmonds. London, Heineman, 1915. Tr.
of Campos de batalla y campos de ruinas. Madrid, Hernando, 1915.
In the Heart of the Tragedy. New York, Hodder, 1917.

HONDURAS

Soto, Marco Aurelio, 1846-1908.
"Santa Lucía and Los Angeles valley", from Lecturas nacionales, 1931.
In Pan American bulletin, v. 68, p. 190.

MEXICO

Agüeros, Victoriano, 1854-1911.
"The day of the dead", in Starr, p. 218.
"The student at home", idem.
"Criticism of the new school of Mexican writers", idem.
"Peón y Contreras and his Romances dramáticos", idem.

Altamirano, Ignacio Manuel, 1834-1893.
"Genius and obstacles", from Revistas literarias de Mexico, 1861-1868, in
Starr, p. 207.
Plea for a Mexican school of writing, idem.
Procession of the Christs, from Paisajes y leyendas, 1884, in Starr, p. 21

Chavero, Alfredo, 1841-1906.
The chroniclers, in Starr, p. 59. Tr. of México a través de los siglos.

Chávez, Carlos, 1899-
Toward a new music: music and electricity; tr. by Herbert Weinstock.
New York, Norton, 1937.

Cruz, Martín de la, 16th cent.
Book of Aztec medicine, written in 1542 by graduate of first mission
school of the new world; tr. from Aztec to Latin by Juannes Badianus;
tr. from Latin by E. W. Emmart, the Badianus manuscript. Baltimore,
Johns Hopkins university, 1940.
_____ _____ Tr. by William Gates: The de la Cruz-Badiano Aztec
herbal, 1939.

Dávalos, Balbino, (1866 ?/1870?)
The great North American poets; tr. by O. W. Gillpatrick. México, Oficina
impresora del timbre, 1901. (With Spanish text). Tr. of: Los grandes
poetas norteamericanos, 1901.

Galindo y Villa, Jesús, 1867-1937.
D. J. Icazbalceta: His life works, in Inter-America, v. IX, 1926, p. 331-344. Tr. of: Don Joaquin García Icazbalceta. Mexico, Imprenta del Museo Nacional, 1904.
—————— —————— In: Anales del Museo v. VI, p. 520-562.

Gamio, Manuel, 1883 -
The Mexican immigrant: his life story; tr. by R. C. Jones. Chicago, 1930.

García Cubás, Antonio, 1832-1912.
The republic of Mexico in 1876; tr. by G. F. Henderson. Mexico, La Enseñanza, 1876.
"Indians of Mexico", in Starr, p. 15; tr. from Escritos Diversos.
Mexico, its trade, industries and resources; tr. by William Thompson.
Mexico, Department of fomento, colonization and industry, 1893.

Rodrigues Cabrillo, Juan, d. 1543.
Discovery of California and northwest America; tr. by A. S. Taylor. San Francisco, Le Count and Strong, 1853. Account of his voyage of 1542 found in manuscript in Archives of the Indies.
—————— —————— In San Francisco Herald, 1853.
—————— —————— Tr. by R. S. Evans, in United States geographical surveys, v. VII, 1879.
Reprinted in: Report of Supt. of U. S. Coast and geodetic survey. Washington, 1886.
—————— —————— Tr. by G. H. Bolton, in Spanish exploration of the Southwest, 1916.

García Icazbalceta, Joaquín, 1825-1894.
The Early Missionaries, in Starr, p. 26, tr. of "La Instrucción Pública en México durante el siglo XVI".

González Obregón, Luis, 1865-1938.
Changes in Mexico, in Starr, p. 120. Tr. of México viejo. México, Escuela correccional, 1891-5.
Luis A. Martinez. idem.
Sor Juana Inéz de la Cruz. idem.
The inquisition. idem.
The streets of Mexico; tr. by Blanche Collet Wagner. San Francisco, 1937.
Tr. of: Calles de México.

González Peña, Carlos, 1885-
A history of Mexican literature; tr. by Mrs. Gusta Barfield Nance and Dr. Florence J. Dunstan. Southern Methodist university press, 1942.
Tr. of: Historia de la literatura mexicana desde los orígenes hasta nuestros días. México, Cultura, 1928.
The wandering bard: Efrén Rebolledo, in Mexican life, v. VI, April 1930, p. 25.
The Paseo in Plateros, idem, (July, 1930).

Guerrero, Julio, 1862-
The Mexican atmosphere, in Starr, p. 152. From: Génesis del Crimen.
Governmental difficulties. idem.
Atavisms. idem.
Mexico's lowest class. idem.

Jiménez Rueda, Julio, 1896 -
    With a great man of letters: Zorilla de San Martín, in Inter-America,
    v. IV, 1921, p. 225-7.

Longinos Martínez, José, d. 1803.
    California in 1892.; tr. by L. B. Simpson, from Mss. in Huntington library
    San Moreno, California. Huntington, library, 1939. (Diary of a botanist
    sent by Charles III to report on trees and shrubs in California).

Méndez, Santiago, 1798-1872, and others.
    Report on the Maya Indians of Yucután; tr. by Marshall H. Saville (The
    American Indian, Heye foundation, 1921).

Miranda, Ignacio de ("George Baset")
    The Don Quijotes of Lorenzo R. Gómez, in Mexican life, v. VI, April 1930,
    p. 33.

Montes de Oca y Obregón, Ignacio, abp., 1840-1921.
    José García Icazbalceta, in Starr, p. 192.
    Mexico's protomartyr, idem.

Noriega, Eduardo, 1853 -
    Climatic zones of Mexico, in Starr, p. 1. Tr. of Geografía de México.
    México, Bouret, 1898.

Olvera, Agustín, d. 1875. (judge who gave his name to Olvera St., Los Angeles
    City of Pamplona; tr. by M. E. Davis, in Overland and Out West monthly,
    v. 89, August 1931, p. 9-10.
    Which one of them? idem.

Paz, Ireneo, 1836-1924.
    The agreement of el Zacate Grullo, in Starr, p. 304. Tr. of: Algunas
    campañas.

Peña, Rafael Angel de la, 1837-1906.
    The Mexican academy, in Starr, p. 183. From his Obras. Mexico, Agüeros,
    1900.

Peza, Juan de Dios, 1852-1910.
    Manuel Acuña, in Inter-America, v. I, 1917, p. 126-128.

Revilla, Manuel Gustavo Antonio.1863 -
    The fine arts in Mexico, in Starr, p. 230. Tr. of: El arte en México
    en la época antigua. México, Secretaría de Fomento, 1893.

Reyes, Alfonso, 1889 -
    Modern poetry of America hispana; tr. by Waldo Frank in Nation, v.   152,
    March 29-April 5, 1941. p. 376-9, 411-2.
    Regulative silence, in Pan American magazine, v. 27, 1918, p. 152. Tr. of
    Silencio reglamentario.
    America's road; tr. by J. L. Grucci, in Amer. pref., v. VII, winter, 1942,
    p. 102-3.

Rinaldini, R.
　　Nervo. In Inter-America, v. I, 1917, p. 67-72.

Riva Palacio, Vicente, 1832-1896. (Rosa Espina)
　　Criticism of Chavero, from Los Ceros. in Starr, p. 72.

Rivera, Agustín, 1824-1916.
　　Backwardness of Mexico in Viceregal-times, in Starr, p. 43. Tr. of
　　Filosofía en Nueva España. Lagos, Veloz, 1885.

Rivera Diego, 1886-

　　La enseñanza del dibujo en las escuelas primarias desde 1920; tr. by
　　J. Castellanos, J. J. Olaguibel, D. Rivera, C. Mérida; in Mexican
　　folkways (special number) November 1934, p. 5-29.

Salado Alvarez, Victoriano, 1867-1931.
　　De autos, in Starr, p. 290.
　　Federico Gamboa, in Starr, p. 296. From: De Mi Cosecha.

Sosa, Francisco, 1848-1925.
　　Statutes on the reforma, in Starr, p. 135. From: El Partido Liberal, 1887.
　　Malintzin, from Biografías de mexicanos distinguidos, in Starr, p. 135.
　　Coronel Gregorio Méndez. idem.
　　Francisco Tres Guerras. idem.

Torres Bodet, Jaime. 1902-
　　Perspective of present day Mexican literature; tr. by A. Plenn, in Mexican
　　life, v. VI, August, 1930, p. 131.

Vasconcelos, José, 1882.
　　Latin America, an interpretation and a prophecy, in Living Age, May 1, 1927.

Velázquez, Primo Feliciano, 1860 -
　　The Tlaxcalan settlements, in Starr, p. 95. From: Documentos para la
　　historia de San Luis Potosí. San Luis Potosí, Imp. del autor, 1897.
　　Andrés de Olmos. idem.
　　Diego Ordoñez. idem.
　　Antonio de Roa. idem.

Velázquez Chávez, Agustín.
　　Contemporary Mexican artists. New York, Covici Friede, 1937. 204 p.
　　illus. with 100 reproductions of paintings of 25 significant artists.

Vigil, José María, 1829-1909.
　　Death of Maximilian, from Mexico a través de los siglos, in Starr, p. 90.

Villaseñor Angeles, Eduardo.
　　An apology for the dilettante, in Mexican life, v. III, June, 1927, p. 40.

Villaseñor y Villaseñor, Alejandro, 1864-1912.
　　Antón Lizardo, from Estudios históricos, in Starr, p. 170.
　　Policy of the United States. idem.

Zarate, Julio, 1844 —
     Death of Hidalgo, from Mexico a través de los siglos, in Starr, p. 79.
     General Nicolás Bravo. idem.

Zayas Enríquez, Rafael de, 1848-1932.
     The case of Mexico; tr. by A. Tridón. Boni, 1914. Tr. of El Caso de
     México y la Política del Presidente Wilson. Mexico, 1914.

PANAMA

Alfaro, Ricardo Joaquín, 1882—
     The liberator, in Pan American bulletin, v. 68, p. 190.

PARAGUAY

Alborno, Pablo, 1877 -
     A colonial church in Paraguay, from Revista de la Sociedad científica
     del Paraguay. In Pan American bulletin, v. 68, p. 195.

PERU

Belaúnde, Victor Andrés, 1883 —
     Bolívar and the political thought of the Spanish American revolution.
     John Hopkins press, 1938. 451 p.

Cornejo, Mariano H.
     The balance of the continents. Oxford university press, 1932.

Gálvez, José, 1885 —
     Arequipa and Lake Titicaca, in Pan American bulletin, v. 68, p. 190.
     From: De Lima a Buenos por Arequipa y La Paz, in La Prensa, Buenos Aires
     August 13, 1933.
     Yuletide in Lima, in Inter-America, v. IX, 1926, p. 350.

Haya de la Torre, Victor Raúl, 1895—
     Internationalism and nationalism; politics and economics, in Latin
     American digest, El Panamá americano, October 2, 1933, p. 4.

García Calderón, Francisco, 1883—
     Latin America, its rise and progress; tr. by Bernard Miall. London,
     Unwin, 1913; New York, Scribners, 1913.

Ibérico y Rodríguez, Mariano, 1892—
     A. O. Deustua and his work, in Inter-America, v. IX, 1926, p. 407-415.
     From El nuevo absoluto. Lima, Minerva, 1926.

Ribero, Mariano Eduardo de, 1795-1857, and, Tschudi, John J. von.
     Peruvian antiquities; tr. by Francis Hawks. New York, Barnes, 1853.
     Tr. of: Antigüedades peruanas. Vienna, Imp. Imperial, 1851.

Riva Agüero, José de la, 1886-
  Peruvian landscapes, in Inter-America, v. III, 1920,
    p. 195.

Sánchez, Luis Alberto, 1900-
  The novel in Indo-America; tr. by Waldo Frank, in Nation,
    v. 152, March 22, 1941, p.323-326.
  Northern exposure: U. S. literary habits, tr. by J. I. B.
    McCulloch; in Inter-American monthly, v. I, 1942, p.
    12-13.

PUERTO RICO

Fernández y García, Eugenio, 1888-
  El libro de Puerto Rico. San Juan, El Libro Azul Publishing
    Company, 1923. English by F. W. Hoadley on opposite sides
    of the page.

Hostos, Eugenio María de, 1839-1903.
  An essay on Hamlet; tr. by M. D. Howland and G. Rivera; in
    Puerto Rico bulletin, No. 12, 1940.

Monteagudo Escámez, Antonio M.
  Golden album of Puerto Rico; pictures and brief articles
    in both Spanish and English. Tr. of: Album de oro de
    Puerto Rico, Cuba, Artes Gráficas, 1939.

URUGUAY

Gallinal, Gustavo, 1889-
  Juan Zorrilla de San Martín; his most recent book: La Epopeya
    de Artigas, in Inter-American, v. VIII, 1924, p. 117-
    122.

Rodó, José Enrique, 1872-1917.
  Ariel; tr. by F.G. Stimson. Houghton Mifflin, 1922. Tr.
    of Ariel. Montevideo, 1900.
  Dialog between bronze and marble, in Inter-America, v. I,
    1918, p. 197-201.
  Motives of Proteus; tr. by Angel Flores. Brentano, 1928.
    Tr. of: Motivos de Proteo. 1909.

Salaverri, Vicente A., 1887-
  Florencio Sánchez; the man and the dramatist, in Inter-
    America, v. IV, 1921. p. 346-352.
  Juana de Ibarbourou, in Inter-America, v. V, 1921, p. 106-
    107.

Zaldumbide, Gonzalo, 1885-
  José Enrique Rodó, in Inter-America, v. II, 1918, p. 44-
    45.
  A Peruvian author who died for France (J. G. Calderón), idem.

Zum Felde, Alberto, 1888-
 José Enrique Rodó: His place among the thinkers of America, in Inter-
America, v. VII, 1924, p. 261-274.
 Contemporary Uruguayan poetry, in Inter-America, v. IX, 1925, p. 62-84.

VENEZUELA

Coll, Pedro Emilio, 1872 -
 The divine persons, in Inter-America, v. IX, 1926, p. 281-293.

Parra-Pérez, Caracciolo, 1888-
 Bolívar: a contribution to the study of his political ideas; tr. by
N. A. N. Cleven. Paris, 1929.

Rangel Báez, Carlos.
 The poetry of ideas in Darío and Nervo, in Inter-America, v. VIII, 1924,
p. 29-38.

Uslar Pietri, Arturo, 1906 -
 The Spanish American novel declares its independence, in Mexican life,
v. XV, February 1939, p. 27.

Vizcarrondo Rojas, Fernando.
 Pan American commercial guide. New York, Abington, 1931 (in Spanish and
English). Tr. of: Manual de correspondencia comercial. Caracas, Opinión
1888.

P O E T R Y

ARGENTINE REPUBLIC

Vidalita, tr. by Muna Lee, in Torres-Rioseco, p. 140.

Almafuerte, see Palacios, Pedro Bonifacio.

Andrade, Olegario Víctor, 1841-1882.
The Condor's nest, in Blackwell, p. 314-326.
Atlántida, idem; also excerpts tr. by E. C. Hills, in Colorado
College Publication Language series II, no. 30, 1915; E. C.
Hills' Hispanic studies. Stanford U. press, p. 120-121.

Arriera, Rafael Alberto, 1889-
Rain, tr. by Alice Jane McVan, in Hispanic poets, p. 191.
Noche de Enero (January Night), tr. by Muna Lee, in APLC, p. 465.

Banchs, Enrique, 1888-
Tiger, tr. by Elizabeth du Gué Trapier, in Hispanic poets, p. 190.
Balbuco (Faltering utterance), tr. in Modernist trend, p. 178-81.
La Estatua (The statue), idem.
Espiritu gentil (Thou gentle spirit), idem.
Cuatro caminos (The four roads), idem.

Bietti, Oscar, 1813?-
Ballad of the dead love, tr. by Helen Eldrige Fish, in Hispanic
poets, p. 195.

Blomberg, Héctor Pedro, 1890-
Two Irish girls, tr. by E. W. Underwood, in West Ind. rev., V,
March, 1931, p. 28.

Borges, Jorge Luis, 1900-
Calle desconocida (An unknown street), in Modernist trend, p. 294-7.
La guitarra (The guitar), idem.
Dulcia Linquimus arva (Sweet vanished land), tr. by Mary and C. V.
Wicker, in Fantasy, no. 26, 1942, p. 71.
Remordimiento por cualquier defunción (Remorse for any death), tr.
by Mary and C. V. Wicker, in Modern verse, Oct., 1941.
Inscripción sepulcral, tr. by Robert Stuart Fitzgerald, in APLC, p.53.
"A Rafael Cansinos Assens" idem, p. 53.
Antelación de Amor, (Love's Priority), idem, p. 55.
Casas como angeles, (Houses like angels), idem, p. 57.
Un patio, idem, p. 57.
La noche que en el Sur lo velaron, idem, p. 59.

Bravo, Mario, 1882-
Song of the general strike, in Blackwell, p. 386.

Cané, Luis, 1897-
Oración de cada despertar, (Prayer for each awakening) tr. by
Dudley Fitts, in APLC, p. 495.

Castellanos, Joaquin, 1861-1932.
    Columbus, in: Blackwell, p. 378.

Cruz Varela, Juan, 1791-1839.
    The 25th of May, 1838, in Buenos Aires, tr. literally, in:
        Green and Lowenfels, p. 294-303.

Dessein Merlo, Justo G.
    Amarga, tr. by Lloyd Mallan, in: New Mexico quarterly review,
        (Aug., 1941).
    Tres paginas, tr. by Lloyd Mallan, in: Modern verse, (Fall,
        1941).
    Hermanos, (Brothers), tr. by Lloyd Mallan, in: Amer. pref.,
        VIII, (Winter, 1912), p. 142-144.

Dominguez, Luis L., 1810-1898.
    The Ombu, in: Blackwell; also in: Christian science monitor,
        (Aug. 12, 1925).

Echeverria, Esteban, 1805-1851.
    The pansy, tr. by A. B. Poor, in: Pan American poems.
    Twilight on the ocean, tr. literally in: Green and Lowenfels,
        p. 378-381.

Fernandez Moreno, Baldomero, 1886-
    On certain things, tr. by Muna Lee, in: Poetry, XXVI, (1925),
        p. 118.

Franco, Luis L., 1898-
    Aprisco, (Goat pen), tr. by Muna Lee, in: APLC, p. 183.

Galindez, Bartolome, 1896-
    In the azure night, tr. by Thomas Walsh, in: Catholic anthology,
        p. 443.
    Sancho's love affair, in: Inter-Amer., IX, (1926), p. 263-280.

Garcia Games, Julia.
    Ode to England, tr. by Lloyd Mallan, in: Poetry, LXII,
        (May, 1943), p. 73.

Ghiraldo, Alberto, 1874-
    For thee, in: Blackwell, p. 338.

Gimenez Pastor, A   , 1872-
    Homage to Dario, tr. by A. B. Poor, in: Pan American Poems.

Girondo, Oliverio, 1891-
    Calle de las Sierpes, (Las Sierpes St.), tr. by M. B. Davis,
        in: APLC, p. 429.

Godoy, Juan, 1873-
    Song to the cordilleras of the Andes, tr. literally in: Green
        and Lowenfels, pp. 260-279.
    Intimate, tr. by Dorothy Conzelman, in: Fantasy, No. 26, (1942),
        p. 51-53.

Godoy, Juan, 1873 - (continued)
Drops of gall, idem.

Guido y Spano, Carlos, 1827-1918.
Funeral song, tr. by P. H. Goldsmith, in Inter-Amer. III, 1920,
p.324.

Gutiérrez, Ricardo, 1836-1896.
Tears, in Blackwell, p. 384.

Hernández, José, 1834-1886.
Martín Fierro, (1872), and La vuelta de Martín Fierro, (1879).
The gaucho Martín Fierro, tr. by Walter Owen, Oxford, Blackwell, 1935, and New York, Farrar and Rinehart, 1935; also
first 26 cantos tr. by Joseph Auslander, in Hispanic notes
and monographs, New York, 1932.

Lastra, Juan Julián.
The thief of songs, tr. by S. de la Selva, in Pan Amer. mag.,
XXVII, (1918), p. 105 (Spanish on opposite page)

Leguizamón, Martiniano, 1858-1935.
Triste, tr. by Alice Jane McVan, in Hispanic poets, p. 185.

López Merino, Francisco, 1904-1928.
Canción para después, (Song for afterwards), tr. by Richard
O'Connell, in APLC, p. 459.
Mis primas, los domingos... (My cousins, on Sundays), idem.
p. 459.

Lugones, Leopoldo, 1874-1938.
Autumnal sweetness, tr. by Thomas Walsh, in Commonweal, Oct.
16, 1942, p. 605.
El Solterón (The Bachelor), tr. in Modernist trends; also in
Torres-Rioseco, p. 113.
A los ganados y las mieses (To the cattle and harvest fields),
idem.
Desdén (Disdain), idem.
Lied de la boca florida (The lay of the rosy lips), idem.
The light, tr. by A.S. Blackwell, in Christian science monitor,
June 10, 1927.
The journey, tr. by Muna Lee, in: Poetry, XXVI, (1925), p. 118;
also in Pan amer. bul., July, 1925; also in Torres-Rio-
seco, p. 114.
Drops of gold, tr. by Alice Jane McVan, in Hispanic poets,
p. 187.
Morning song, tr. by Beatrice Gilman Proske, in Hispanic
poets, p. 189.
A message, in: Blackwell, p. 326.
The palm tree, idem, p. 328; also in Pan Amer. bul., Feb., 1928;
also in: Good neighbor tour, v.   VI, p. 42.
The serenade, in Blackwell, p. 330.
To thee, idem, p. 332.
How the mountains talk, idem.; also tr. by Blackwell in
Springfield republican, July 4, 1915.

Lugones, Leopoldo, 1874-1938 (continued)
The cult of the flowers. In Inter-American I, (1917), p.123-125.

Marechal, Leopoldo, 1900-
Cortejo (Cortège), tr. by Dudley Fitts, in APLC, p. 537.

Mármol, José, 1818-1881.
To Rosas, 1849, extracts tr. by A. B. Poor, in Pan American
poems.
May twenty-fifth, 1849, idem.
In an album, idem.
The tropics, tr. literally in Green and Lowenfels, p.304-313.

Martínez, Leónidas.
Romance of the little school at Raco, tr. of Romance para la
escuelita en Raco, in Argentine magazine, Buenos Aires, Aug.
1942, p. 5.

Mitre, Bartolomé, 1821-1906.
The gaucho's horse, tr. by Alice Jane McVan, in Hispanic poets,
p. 183.
A flower of the soul, in Blackwell, p. 382.
Excerpts from Santos Vega, in Inter-Amer. V, (1921), idem, p.74-
75.
O patria, o patria, idem. p. 78; also other excerpts, p. 181-195.

Nalé Roxlo, Conrado, 1898-
Nocturno, (Nocturne) tr. by M. B. Davis, in APLC, p.497.
Partida, (The game), idem. p. 497.
Lo imprevisto, (The unforeseen), idem. p. 499.

Naón, P. J., d. 1913.
Bubbles, tr. by A. B. Poor, in Pan American poems.
The fugitive, idem.

Obligado, Rafaél, 1851-1920.
Santos Vega, tr. in Blackwell, including: The soul of the
singer, The singer's sweetheart, The singer's hymn, and The
death of the singer.
Excerpts in Inter-Amer. IV, (1920), p.85-94.

Palacios, Pedro Bonifacio, 1854-1917.
Very far ahead, tr. in Blackwell, p. 392.

Rivera Indarte, José, 1814-1845.
To——; verses written in the Mexican gulf, tr. literally in
Green and Lowenfels, p. 382-385.
To——; tr. by A. B. Poor, in Pan American poems.

Storni, Alfonsina, 1892-1938.
Inheritance, tr. by Jessie Read Wendell, in Hispanic poets,
p. 192.
Your arrows, tr. by Alice Jane McVan, in Hispanic poets, p.193.
You and I, in Blackwell, p. 386.
The piety of the cypress, idem. p. 390.

Storni, Alfonsina, 1892-1938. (continued)
    She who understands, idem.; also tr. by Blackwell, in Birth
        control rev., Sept., 1925.
    Corta lírica a otra mujer, in Modernist trend, p. 220-5.
    The cypress, tr. by A. S. Blackwell, in Christian science moni-
        tor, May 6, 1926.
    Running water, tr. by Muna Lee in Poetry, XXVI, (1925), p. 117;
        also in Torres-Rioseco, p. 123.
    Mundo de siete pozos, (World of 7 wells), tr. by Dudley Fitts,
        in APLC, p. 502.
    Peso ancestral, (Ancestral burden), tr. by Richard O'Connell,
        in APLC, p. 511.
    Epitafio para mi tumba, (Epitaph for my tomb), tr. by Rolfe
        Humphries, in APLC, p. 511.

Tiempo, César see Zeitlin, Israél.

Varela, Florencio, 1807-1848.
    Peace, tr. by A. B. Poor, in Pan American poems.

Varela, J. C., 1794-1839.
    The twenty-fifth of May, 1838, in Buenos Aires, tr. by A. B.
        Poor, in Pan American poems.

Vignale, Pedro Juan, 1903-
    El granadero muerto, (The dead grenadier), tr. by Donald Walsh,
        in APLC, p. 473.

Zeitlin, Israél ("Oésar Tiempo"), 1906-
    Cementerio israelita, (Israelite graveyard), tr. by Rolfe Humph-
        ries, Donald Walsh and Dudley Fitts, in APLC, p. 233.
    Digo otra muerte joven, (I tell of another young death), tr.
        by Donald Walsh, in APLC, p. 235.
    Arenga en la muerte de Jaim Najman Biálik, (Harangue on the
        death of Chayim Nachman Bialik), idem, p. 239.

POETRY - BOLIVIA

Bustamante, R. J., 1821-1881.
    Prelude to the Mamoré, in Inter-Amer. IV, (1921), p. 274.

Cortés, José Manuel, 1811-1865.
    To the moon, tr. literally, in Green and Lowenfels, p. 356-61.

Dorta Duque, Manuel.
    Dew, in Blackwell, p. 462.

Duque, Manuel, see Dorta Duque, Manuel.

Jaimes Freyre, Ricardo, 1872-1934.
    Inner landscapes, tr. in Blackwell, p. 454.
    The ancestors, idem, p. 456.
    The idol, idem, p. 460.
    Pórtico, (The portal), tr. in Modernist trend.

Jaimes Freyre, Ricardo, 1872-1934 (continued)
    El alba (Dawn), _idem_.
    Las voces tristes (The mournful voices), _idem_; also in Torres-
        Rioseco. p. 100.

    Aeternum vale, (Eternal farewell), _idem_ ; also tr. by Muna Lee,
        in Pan Amer. bull., July, 1925; also in Poetry, XXVI, (1925),
        p. 119.

Lara, Jesús, 1898-
    Maya, tr. by Milton B. Davis, in APLC, p. 441.

Otero Reiche, Raúl, 1906-
    "Se iba la noche——", (The night was going), tr. by Rolfe Humph-
        ries, in APLC, p. 557.
    Romanza del guitarrero, _idem_, p. 557.
    América, tr. by Donald Walsh, in APLC, p. 561-577.

Ramallo, Miguel (General), 1817 -
    Impressions at the foot of Illimani, tr. by A. B. Poor, in
        Pan American poems.

Sanjinés, Jenaro, 1842*-1900*.
    National anthem (tr. of three stanzas) in Bolivia, Sept.-Oct.,
        1941, p. 26.

POETRY - BRAZIL

Almeida, Guilherme de, 1890-
    Brazilian nocturnes Maxixe; Caterete; Samba, tr. by Underwood,
        in West Ind. Rev., IV, (Sept., 1937), p. 20.
    Brazilian day: Yellow, Purple, Red, _idem_, v. IV, (1938),
        p. 31.
    Brazilian night, _idem_.

Almeida Seabra, Bruno, see Seabra, Bruno.

Anjos, Augusto dos, 1884-1913.
    O homen, tr. by Raúl d'Eca, in Pan Amer. bull., v. 72,
        (1938), p. 382.
    Triste, _idem_.
    Sobre historias, _idem_.

Bandeira, Manuél, 1886-
    Very soundly, tr. by H. R. Hays, in Decision, v. I, May, 1941,
        p. 57.
    Evogao do Recife, (Salute to Recife), tr. by Dudley Poore, in
        APLC, p. 108.
    Na Rúa do Sabão, (In Soapsuds Street), _idem_, p. 115.
    Mozart no céu, (Mozart in Heaven), _idem_, p. 117.
    A mata, (The woods), _idem_, p. 117.
    O cacto, (The cactus), _idem_, p. 119.
    A estrada, (The highway), _idem_, p. 121.
    Noite morta, (Dead night), _idem_, p. 121.

Bilac, Olavo dos Guimarães, 1865-1918.
  Caçador de esmeraldas, excerpts tr. by Thomas Walsh, in His-
    panic anthology, p. 572-577.
  Emerald hunter, tr. by L. E. Elliott, in Pan Amer. mag. XXIV,
    (1916), p. 209, and v , XXVII, (1918), p.150-3 (epic
    about the 7 year search of Fernão Dias)
  Excerpts tr. by Frances E. Buckland, in Torres-Rioseco, p.234.

Bruno, Seabra, see Seabra, Bruno.

Bulhão Pato, Raymundo Antonio de, 1829-1912.
  The two mothers, tr. by Thomas Walsh, in Hispanic anthology,
    p. 697-8.

Carvalho, Ronald de, 1893-1935.
  Mercado de Trinidad, (Trinidad market), tr. by Dudley Poore,
    in APLC, p. 129.
  Interior, idem, p. 129.
  Brazil, idem, p. 131.

Correia, Raymundo, 1860-1911.
  Saudade, tr. by Frances E. Buckland, in Torres-Rioseco, p.235.

Del Picchia, Paulo Menotti, 1892-
  Land of Nostalgia, tr. by Underwood, in West Ind. Rev., IV,
    Oct., 1937, p. 20.
  O beco (The narrow Street), tr. by Dudley Poore, in APLC,
    p. 137.
  Baía de Guanabara, idem, p. 137.

Drummond de Andrade, Carlos, 1902-
  Infância, (Childhood), tr. by Dudley Poore, in APLC, p.165.
  Fantasia, idem, p. 167.
  Jardin de Praça da Liberdade, (Garden in Liberty Square),
    idem, p. 169.

Fagundes Varella, Luiz Nicolau, 1841-1875.
  A Roça, (Life in the interior), tr. by Thomas Walsh, in His-
    panic anthology, p.695-696; also tr. by L. E. Elliott in
    Pan American mag., XXIV, (1916), p. 210 (with Portuguese
    on opposite page).

Ferreira de Lacerda, Bernardo, c. 1634.
  Soneto al desierto de Buçaco (Deserted garden of Busaco) tr.
    by L. E. Elliott in Pan Amer. mag., XXXV, July, 1922, p.34 (with
    original on opposite page).

Gama, Basilio de.
  Uruguay, 1760 (excerpt, Death of Lindoya) tr. by L. E. Elliott,
    in Pan Amer. mag., XXVIII, (1919), p. 250.

Gonçalvez Dias, A., 1823-1864.
  Marabá, tr. by A. B. Poore, in Pan American poems; also in Poet
    lore, XV, Spring, 1904, p. 43.

Gonçalvez Días, A., 1823-1864. (continued)
    Canção do exilio (Song of the exile), tr. by L. E. Elliott, in
        Pan Amer. mag., XXIV, 1916, p.210; also tr. by Frances
        E. Buckland in Torres-Rioseco, p.227.
    Excerpts, tr. by F. Buckland in Torres-Rioseco, pp.227-9.

Guerreiro Ramos, A.
    O canto da Rebeldia, excerpts, (My gigantic hand, prose poem),
        tr. by d'Eça, in Pan Amer. bull., v. 72, (1938), p.385.

Guimarrães, Luis, 1878-1940.
    St. John's eve, tr. by L. E. Elliott, in Pan Amer. mag., XXV,
        (1917), p. 86.

Lima, Jorge, 1895-
    Tempo e eternidade, excerpts, tr. by d'Eça, in Pan Amer. bull.,
        v. 68, 1934.
    Songs, tr. by Ruth Matilda Anderson, in Hispanic poets, p.197.
    The poet was born, excerpt, in Pan Amer. bul., v. 72, 1938,
        p. 355.
    Old Joe, tr, by Angel Flores, in Amer. pref. VII, winter, 1912,
        p. 162.
    Pae João, (Daddy John), tr. by Dudley Poore, in APLC, p.63.
    A Ave, (The bird), idem. p. 65.
    Poema de Qualquer Virgem, (Any virgin), idem, p. 67.
    O grande circo mystico, (Big mystical circus), idem, p. 69.
    Espirito Paraclito, (Paraclete), idem, p.73.
    Poema do Christão, (Christian's Poem), idem, p.77.
    The negress Fulô, tr. by Frances E. Buckland, in Torres-Rio-
        seco, p. 239.

Machado de Assis, Joaquim Maria, 1839-1908.
    Blue Fly, tr. by Frances E. Buckland, in Torres-Rioseco,
        p. 232.
    Vicious circle, idem, p. 232.

Mendes, Murilo, 1901*-
    E ensenada de Botafogo, excerpt, including: Lord Jesus and
        There is a woman, tr. by d'Eça, in Pan Amer. bull., v.
        72, (1938), p.385;
    Psalmo, (Psalm), tr. by Dudley Poore, in APLC, p. 85.

Moreyra, Alvaro, 1888-
    A mangueira e a sabia, excerpt, tr. by d'Eça, in Pan Amer. bull.,
        1938, p. 383.
    O Bau, idem.

Nery, Ismael.
    Oração de I.N. (Prayer of Ismael Nery), tr. by Dudley Poore,
        in APLC, p. 83.

Octavio, Rodrigo.
    Rhapsodies, tr. by Louis K. Sparrow, in Two translations from
        Brazilian authors. (Typewritten with comments by Pan Amer.
        union. 65.p.)

Oliveira, Alberto de, 1859-1937.
    Selva, verses, tr. by L. E. Elliott, in Pan Amer. mag., XXIV,
        (1917), p. 211.
    Em plena luz, (In the light) tr. by L. P. Hill, in Pan Amer.
        mag., XXVII, (1918), p. 98.
    Previsão, (Prevision), tr. by L.P.Hill, idem, (Portuguese on
        opposite page).
    A vela (The candle), tr. by L.E.Elliott, in Pan Amer. mag.,
        XXVII, (1918), p.46; also tr. by Walsh in Hispanic antho-
        logy, p.694-5.
    Sky of Curitiba, tr. by Frances E.Buckland, in Torres-Riose-
        co, p. 236.

d'Oliveira, Felippe, 1891-1933.
    Lanterna verde (Point of convergence), excerpts, tr. by d'Eça,
        in Pan Amer. bull., v. 72, (1938), p.386.

Pato, Bulhão, see, Bulhão Pato, Raymundo Antonio de.

Picchia, Menotti del, see, del Picchia, Paulo M.

Ribeiro Couto, Ruy, 1898-.
    (Noroeste e outras poemas; São Paulo, Editora nacional, 1933),
        excerpt from The gentle rain, tr. by d'Eça in Pan Amer. bull.,
        v. 72, 1938.

Rosas, Nöel (contemporary writer of Sambas).
    Philosophia, tr. by Arthur Goodfriend, in New York Times,
        Jan. 11, 1942, Sect. X, p. 1.

Schmidt, Augusto Frederico, 1899-.
    Canto de noite (Like the wind tonight) excerpt, tr. by d'Eça,
        in Pan Amer. bull., v. 72, (1938), p.384.

Seabra, Bruno, 1837-1876.
    Moreninha, (Dark maiden), tr. by L. E. Elliott, in Pan Amer.
        mag., vol. 27, (1918), p. 160.
    Theresa, tr. by A. P. Poor, in Pan American poems.

Verissimo de Mattos, José, 1857-1915.
    (Interesses da Amazonia, Rio: Jornal do commercio, 1915).
    Going after rubber, tr. by Linker, in Poet lore, vol. 39,
        (1928) p. 154-8.
    Returning from rubber gathering, idem, p. 467-72.

Villela, Iracema.
    Teatime; or, Over the teacups, tr. by L. K. Sparrow, in Two
        translations from Brazilian authors, (Typewritten by Pan
        Amer. Union, 65 p.)

POETRY — CHILE

Anguita, Eduardo, 1914-
    Tránsito al fin, (Passage to the end), tr. by Lloyd Mallan, in
        APLC, p.547.

Anguita, Eduardo, 1914- (continued)
    Oficio, (Service), idem, p.545.

Castro Z., Oscar, 1910-
    Responso a García Lorca, (Response for García Lorca), tr.
      by Dudley Fitts, in APLC, p.519.

Contardo, Luis Felipe, 1880-1922.
    Evening, in Blackwell, p.304, from Cantos del camino. San-
      tiago, Universo, 1918.
    Home of peace and purity, idem; also in Hispanic anthology,
      p. 708-710.
    The calling, idem.
    My sister's death, tr. by Blackwell, in Stratford journal,
      IV, March, 1919, p. 140.

Contreras, Francisco, 1877-1933.
    Luna de la patria. Santiago, Victoria, 19--? from The Charm
      of the rains, in Blackwell, p.304; also, in Stratford jour-
      nal, IV, March, 1919, p.139.

Cruchaga Santa María, Angel, 1893-
    La oración antes del sueño, from La selva prometida, tr. by
      Henry A. Holmes, in Vicente Huidobro and Creationism,
      Colombia Univ. press, 1934, p.42.

Díaz Loyola, Carlos ("Pablo de Rokha") 1894 -
    Alegoría del tormento (Allegory of torment), tr. by H. R.
      Hays, in APLC, pp.399-403.

Duble Urrutía, D., 1877-.
    The mines, selections. tr. by Muna Lee, in Poetry XXVI,
      (1925), p. 121-2.

Ercilla y Zúñiga, Alonso de, 1533-1594.
    La Araucana, pt. I, 1569; complete 1589.
    La Araucana, excerpts tr. by Thomas Walsh in Hispanic anthology;
      also excerpts by Willis Knapp Jones and Read Bain, in Poet
      lore, v. 48, 1942; also excerpts from 1st Canto, tr. in
      prose by L. E. Elliott, in Pan Amer. mag., v. 28, (1919),
      p. 249; also excerpts tr. by R. Alsop in Geographical, na-
      tural and civil history of Chili, Middletown, Conn.,1890,
      and London, Longman, Hurst, 1809; also tr. by P.T.Manches-
      ter and C.M. Lancaster, unrimed stanzas from Cantos I,II,
      III, and VII, in World affairs, v. 104, Sept. 1941, p.
      180-2.

Escuti Orrego, Santiago, 1855-1929.
    After the duel, tr. by A. B. Poor, in Pan American poems.

Fernández Montalvo, Ricardo, 1866-1899.
    Su cabellera suelta (Her flowing tresses), tr. by Blackwell
      in Pan Amer. mag., v. 28, (1919) p.158; also in Stratford
      Journal, IV, March, 1919, p.138,

Godoy Alcayaga, Lucila ("Gabriela Mistral"), 1889-
 Hymn to the tree, in Blackwell, p.236; also in A Spanish
  American poet (G.Mistral,) tr. anon. in Lexington, Ky.
  Herald, May 11, 1924; also tr. by Blackwell in Pan Amer.
  bull, Jan., 1926; also in Good neighbor tour, v. VI, p.
  41; also in Torres-Rioseco, p.121.
 The enemy, in Blackwell, p.240; also in Lexington, Ky. He-
  rald, May 11, 1924; also in Pan Amer. bull., vol.68, p.197.
 Prayer for the nest, in Blackwell, p.252; also in Lexington, Ky.
  Herald, May 11, 1924.
 White clouds, in Blackwell, p.262; also in Lexington Herald.
 The thorn tree, idem; also in Stratford monthly, v. I, new
  series, May, 1924, p. 136.
 Changes, tr. by A.S.Blackwell, in Chile (New York) v. X,
  (1931), p. 75.
 Poems of the mother, in Inter-Amer., IV, (1921), p.363-365.
 The dream, tr. anon. in Republic, May 17, 1924.
 Poems of the home, including: The Brazier, The Lamp, and
  The earthen jar, in Blackwell, p.256; also in Christian
  register, May 22, 1924.
 The teacher's prayer, tr. anon. in Journal of education (Boston)
  (May 29, 1924); also tr. by Isabel K. MacDermotte in Pan Amer.
  bull., July 1924.
 Ecstasy, tr. by Muna Lee in Poetry, XXVI, (1925), p. 121; also
  in Mexican life, vol. I, 1924, p.10; also in Pan Amer. bull.
  July, 1925.
 La Manca, (The little girl that lost a finger), tr. by Muna
  Lee in APLC, p.39.
 El Ruego, (The prayer), tr. by Isabel MacDermotte in Pan Amer.
  bull., July 1924; also tr. by Donald Walsh in APLC, p.39.
 God wills it, tr. by K.G.Chapin, in Poetry, v. 59, Dec.,
  1941, p. 123.
 Sonnets of death, including From that cold ledge where they
  have laid you by, My weariness shall know [sic] one day increase,
  and The hands of evil have been on your life, tr. by
  Thomas Walsh in Hispanic anthology, p.735; also in Com-
  monweal, v. 35, Dec. 26, 1941, p.244.
 Ballad of the star, tr. by Alice Jane McVan, in Hispanic
  poets, p. 199.
 Night, idem.
 The Jars, in Blackwell, p. 244.
 Vessels, idem , p.246.
 Thirst, idem.
 The thistle, idem. p. 248.
 The sad mother, idem , p. 254.
 Little hands, in Blackwell, p. 266; also tr. by Isabel K.
  MacDermotte, in Pan Amer. bull., July, 1924.
 The children dance, in Blackwell, p. 266.
 Little feet, idem, p. 264.
 To the children, idem , p. 240; also in Books abroad, V.
  (1931), p. 365.
 In memoriam, tr. by Isabel K. MacDermotte, in Pan Amer.
  bull., July, 1924.

Godoy Alcayaga, Lucila, 1889- (Gabriela Mistral) (Continued)
    My earthen pitcher, idem.
    My lamp, idem.
    Charity, idem.
    Intima (Intimate) idem.
    Balada (Song) idem.
    La Maestra rural, (The rural teacher) idem.
    Poems in ecstasy; I am weeping; Hide me; Waiting for thee,
        in Mexican life, vol. I, 1924, p. 10.
    Perchance my loss, tr. by A. Ortiz-Vargas, in Poet lore, v.
        46, 1940, p. 339-352.
    He passed with another, idem.
    Here I am, O God, idem.
    Poem of the sun, idem.
    Alone in the plain, idem.
    Where shall we dance? idem.; also tr. by Blackwell, in Poet
        lore, v. 46, 1940, p.351.
    Many years hence, tr. by Blackwell, in Books abroad, V,
        (1931), p.366.

González, Pedro Antonio, 1863-1903.
    The candle, tr. by Willis Knapp Jones, in Poet lore, v. 32,
        autumn, 1921, p.406.

González Bastías, Jorge, 1879-
    The song of the road, tr. by L. E. Elliott, in Pan Amer.
        mag., XXVI, (1917), p.68.
    To the old guitar, in Blackwell, p. 306; also in Stratford
        journal, IV, March, 1919, p. 137.

Guzmán Cruchaga, Juan, 1896-
    Lejana (Distant), in Modernist trend.

Hübner, Jorge, 1892-
    The river, in Blackwell, p.294; also in Pan Amer. bull.,
        Feb., 1928; also in Boston Evening transcript, June 8,
        1927; also in Books abroad, V, 1931, pp.366-7.
    The wind, in Blackwell, p. 296; tr. by Blackwell in New
        leader, April 3, 1926.

Huidobro, Vicente, 1893-.
    Arte poética, tr. by M.B.Davis, in APLC, p.347.
    Ronda, tr. by Donald Walsh, idem, p.347.
    Day and night, tr. by H.R.Hays, in Decision I, May, 1941,
        p.54-55.
    Adios,(Adieu), tr. in Modernist trend, p.236-43.
    Horizonte, (Horizon) idem.
    Mañana primaveral, (Spring morning), idem.
    La senda era tan larga, (The path was so long), idem.
    Campanario, (Bell tower), idem.
    Hijo (Son), idem; also tr. by Henry A. Holmes, in Vicente Hui-
        dobro and Creationism, Columbia univ. press, 1934, p. 20.

Huidobro, Vicente, 1893- (continued)
    Ecuatorial, tr. by Henry A. Holmes, idem , p. 21.
    Altazor, idem.Selections, p.28-32, 46-47.
    Vermouth, idem , p. 51.
    Maison, both French and Spanish versions, idem, p.54.
    Balandre, idem, p.55.
    Luna, idem, p.56.
    Apportez des jeux (Bring games), tr. by Joseph Staples, in
        APLC, p.341.
    Je suis un peu lune (I am partly moon), idem, p.341.
    Tu n'as jamais connu (You have never known the tree of ten-
        derness), idem, p.343.
    Noyé charmant (Bewitching drowned) idem, p.345.
    Naturaleza viva (Natural vive), tr. by Dudley Fitts, idem,
        p.349.
    Ella (She), idem, p.351.
    Landscape, tr. by Torres-Rioseco, in Torres-Rioseco, p.124.

Irisarri y Trucio, Hermógenes, 1819-1886.
    Love, tr. by A.B. Poor, in Pan American poems.

Lillo, Samuel A., 1870-
    To Vasco Núñez de Balboa, tr. by Thomas Walsh in Hispanic
        anthology, p.699-701; also tr. by L. E. Elliott, in
        Pan Amer. mag., XXVI, 1917, p.69; also tr. by Willis
        Knapp Jones, in Poet lore, v. .32, autumn, 1921, p.407-8.
    The abandoned time, tr. by L. E. Elliott, idem , p. 70.

Magallanes Moure, Manuel,1875-
    Hymn to love, in Blackwell, p.298-301.
    The rendezvous, tr. by Thomas Walsh, in Hispanic anthology,
        p.689-691.
    My mother, idem; also tr. by L. E. Elliott, in Pan Amer.
        mag., XXVI, (1917), p.71.
    Table talk, tr. by Muna Lee, in Poetry, XXVI, (1925), p.122.

Marín de Solar, Mercedes, 1804-1868.
    To Manuel Rodríguez, tr. in Blackwell, p.306.

"Mistral, Gabriela", pseud. see Godoy Alcayaga, Lucila.

Mondaca, Carlos R., 1881-1928.
    Fatigue, tr. by L. E. Elliott, in Pan Amer. mag., XXVI,
        (1917), p.68.
    Amor, tr. by D. Hipp (A.R.González, pseud.) in Poetry,
        XXXVIII, (1931), p.309.

Montenegro, Ernesto, 1885-
    To modern poets, tr. by Thomas Walsh, in Hispanic anthology,
        p.740-741.
    Plazas de Chile, tr. by A. S. Blackwell, in Christian science
        monitor, Aug. 8, 1925.

"Neruda, Pablo" pseud. see, Reyes, Neftalí Ricardo.

Pezoa Véliz, Carlos, 1878-1908.
    Age, tr. by Thomas Walsh, in Hispanic anthology, p.702.
    The hospital, one afternoon, idem ; also, Afternoon in
        the hospital, tr. by Alice Jane McVan, in Hispanic
        poets, p.198;also Hospital one afternoon, tr. by L.
        E. Elliott, in Pan Amer. mag., XXVI, (1917), p.71,
        also Tarde en el hospital, in Modernist trend.
    Nada, in Modernist trend.
    Fecundidad, (Fecundity), tr. by J. Crowhurst-Rand, in Pan
        Amer. mag., XXVI, (1917), p.326.

Prado, Pedro, 1886-.
    Lazarus, tr. in Blackwell, p.278; tr. by Blackwell in Zion's
        Herald, July 25, 1926; also in Modernist trend; also ex-
        cerpts tr. by Willis Knapp Jones in Poet lore, vol. 32,
        autumn, 1921, p. 407.
    Our mountain, tr. in Blackwell, p. 286.
    Los pájaros errantes (The birds of passage), tr. in Moder-
        nist trend.
    Las manos (The hands of my beloved), idem.
    The three Marys, tr. by Blackwell, in Stratford journal, IV,
        March, 1919, p.138.
    Poems in prose, tr. anon, in Inter-Amer., VIII, Dec., 1924.
        p.123-125.

Préndez Saldías, Carlos, 1892-
    My shadow, tr. by Thomas Walsh, in Commonweal, Oct. 16,
        1942, p. 605.

Reyes, Neftalí Ricardo, 1904-
    Maestranzas de noche (Arsenal by night), in Modernist trend.
    Poemas de amor; idem.
    Canto general de Chile, tr. by J. L. Grucci, in Amer. Pref.
        VII, winter, 1912, p.140-141.
    Es cierto, amada mía, hermana mía, es cierto, (It is sure, my
        love), tr. by J. L. Grucci, in Fantasy, no.XXVI, 1942, p.
        55; also in Chilean Gazette I, 5, (Dec. 1942), p. 7.
    Canto para Bolívar, tr. by J. L. Grucci, in Three Spanish
        American poets.
    Tres cantos materiales, idem.
    Madrid, tr. by J. Hambleton in Canadian forum, XXI, June,
        1941. p. 86.
    Dish of blood from Almería, idem.
    I am on my way, tr. by H. R. Hays, in Decision I, May, 1941,
        p.49-50.
    Ode with a lament, idem. p. 55-56.
    Walking around, tr. by H. R. Hays, in APLC, p.303.
    Entierro en el este, tr. by Angel Flores, idem, p. 311.
    Ritual de mis piernas, tr. by Dudley Fitts, in APLC, p.305.
    7 de Noviembre: Oda a un día de victorias, (November 7: Ode
        to a Day of victories), tr. by Dudley Fitts, in APLC, p.
        311.

Reyes, Neftalí Ricardo, 1904-(continued)
Residencia en la tierra, tr. by Maurice Halperin, in Books
abroad, v.   XV (1941), p.165.

Ried, Alberto, 1884-
Mi Jardín (My garden), tr. by Lilian Elwyn Elliott, in Pan
Amer. mag. XXVI, (1917), p. 121 (Spanish on opposite page).

Rojas, Manuel, 1896-
El vaso de leche, tr. by J. L. Grucci, in Amer. Pref., winter, 1941.

Rokha, Winette de (Luisa Anabalón Sanderson) ("Juana Inés de la
Cruz"), 1894*-
Vals en la plaza de Yungay, (Waltz in Yungay Sq.), tr. by
H. R. Hays, in APLC, p.145.
Canción de Tomás, el ausente, (Song of Thomas, departed),
idem, p.145.
Figura de invierno, (Winter figure), idem, p. 147.

Silva, Víctor Domingo,1882-
Music in the square, in Blackwell, p.290.
Cain, idem, p.292; also in Stratford journal IV, March,
(1919) p.139.
The return, tr. by Thomas Walsh, in Hispanic anthology,
p.723-6.
Ballad of the violin, idem., also in Modernist trend; also
tr. by L. E. Elliott, in Pan Amer. mag., XXVI, 1917, p.71.

Tondreau Valín, Narciso, 1861-
Yesterday and today, tr. by A. B. Poor, in Pan Amer. poems.

Torres-Rioseco, Arturo, 1897-.
Campanita nocturna, (Bells by night), in Modernist trend.
Versos de profecía,(Prophetic verses), idem.
Cuando me muera, (When I am dead), idem.
Ausencia, (Absence), idem.
Poems to living Spain, tr. by J. L. Grucci, in Amer. Pref.
VII, winter, 1912, p.158-159.

Valle, Rosamel del, 1900-
Shadow of the fish, tr. by Lloyd Mallan, in Poetry, v.
LXII (May, 1943), p. 76.

Vega, Daniel de la, 1892-
In the master's footsteps, in Blackwell, p.302.
The door, idem; also tr. by L. E. Elliott, in Pan Amer.
mag., XXVI, 1917, p.67.

Velgas, Juan José.
The azure sky, tr. by Thomas Walsh, in Hispanic anthology,
p.757-758.

Véliz, Carlos Pesoa, see Pezoa Véliz, Carlos.

Zamora, Luis A., 1879-
>A secret, tr. by Blackwell, in Boston Record, Oct. 1, 1915;
also in Las novedades, Oct. 7, 1915; also in Stratford
journal, IV, March, 1919, p.140.

POETRY - COLOMBIA

"Alas, Claudio de", pseud. see Escobar Uribe, Jorge.

Alvarez Henao, Enrique, 1871-1914.
>The bee, in Blackwell, from Poesías, Barcelona: López, 19—?

Caro, José Eusebio, 1817-1853.
>Words of the last Inca, in Blackwell, p. 414-416; also in
Las novedades, Aug. 19, 1915, from Obras escogidas,
Bogotá, El Tradicionista, 1873.

Carranza, Eduardo, 1915-
>Domingo, (Sunday), tr. by Donald Walsh, in APLC, p. 161.

Carrasquilla, Ricardo, 1827-1886.
>Spain and America, tr. by Thomas Walsh, in Hispanic antho-
logy, p. 465.

Casas, José Joaquín, 1866-
>The secret, tr. by Thomas Walsh, in Catholic anthology,
from Poemas criollos, Bogotá: C. de Jesús, 1932.

Castillo y Guevara, Francisca Josefa de, 1671-1742.
>Christmas carol, tr. by Thomas Walsh, in Catholic anthology,
p. 220.

Escobar Uribe, Jorge, (Claudio de Alas, pseud.), 1886-1918.
>Poet of gloom, tr. by Willis Knapp Jones, in Poet lore,
XXXV, 1924, p. 456-463, containing translations of
his Ante un cráneo, Fiat lux, Cuando escucho el Vals
Francia.

Fernández Madrid, José, 1789-1830.
>To the liberator, on his birthday, tr. literally in
Green and Lowenfels, p. 362-367.

Flórez, Julio, 1867*-1923.
>Apoteosis en la muerte de una niña (Apotheosis on the
death of a young girl), tr. by L. E. Elliott, in Pan
Amer. mag., XXIV, (1917), p. 238. (With Spanish on opposite page).
>Oro en polvo, (Gold dust), tr. by Thomas Walsh in Pan
Amer. mag., XXVII, (1918), p. 213.
>Love's message, in Blackwell, p. 416.
>Danger, idem, p. 418.
>Hymn to Aurora, tr. by Thomas Walsh, in Hispanic antho-
logy, p. 687.

Francisca Josefa de la Concepción, Madre, see Castillo y
Guevara.

García Tejada, Juan Manuel, 1774-1845.
To Jesus on the cross, tr. by Thomas Walsh, in Catholic
anthology, p. 233.

Gómez Jaime, Alfredo, 1878–
Pinceladas (A sketch), in Blackwell; also in Pan Amer.
mag., XXX V, July, 1922, p. 32, (Spanish on opposite
page).
Problem, tr. by Muna Lee, in Pan Amer. bull., July, 1925;
also in Poetry, v. 26, 1925, p.127.
I come for a soul, in Inter-Amer., VIII, (1924), p. 55-
64.

Gómez Restrepo, Antonio, 1869–
Eyes, tr. by Thomas Walsh, in Hispanic anthology, p. 119-
120.
The general life, idem, p. 620.
Toledo, idem, p. 620; also in Catholic anthology, p. 362,
from Poesías publicadas por la Academia colombiana,
Bogotá, 1940.

González Manrique, Mariano, 1829-1870.
Barcarole, tr. by A. S. Blackwell, in The Public, Chicago,
Oct., 22, 1909.

Isaacs, Jorge, 1837-1895.
The mima, tr. by Alice Jane McVan, in Hispanic poets, p.
201.
A Cali, (To Cali), tr. by J. M. Saavedra Galindo, in
Pan Amer. mag., XXXIX, (1926), p. 223, (Spanish on
opposite page); also tr. by Underwood, in West Ind.
rev., IV, March, 1928, p. 28.
Tomb of Belisario, tr. by Underwood, in West Ind. rev.,
IV, March, 1928.

Ivanovitch, Dimitri, 1888-
The child's asleep, tr. by Thomas Walsh, in Hispanic
anthology, pp. 749-50.

López, Luis Carlos, 1885*-
From my farm, tr. by Alice Jane McVan, in Hispanic
poets, p. 212.

López, Luis Carlos, 1885*— (continued)
    River folk, tr. by Thos. Walsh, in Hispanic anthology, p.
        711-14.
    Verses to the moon, idem.
    The village mayor, tr. by Thos. Walsh, in Literary digest,
        LXIX, 1921, p.34.
    Sonnet: To my native city, tr. by H.R. Hays, in Decision I,
        May, 1941, p.48.
    Campesina, no dejes, (Country girl, don't stay away), tr. by
        Donald Walsh, in APLC, p. 199.
    Siesta del trópico, (Tropic siesta), idem, p. 201.
    Toque de oración, (Vespers), idem, p.203.
    Tarde de verano, (Summer afternoon), idem, p.205.
    Noche de pueblo, (Village night), idem, p.201, also Village
        night, tr. by Muna Lee, in Poetry, XXVI, (1925), p.126-7.

Madiedo, Manuel María, 1818*-1900.
    The Guaili, tr. by A. B. Poor, in Pan American poems.

Maya, Rafaél, 1898-
    Allá lejos, (Far over yonder), tr. by Rolfe Humphries, in
        APLC, p. 443.

Osorio, Miguel Angel, 1883-1942. (Ricardo Arenales, Porfirio Barba
    Jacob, pseud).
    The lament of October, in Anthology of Mex. poets, p.71; also
        tr. by Underwood, in West Ind. rev., IV, May, 1938, p.30.
    Stanzas, idem.
    Song of La vida profunda, idem.

Pardo García, Germán, 1902-
    El instante, (The moment), tr. by Rolfe Humphries, in APLC, p.449.
    La lejanía, (Remoteness), idem. p.449.

Pérez, Felipe, 1834-1891.
    Dewy blossoms, tr. by A.S. Blackwell, in New York Evening post,
        June 17, 1915.

Pombo, Rafaél, 1833-1912.
    To Bolívar, in Blackwell, p.394; also Fragmento del himno a
        Bolívar, (Fragment to the hymn to Bolivar), tr. by Blackwell,
        in Pan Amer. bull., Sept.,1926; also in Pan Amer. p.66.
    Woman, in Blackwell, p.394.
    The two Americans, idem, also tr. by Blackwell, in Boston trans-
        cript, April 8,1926; also in Pan Amer.,p.10.
    At Niagara, tr. by Thomas Walsh, in Hispanic anthology, p.471-483.
    Our madona at home, idem; also in Catholic anthology, p.274.

Silva, José Asunción, 1865-1896.
    A citizen of the twilight, tr. by G. G.King, Longmans, 1921.
    Art, tr. by Thos.Walsh, in Catholic anthology, p.339.
    Egalité (Equality), in Modernist trend.
    The day of the dead, in Blackwell, p. 404.
    Stars, idem, p.402.
    Serenade, idem, p.402; also in Las novedades, July 1,1915.
    A poem, tr. by Alice Jane McVan, in Hispanic poets, p.207.
    Nocturne, idem; also in Modernist trend; also tr. by Muna

Silva, José Asunción, 1865-1896 (continued)
Lee, in Pan Amer. bull., Sept.,1926; also in Poetry,
XXVI, 1925; p.123-5; also in Pan Amer. mag., v.41, 1928,
p.116 (with Spanish on opposite page); also in Torres-
Rioseco, p.98, tr. by I.Goldberg, "?"; tr. by A. S. Black-
well, in Pan Amer. bull., Sept.,1926.
Excerpts in Inter-Amer. IV, 1920, p.108-116.

Talero Nuñez, Eduardo.
Blood, tr. by A. S. Blackwell, in New York Call, July 18, 1915.

Uribe, Diego, 1867-
In pursuit of the dream, in Blackwell, p. 420.

Valencia, Guillermo, 1873-1943.
Los camellos (The camels), tr. by Beatrice Gilman Proske,
in Hispanic poets, p. 209; also in Modernist trend.
To the Andes, in Blackwell, p.412; also in Pan Amer. bull.,
LXII, 1920.
She, in Blackwell, p.414; also in Good neighbor tour, VI, p.39.
Sursum, tr. by Thomas Walsh, in Hispanic anthology; also in
Catholic anthology, p.386.
The two beheadings, tr. by Thos. Walsh, in Hispanic anthology;
also in Pan Amer. mag., XXVI, 1918, p.332-334.
White storks, tr. by Blackwell, in Poet lore, XXXVII, p. 616-622.
Leyendo a Silva, (Reading Silva), in Modernist trend.
Anarchs, selections, tr. by Muna Lee, in Poetry XXVI, (1925),
p.125-126.
Turris Eburnae, tr. by Thomas Walsh, in Pan Amer. mag., XXVII,
(1918), p.208.

POETRY - COSTA RICA

Brenes Mesén, Roberto, 1874-
Condor's eyes, in Blackwell, p. 480.

Estrada, Rafaél, 1901-1934.
Soldados, (Mexican soldiers), tr. by Donald Walsh, in APLC, p.157.
Huellas, (Traces), idem, p.157.
Atardecer, (Twilight), idem, p.159.

González Rucavado, Claudio, 1879-1929.
Scenes from Costa Rican life; Public holiday, The ball, Fireworks,
in Pan American mag., XIV, (1912).

Hine, David, 1858-
The bright star, in Blackwell, p. 480.

Luján, Fernándo, 1912-
Song of the long drouth, tr. by Alice Jane McVan, in Hispanic
poets, p. 214.

Sáenz, Carlos Luis, 1899-
As a petal, tr. by Elizabeth du Gué Trapier, in Hispanic poets,
p. 213.

Arguere y Arguere, Brígida.
     The beautiful, tr. by Underwood, in West Ind. rev., III,
          Sept., 1936, p.36.

Ballagas, Emilio, 1908*-
     Pregón, tr. by J. L. Grucci, in Torres—Rioseco, p.128.
     Rhumba: The negress, tr. by H. R. Hays, in Decision I,
          May, 1941, p. 51.

Bernal, Emilia, (1885?)
     Wishes, tr. by Underwood, in West Ind. rev., III, Sept.,
          1936. p.37.
     Violets, idem.

Bobadilla, Emilio ("Fra Candil"), 1867—1919.
     Spring, tr. by Underwood, in West Ind. rev., III, Jan.,
          1937, p.35.

Borrero de Luján, Dulce Maria, 1883—
     The singing rose, in Blackwell, p.490.
     Song, idem. p. 494.
     The song of the palms, in Pan Amer. bull. LXII, (1928),
          p.1214—19; also tr. by Underwood, in West Ind. rev.,
          III, Sept., 1936, p. 37.

Brull, Mariano, 1891—
     Interior, tr. by Thomas Walsh, in Hispanic anthology, p.
          759—762.
     To the mountain, idem.
     Mi corazón, tr. by O. Tenney, in Pan Amer. mag., XXVII,
          1918, p.40. (With Spanish on opposite page)
     Pax Animae, idem.

Buesa, José Angel, 1910-
     Elegy, tr. by Underwood, in West Ind. rev., V, Nov., 1938,
          p.31.
     Sonnet, idem.
     Elegy II, idem.
     Nocturn, idem.
     Nocturn VI, idem.

Byrne, Bonifacio, 1861—1937.
     The Spanish tongue, in Blackwell, p. 498—500; also in Bos-
          ton Record, June 25, 1915.
     Our language, tr. by Underwood, in West Ind. Rev., IV, July,
          1938, p.27.

Carbonell y Rivero, José Manuel, 1880-
     One grieving dusk, tr. by Underwood, in West Ind. rev., III,
          Feb., 1937, p.36.

Casal, Julián del, 1863—1893.
     Scene in the tropics, tr. by Ruth Matilda Anderson, in His-
          panic poets, p.219.

Casal, Julián del, 1863–1893. (continued)
    The friar, tr. by Thomas Walsh, in Catholic anthology, p.337.
    To my mother, tr. by Thomas Walsh, in Hispanic anthology,
        p.564–568.
    My loves, idem.
    Confidences, idem.
    The pearls, idem; also in Goldberg, Studies in Spanish Amer.
        lit., p.52.
    Nostalgia, tr. by Underwood, in West Ind. rev., II, July,
        1936, p. 24.
    Memory of childhood, tr. by Underwood, in West Ind. rev.,
        II, Aug., 1936, p. 43.
    The sad virgin, idem.
    Enchantress, idem.
    Pax Animae, idem.
    Rhyme, idem.

Castellanos, Jesús, 1879–1912.
    An idyl in a minor key, in Blackwell.

Castillo de González, Amelia (name also given as Aurelia),1842-1920.
    The Alps, tr. by Underwood, in West Ind. rev., III, Sept.
        1936, p.37.

Collado, María, see, García Collado, José María.

Doreste, Arturo, 1896–
    To Fabio Fiallo, a sonnet, tr. by Underwood, in West Ind.
        rev., II, March, 1936.
    Aquarelle, idem, IV, July, 1938, p.27.

Estenguer, Rafael, 1899 –
    Ay mi madre, Ay mi madre, adaptation by Benjamin F. Carru-
        thers, in Amigos, I, Jan., 1942, p.38–39 (with Spanish
        on opposite page).

Florit, Eugenio (born in Madrid, 1903, but considered Cuban).
    La niña nueva, (The baby girl), tr. by Donald Walsh, in APLC,
        p.29.
    Martirio de San Sebastián, (Martyrdom), idem, p.33.
    Estrofas a una estatua, (Strophes to a statue), idem, p.35.
    A la mariposa muerta, (To the dead butterfly), tr. by Richard
        O'Connell, in APLC, p. 31.
    En la muerte de alguien, (On someone's death), tr. by Muna Lee,
        in APLC, p.31.

Fornaris, José, 1827–1890.
    From banks of Seine, tr. by Underwood, in West Ind. rev.,
        III, Feb., 1937, p. 36.

García Collado, José María, 1890–
    Dead leaves, tr. by Underwood, in West Ind. rev., III, Sept.,
        1936, p. 37.

Gómez de Avellaneda, Gertrudis, 1816-1873.
> To hope, tr. literally in Green and Lowenfels, p.280-293.
> To youth, idem. p.324-333.
> The final day, idem, p.300-355.
> To Washington, idem; also tr. by A. B. Poor, in Pan Amer.
> poems.
> To the sun, idem.
> To a butterfly, idem. p.388-395.
> Return to my fatherland, tr. by Underwood, in West Ind. rev.,
> II, May, 1936, p. 34.
> On leaving Cuba, idem; also in Blackwell, p.490.
> To him, tr. by Thomas Walsh, in Hispanic anthology, p.434-436.
> On the Betis, tr. by Alice Jane McVan, in Hispanic poets, p.215.

Guillén, Nicolás, 1904-
> No sé por que piensas tú, (Soldier, I can't figure why), tr.
> by H. R. Hays, in APLC, p.245, also tr. by J. L. Grucci,
> in Amer. Pref. VII, winter, 1941-42, p.160-161.
> Fusilamiento, (Execution), tr. by Langston Hughes, in APLC,
> p.247; also tr. by J. L. Grucci, in Fantasy, XXVI, (1942),
> p.69.
> Riesgo y Ventura de dos soldados, tr. by J. L. Grucci, in
> Torres-Rioseco, p. 129.
> Mis dos abuelos, tr. by J. L. Grucci, in Amer. Pref., VII,
> winter, 1942, p. 160-161.
> Metal and Rock, in their glances, tr. by R. Humphries, in
> Nation, v.   153, Dec, 27, 1941, p.671.
> Canto negro, one stanza, tr. by Underwood, in West Ind. rev.,
> II, Sept., 1935, p. 41.
> The arrival, idem.
> I've seen Sabas, tr. by H. R. Hays, in Decision I, May, 1941,
> p.50-51.
> Dos niños, (Two children), tr. by H. R. Hays, in APLC, p.249.
> Soldado muerto, (Dead soldier), tr. by Langston Hughes, in
> APLC, p.249.
> Cantaliso en un bar, idem, p. 251.
> Velorio de Papá Montero, (Wake for papa Montero), idem, p.259.
> Visita a un solar, (Visit to a tenement) tr. by Dudley Fitts,
> in APLC, p.255.
> Reveille of dawn, tr. by H. R. Hays, in Decision I, May, 1941,
> p.56.

Heredia y Campuzano, José María, 1803-1839.
> Ode to Niagara, tr. by Thomas Walsh, in Hispanic anthology.
> p.405-414; also Niagara, tr. by William Cullen Bryant, in
> U. S. rev. and lit. gazette, Boston, (1827), I, p.283-286;
> also tr. by Bryant, in Longfellow's Poets and poetry of
> Europe; also in Hills, Odes; also in Pan Amer. bull., v.
> 73, June, 1939, p.349-352; also tr. by Bryant in Selections
> of best Spanish poets; also in Joyas.(This was the first
> Latin America poem published in English translation in the
> United States).
> Hurricane, tr. by Thomas Walsh, in Hispanic anthology; also
> tr. by W.C.Bryant, in Poor's Pan American poems; also tr.

Heredia y Campuzano, José María, 1803-1839. (continued)
    anon. in The talisman I, New York, p.114-114; also in poems
        trans. by W. C. Bryant, New York: Bliss; also tr. by
        Francisco González del Valle, in Poesías de Heredia;
        also in Selections of best Spanish poets; also in Joyas.
    To the sun, tr. in Blackwell, p.486.
    Atlántida, tr. by E. J. Hills, in Hispanic American studies,
        Stanford univ. press, 1929.
    The exile's hymn, tr. by James Kennedy, in North American
        rev. LXVIII, 1849, p.129; also a fragment in González de
        Valle; also fragment in Selections from the Best Spanish
        poets.
    The season of the northers, in North Amer. rev. LXVIII, p.
        129-160; also, in Selections of best Spanish poets;
        also in Joyas; also in Selections from the poems of
        Heredia, with translations in English verse, Habana,
        1844, by James Kennedy; also in González del Valle.
    On the temple mound of Cholula, tr. by Underwood, in West
        Ind. rev., II, April, 1936, p.43.
    Immortality, idem; also in Joyas; also in González del
        Valle.
    To Emilia, tr. by E. C. Hills, in Colorado College pub-
        lications: Language series, v. II, no. 30, 1915; also
        in Hills Hispanic studies, Stanford univ., press, 1929,
        p. 117.
    Ode to the night, tr. by James Kennedy, in Selections of
        best Spanish poets; also in Joyas; also in Modern poets
        and poetry of Spain, by James Kennedy (London: Longmans,
        1852); also in González del Valle.
    Poesy, tr. by James Kennedy, in Selections of best Spanish
        poets; also in Joyas.
    To the star of Venus, tr. by G. F. Vingut, in Selections,
        etc; also in Joyas.
    To my horse, tr. by James Kennedy, in Selections, etc; also
        in González del Valle.
    In a lady's album, tr. by James Kennedy, in Selections, etc.
    On the anniversary of the 4th of July of 1776, tr. by Minna
        C. Smith, in González del Valle.
    In a tempest, tr. literally in Green and Lowenfels, p.668-
        673.

Hernández Miejares, Enrique, 1854-1914.
    The most beautiful, in Blackwell, p.498; also in Pan Amer.
        bull., LXII, Feb. 1928, p.146-157; also The fairest one,
        tr. by A. Coester, in Hispanic anthology, p.538; also,
        The most fair, tr. by Muna Lee in Poetry XXVI, (1925),
        p.128, from Obras completas, Havana: Avisador Comercial
        1915-1916.

Leynaz y Muñoz, Dulce María.
    Opium smoke, tr. by Underwood, in West Ind. rev., III, Sept.,
        1936, p.38.

Lles, Fernando, d. 1883–
    You will become the rhythm of rhapsody, tr. by Underwood,
       in West Ind. rev., III, Nov., 1936, p.32.

Lles, Francisco, 1892–1921.
    Live I, tr. by Underwood, in West Ind. rev., III, Nov., 1936.
       p.31.
    Live II, idem.

López, René, 1884–1909.
    The sculptor, tr. by Thomas Walsh, in Hispanic anthology,
       p.746–747.

López de Briñas, Felipe, 1822–1877.
    Sapphic song, tr. by Gertrudis F. de Vingut, in Selections
       of best Spanish poets; also in Joyas, p.29–32.

Luaces, Joaquín Lorenzo, 1827–1867.
    La salida del cafetal, (On leaving the coffee plantation),
       tr. by Willis Knapp Jones and Read Bain, in World af-
       fairs, Sept., 1942.

Mariño, José Julián, 1853–1895.
    Simple stanzas, tr. by Beatrice Gilman Proske, in Hispanic
       poets, p.218; also in Goldberg, Studies in Spanish Amer.
       lit,; also in C. Charles Fuya... New York, 1898.
    Little rose shoes, first 3 stanzas, tr. by Underwood, in
       West Ind. rev., II, June, 1936, p.34.

Martínez Villena, Rubén, 1899–1934*.
    Allegro Vespertina, tr. by Underwood, in West Ind. rev., III,
       Feb., 1937, p. 36.

Mendive y Daumy, Rafaél María, 1821–1886.
    The virgin smile, tr. by G. F. Vingut, in Joyas, p.33–34;
       also in Selections from the best Spanish poets; also tr.
       by Thomas Walsh, in Hispanic anthology, p.457–460.
    To Pepilla, a fair young girl of Havana, tr. by W. H. Hurl-
       burt, in North Amer. rev., v. 68, (1849), p.152.
    The brook, tr. by Thomas Walsh, in Hispanic anthology, p.
       457–60.
    The breath of love, tr. literally in Green and Lowenfels,
       p.374–377.

Milanés y Fuentes, José Jacinto, 1814–1863.
    To my wife, tr. by W. H. Hurlburt, in North American rev.,
       v. 68, (1849), p. 144.
    Flight of the turtle dove, tr. by Underwood, in West Ind.,
       rev., May, 1936, p.34.

Montagú y Vivero, Guillermo de, 1882–,
    The old man's song, tr. by Underwood, in West Ind., rev.,
       III, Feb., 1937, p.36.

Orgallez, Manuel.
    On the mournful and early death of Isabel Leonora de Mar-
        tiarta, tr. by W. H. Hurlbert, in North Amer. rev., vol.
        68, (1849), p.155.

Palma y Romay, Ramón de, 1812-1860.
    The Cuban dance, in Blackwell, p.494.

Pedroso, Regino, 1896*-
    And we shall inherit the earth, tr. by Underwood, in West
        Ind. rev., I, June, 1935, p.42.
    Mañana (Tomorrow), idem, vol. II, Sept., 1935, p. 40; also
        tr. by Dudley Fitts, in APLC, p.227.
    Five o'clock tea, idem. p.42.
    Conceptos del nuevo estudiante, (Opinions of the new stu-
        dent) tr. by Langston Hughes, in APLC, p.229.

Perés y Perés, Ramón Domingo, 1863-
    The Aeolian harp, tr. by Thomas Walsh, in Hispanic anthology,
        p.570.

Pichardo, Manuél Serafín, 1869-
    Toledo, tr. by Underwood, in West Ind. rev., III, Feb., 1937,
        p.36.

Pierra de Poo.
    Love's mirror, tr. by Thomas Walsh, in Hispanic anthology,
        p.747.

"Plácido" pseud. see Valdés, Gabriel de la Concepción.

Pons, José B.,
    Past hours, tr. by L. E. Elliott, in Pan Amer. mag., XXXIV,
        April, 1922, p.23, (with Spanish on opposite page).

Poveda, José Manuel, 1888-1926.
    The manuscript, tr. by Thomas Walsh, in Hispanic anthology,
        p.742.
    Songs of the creative voice, idem.
    Prayer, tr. by Underwood, in West Ind. rev., III, Feb., 1937,
        p.49.
    Withdrawal, tr. by Muna Lee, in Poetry XXVI, 1925, p.129,
        from Versos precursores, (Manzanillo, Cuba: El Arte, 1917).

Rodríguez Embil, Luis, 1876-
    Farewell to Austria, tr. by Underwood, in West Ind. rev.,
        VI, Nov., 1939, p.30.

Salas Aloma, Mariblanca.
    I-criminal, tr. by Underwood, in West Ind. rev., III,
        Sept., 1936, p.38.

Salom, Diwaldo, 1879-
    I know not, tr. by Muna Lee, in Poetry, XXVI, (1925), p.129.

Sansores Pren, Rosario ("Crisantema").
  Sonnet, tr. by Underwood, in West Ind. rev., III, Sept.,
    1936, p.38.

Sarrett, Cecilio V.
  Tatuaje, tr. by Underwood, in West Ind. rev., IV, July,
    1938, p.27.

Sellén, Antonio, 1840-1888.
  The broken branch, tr. by Thomas Walsh, in Hispanic antho-
    logy, p.519.

Tallet, José Zacarías, 1893-
  La rhumba, tr. by J. L. Grucci, in Torres-Rioseco, p.127.

Tejeda, Diego Vicente, 1848-1903.
  Juliet, tr. by Thomas Walsh, in Hispanic anthology, p.521-
    523.
  To thee, idem.

Tolón, Miguel Teurbe, 1820-1858.
  Last song of exile, tr. by author, in Joyas; also in Se-
    lections from best Spanish poets.
  Mother's love, tr. by Tolón, idem.

Trujillo Arrendondo, Rosa, (Rosa Té).
  Kings of the East, tr. by Underwood, in West Ind. rev.,
    III, Sept., 1936, p.38.

Uhrbach, Carlos Pío, 1872-1897.
  Silver rhyme, tr. by Underwood, in West Ind. rev., III, Nov.
    1936, p.32.

Uhrbach, Federico, 1873-
  Retrogression, tr. by Underwood, in West Ind., rev.,III,
    Nov., 1936, p.33.

Valdés, Gabriel de la Concepción, ("Plácido") 1809-1844.
  Prayer to God, tr. by Thomas Walsh, in Hispanic anthology,
    p.431-433; also in Catholic anthology, p.256; also tr.
    by W. H. Hurlburt, in North American rev., no.68,(1849),
    p.152; also in Selections of best Spanish poets; also in
    Joyas; also reported published in 1844, in several anti-
    slavery magazines.
  Prayer, tr. by María W. Chapman, in The Liberty bell, p.67-
    71.
  Sonnet to Greece, tr. by Dr. Wurdeman, London Quarterly rev.,
    Jan., 1848; also in North Amer. rev., vol.68, (1849),
    p.146-147.
  Hymn to liberty, tr. anon, in North Amer. rev., v. 68, (1849),
    p.129-160; attributed to anon. translator in New York
    Tribune, and also appearing in 1844 in several anti-slavery
    publications.
  Farewell to my mother, tr. by Vingut, in Selections of best
    Spanish poets; also in Joyas; also in North Amer. rev.,
    v. 68, (1849), p.146.

Valdés, Gabriel de la Concepción, ("Plácido") 1809-1844. (cont.)
  The crucifixion, tr. by E. W. Underhill, in West Ind. rev.,
    II, May, 1936, p.33-34.
  Excerpts in Inter-Amer., VIII, Dec., 1924, p.160-165.

Valdés Mendoza, Mercedes, 1822-1896.
  Hope, excerpt tr. by Underwood, in West Ind. rev., III,
    Sept., 1936, p.39.

Valle, Margarita del,
  Bird song, tr. by Underwood, in West Ind. rev., III, Sept,
    1936, p.39.

Villar Buceta, María, 1898-
  Twilight and autumn, tr. by Underwood, in West Ind. rev.,
    III, Sept., 1936, p.39.

Villarronda, Guillermo, 1912-
  Tengo miedo perderte, tr. by Underwood, in West Ind. rev.,
    IV, July, 1938, p.27.

Zenea, Juan Clemente ("Adolfo de la Azucena") 1831-1871.
  In days of slavery, tr. by Underwood, in West Ind. rev.,
    II, May, 1936, p.34.

POETRY - DOMINICAN REPUBLIC

Bazil, Osvaldo.
  Idyl, tr. by Muna Lee, in Pan Amer. bull. July, 1925; also,
    in Poetry, XXVI, (1925), p.147.

Bermúdez, Federico.
  The washerwoman, tr. by Underwood, in West Ind. rev., II,
    Feb., 1930, p.34.

Fiallo, Fabio, 1865-
  Seduction, tr. by Underwood, in West Ind. rev., III, March,
    1936, p.3.
  Hebe, idem.
  Dear star, idem. also by Blackwell, idem, May, 1938, p.43.
  Golgotha Rosa, idem, II, Feb., 1936, p.35.
  Full moon, idem; also tr. by Muna Lee, in Poetry, XXVI,
    (1925), p.148.
  Would I were thy mirror, in Blackwell, p.502.
  The roses of my rose tree, idem.
  Broken wings, idem, p.506.
  The bells ring Gloria, idem; also tr. by Blackwell, in
    West Ind. rev., III, Dec., 1936, p.43.
  Nostalgia, tr. by Muna Lee, in Hispanic anthology, p.591.
  Little girl in heaven, tr. by Margaret B. Hurley (Trujillo
    City: La Opinion, 1937).
  In her track, tr. by Blackwell, in West Ind. rev., IV, April,
    1938, p.30.
  The mystery, tr. by Muna Lee, idem, IV, May, 1938, p.21.

Fiallo, Fabio, 1865- (continued)
    Three gifts, tr. by Blackwell, idem., IV, May,1938, p.43.
    The arrow, tr. by Muna Lee, idem, V, April, 1939, p.18.

Guerrero, Miguel. A.
    The old convent, tr. by Underwood, in West Ind. rev., II,
        Feb., 1936, p.34.

Henríquez Ureña, Max, 1885-
    Provincial idyll, tr. by Underwood, in West Ind. rev., II,
        Jan., 1936, p.35.

Herrera, Manuel de J.
    The fountain, tr. by Underwood, in West Ind. rev., II,
        Feb., 1936, p.34.

Mejía, Juan Tomás.
    To a beautiful woman, tr. by Underwood, in West Ind. rev.,
        II, Feb., 1936, p.34.

Ovando, Leonor de (late 16th century).
    Sonnet, tr. by J. C. Bardin, in Pan Amer. bull., LXXIV,
        Dec., 1940, p.828.

Pellerano Castro, Arturo B., 1865-1916.
    Americana, tr. by Underwood, in West Ind. rev., II, Feb.,
        1936, p.33.

Pérez, José Joaquín, 1845-1900.
    Home coming, tr. by Underwood, in West Ind. rev., II, Feb.,
        1936, p.33.

Thaly, Daniel, 1880-
    Sonnet, tr. in West Ind. rev., II, Oct., 1935, p.36,
    To the Antilles, idem.
    Palms, idem.
    Romantic dream, idem.
    Melopée Africaine, idem., III, Oct., 1936, p.48.
    Chant de la nostalgia, idem.
    Hurricanes, idem, III, Feb., 1937, p.31.
    Street cries of Martinique and Dominica, idem, III, April,
        1937, p. 33.
    Poetic legends of Dominica, idem, III, May,1937, p.35.
    My West Indian home, idem, IV, July, 1940, p.36-37.
    The West Indies before Columbus, idem.

Ureña de Henríquez, Salomé, 1850-1897.
    The glory of progress, in Blackwell, p.508.
    The bird in the nest, idem, p.514.
    The revolution and culture in Mexico, tr. anon. in Inter-
        Amer., VIII, 1925, p.387-394.
    Coming of winter, tr. in West Ind. rev., II, Jan., 1936,
        p.34.

Vizardi, Ligio.
    The road, tr. in West Ind. rev., II, March, 1936, p.3.
    Dolor antiguo, _idem_, II, Feb., 1936, p.35.

POETRY -- ECUADOR

Borja, Francisco.
    The dead man, tr. by Lloyd Mallan, in Poetry, v.   LXII
        (May 1943), p.70.

Carrera Andrade, Jorge, 1903-.
    Islas sin nombre, tr. by Lloyd Mallan, in Fantasy, no.26,
        1942, p.57-59; also in Three Spanish Amer. poets.
    Soledad y Gaviota, (Gull and solitude), _idem_.
    Elegía a Abraham Valdelomar, tr. by Lloyd Mallan, _idem_.
    Cantón sin nombre, (Nameless neighborhood), _idem_.
    Filosofía del humo (Philosophy of smoke), tr. by Lloyd
        Mallan, in Three Spanish Amer. poets; also in Amer.
        Pref. VII, winter, 1941-42, p.145-146.
    Historia contemporánea, (Contemporary history), _idem_.
    Huésped, (The guest), tr. by Lloyd Mallan, in Three
        Spanish Amer. poets; also tr. by Muna Lee, in APLC,p.11.
    La segunda vida de mi madre, _idem_.
    2° 48' latitude sur, tr. by Lloyd Mallan, in Three Spanish
        Amer. poets.
    Edición de la tarde, _idem_.
    El extranjero, _idem_.
    Nueva York de noche, _idem_.
    Guayaquil, _idem_.
    Paita, _idem_.
    La Habana, _idem_.
    Nassau, _idem_.
    St. Georges, _idem_.
    Vigo, _idem_.
    La Coruna, _idem_.
    Santander, _idem_.
    Barcelona, _idem_.
    La Pallice, _idem_.
    Soledad de las ciudades, _idem_.
    III clase, _idem_.
    Color de La Habana, _idem_.
    Huelga, _idem_.
    Evasión del lunes, _idem_.
    Polvo, cadáver de tiempo, _idem_.
    Viento Nordeste, _idem_.
    2 from Zona Minada, _idem_.
    3, _idem_.
    Nada nos pertenece, _idem_.
    Inventario de mis únicos bienes, _idem_.
    Little girl of Panama, tr. by E. W. Underwood, in West Ind.
        rev., IV, Oct., 1937, p.24.
    Curaçao, _idem_.
    Dawn beside the Island of Trinidad, _idem_.
    This earth is built upon our deaths, tr. by Lloyd Mallan,
        in Amer. Pref. VII, winter,1941-42, p.145-46.

Carrera Andrade, Jorge, 1903- (continued).
    Ballot for green, tr. by Muna Lee, in Poetry, LIX, (1942),
        p.386.
    Movements of nature, _idem_.
    Clock, _idem_.
    Sierra, tr. by Muna Lee, in APLC, p.3.
    Domingo, (Sunday) _idem_, p.5.
    Corte de Cebada, (Reaping the Barley), _idem_, p. 7.
    Ha llovido por la noche, (It rained in the night) _idem_,p.9.
    Vocación del espejo, (Vocation of the mirror), _idem_,p.11.
    La campanada de la una, (The stroke of one), _idem_, p.13.
    Klare von Reuter, _idem_, p.15.
    La vida perfecta, (Perfect life), tr. by Dudley Fitts, in
        APLC, p.7.
    Primavera & cía, (Spring and Co.,) tr. by Richard O'Connell,
        in APLC, p.3.
    Mal humor, (Ill humor), tr. by Donald Walsh, in APLC, p.13,
    Biografía para uso de los pájaros, _idem_, p.19,
    Oda al puente de Oakland bay, tr. by Eleanor L. Trumbull,
        (Stanford Univ. press, 1941).

Carrión, Alejandro, 1915-
    Buen año, (A good year), tr. by Dudley Fitts, in APLC, p.289.

Cordero, Romero, _see_, Romero y Cordero, Remigio.

Escudero, Gonzalo, 1903-.
    Los dolmenes, tr. by Dudley Fitts, in APLC, p.355.
    Dios, _idem_, p.355.
    Zoo, tr. by Richard O'Connell, in APLC, p.357; also tr. by
        Mary and C. V. Wicker, in Amer. Pref., winter 1941-1942.
    Overtones, tr. by Muna Lee, in Poetry, XXVI, (1925), p.131.

Lasso, Ignacio.
    Junto al Rio, tr. by J. L. Grucci, in New Mexico quarterly,
        Aug., 1941, from Escafandra, Quito, Elan, 1934 .

León, Miguel Angel, 1900-
    El agua, (Water), tr. by Mary and C. V. Wicker, in Fantasy,
        XXVI, (1942), p.53.
    Cataclysm, tr. by Mary and C. V. Wicker, in Amer. Pref.,
        VII, winter, 1942, p.154.

Olmedo, José Joaquín, 1790-1847.
    The tree, in Blackwell, p.464; also in Hills, Odes.
    To General Flores, tr. by A. B. Poor, in Pan Amer. poems.

Romero y Cordero, Remigio.
    Música de América, tr. by Mary and C. V. Wicker, in Amer.
        Pref., winter, 1941.

Sánchez, Luis Aníbal.
    Brother dog, tr. by Muna Lee, in Catholic anthology, p.431;
        also in Poetry, XXVI, (1925), p.130.

Silva, Medardo Angel, 1899-1921.
    Detalle Nocturno (Nocturnal detail), tr. by Mary and C. V.
      Wicker, in Fantasy, no. XXVI, 1942, p.55.

POETRY - EL SALVADOR

González y Contreras, Gilberto, 1904-
    Calor (Heat), tr. by Dudley Fitts, in APLC, p.176.
    Iglesia, (Church), idem, p.176.

Lars, Claudia (Carmen Brannon Beers), 1903-
    Cara y Cruz (Heads and Tails), tr. by Donald Walsh, in APLC.
      p.179.
    Dibujo de una mujer que llega, (Sketch of the frontier woman).
      idem, p.179.

POETRY - GUATEMALA

Arévalo Martínez, Rafael, 1884-
    Human wolves, in Blackwell, p.474-476.
    My sister, idem.
    The contemporary Sancho Panza, tr. by Thomas Walsh, in His-
      panic anthology, p.731-734.
    Las imposibles, selections, tr. idem.
    The earrings, tr. anon, in Inter--Amer. I, (1917), p.76.
    Ropa limpia (Clean clothes), tr. by Muna Lee, in APLC, p.485.
    Entrégate por entero, (Give yourself wholly), idem, p.485.
    Our lady of the afflicted, in Living age, vol.321, (1924),
      p.801.
    The panther man, idem, p. 1005.

Asturias, Miguel Angel, 1899-
    Los indios bajan de Mixco (The indians come down from
      Mixco), tr. by Donald Walsh, in APLC, p.141.

Cardoza y Aragón, Luis, 1902-
    Romance de Federico García Lorca, (Ballad of Federico García
      Lorca), tr. by Donald Walsh, in APLC, p.523.

POETRY - HAITI

Borno, Louis, 1865-1942.
    Moonlight, tr. by Underwood, in West Ind. rev., III, May,
      1937, p.34; also in Underwood, Poets of Haiti.

Brierre, John, 1910-
    Black Ghislaine, tr. by Underwood, in West Ind. rev., II,
      Dec., 1935, p.34.
    By this black shore, idem.

Brouard, Carl.
    Sultana, tr. by Underwood, in West Ind. rev., II, Dec.,
      1935, p.35. (with the Spanish).

Casseús, Mauricio A., 1907-
    Plantation, tr. from the French, by Underwood, in Mexican
      life, Aug., 1936, p.12.

Casseús, Mauricio A., 1907- (continued)
    Linés, tr. by Underwood, in Mexican life, Aug. 1934, p.20.
    Rumba, tr. by Underwood, in West Ind. rev., II, Dec., 1935,
        p.34.

Hippolyte, Domique.
    Musa, tr. by Underwood, in West Ind. rev., II, Dec., 1935,
        p.37.

Legendre, Georges.
    Jazz, tr. by Underwood, in West Ind. rev., II, Dec., 1935,
        p.36, (with the original).

Le-Reve-Fort, Abdel Saadi.
    Two Aquarelles of the Haitian sea, tr. by Underwood, in
        West Ind. rev., VI, Oct., 1939, p.29.

Magloire-Fils, Clement, 1912-.
    My glass, tr. by Underwood, in West Ind. rev., II, Dec.,
        1935, p.34.

Mayard, Pierre.
    Lord, Lord, tr. by Underwood, in West Ind. rev., II, Dec.,
        1935, p.36 (with the original).

Morpeau, Pierre Moraviah.
    Beloved, tr. by Underwood, in West Ind. rev., II, Dec.,
        1935, p.37.

Roumain, Jacques, 1906-
    Lorsque bat le tan-tan, (When the tom-tom beats), tr. by
        Langston Hughes, in APLC, p.279.
    Guinée (Guinea), idem, p.279.; also tr. by L. C. Kaplan,
        in Poetry, vol.LXII,(May, 1943), p.61.

Roumer, Emile, 1903-.
    Evening in Haiti, tr. by Underwood, in West Ind. rev., II,
        Dec., 1935, p.35.
    Have a care, idem.
    Declaration paysanne, (The peasant declares his love), tr.
        by John Peale Bishop, in APLC, p.489.

Vaval, Duraciné, 1879-
    Tropic noon, tr. by Underwood, in Mexican life, X, Nov.,
        1934, p.13.
    Les mangos, (The mangoes), tr. by Donald Walsh, in APLC,
        p.447.

Vieux, Damocles, 1876-
    Furcy, tr. by Underwood, in West Ind. rev., II, Nov.,
        Dec., 1935, p.33-36, includes quotations from Casseús,
        Brierre, Brouard, Roumer, Mayard, Moraviah, Morpeau,
        and Hippolyte.

POETRY - HONDURAS

Guillen Zelaya, Alfonso, 1888-
 Lord, I ask a garden, tr. by Thomas Walsh, in Hispanic an-
   thology, p.151.
 Dios te haya perdonado (God have you in his care), tr. by
   E. M. Shores, in Pan Amer. mag., XXVII, (1918), p.206,
 See Others, Chicago, Latin American number, for other trans-
   lations.

Martínez Galindo, Arturo.
 Todo fué tan sencillo (It was all so matter of fact), tr.
   by Donald Walsh, in APLC, p.491.

Membreño, Alberto, 1859-
 Obituary, tr. anon, in Hispania, IV, (1921), p.195.

Molina, Juan Ramón, 1875-1908.
 Autobiography: Una muerta; para un apostol; Ojos de los
   niños, and En la alta noche; tr. by J. W. Chaney,
   in Colorado college. Publication language series, II,
   no.35, 1921.

Reyes, María Francisca, 1835-
 Two poems, tr. in prose by Mariana de Caceres, in "Woman
   of the America", in Pan Amer. bull., LXXIV, p.502.

Suasnavar, Constantino (also sometimes classed as Colombian)
   1912-.
 Números 26, 9, 30, 21, 17, y 43, (Numbers), tr. by Muna
   Lee, and Dudley Fitts, in APLC, pp.221-5.

Turcios, Froilán, 1875-1943
 Blue eyes, in Blackwell, p.478.
 The parricide, tr. anon, in Inter-Amer., I, (1917), p.12-13.

Valle, Rafaél Heliodoro, 1891-
 El ánfora sedienta (Thirsting amphora), tr. by Muna Lee,
   in APLC, p.483.

Zepeda, Jorge Federico, 1883-1932.
 The pine, tr. by A. S. Blackwell, in Christian science monitor, March,22, 1926.

POETRY - MARTINIQUE

Achard, Marcel, 1899-
 The Muse Pérégrine, tr. by Underwood, in Negro poets of
   Martinique, in West Ind. rev., II, Oct., 1935, p.35-36.

POETRY - MEXICO

Acuña, Manuel, 1849-1873.
 To the martyred poet, Juan Díaz Covarrubías, in Blackwell,

Acuña, Manuel, 1849–1873. (continued)
    p. 154; also tr. literally in Green and Lowenfels;
    also in New York Call, Oct. 21, 1917; reprinted in
    Stratford journal, III, Sept., 1918, p. 118.
    Nocturn (To Rosario), in Anthology of Mex. poets, p.
    291., also tr. literally in Green and Lowenfels, p. 80;
    also in Inter-Amer. I, (1918), p. 126–128, with other
    excerpts.
    Ode (To the memory of Gertrudis Gómez de Avellaneda), tr.
    by Underwood, in Anthology of Mex. poets, p. 295;
    also in West Ind. rev., II, May, 1936, p. 34.
    Sonnet, to Manuel Domínguez, in Green and Lowenfels, p. 66–
    69.
    A que más gloria, idem.
    Tears, tr. literally in idem, p. 80–85.
    To the Philharmonic society, idem.
    15th of September, idem.
    Before a corpse, idem.
    Fifth of May, idem.
    Farewell to ___, idem.
    Then and now, idem.
    The illusion of existence, idem.
    Farewell to Mexico, idem.
    Hope, idem.
    To the Mexican nightingale, idem.
    To the fatherland, idem, 175.
    Withered pages, tr. by Goldberg, in Mexican poetry, p.
    16–17.

Alarcón, Juan Ruiz de, see, Ruiz de Alarcón, Juan.

Alpuche, Wenceslao, 1804–1841.
    Fame, in Anthology of Mexican poets, p. 230.

Altamirano, Ignacio M., 1834–1893.
    To Atroyac, in Anthology of Mexican poets, p. 253.

Altolaguirre, Manuel.
    My brother Luis, tr. by Stephen Spender, in Mexican life,
    Dec., 1937, p.18.

Argüellos Bringas, Roberto, 1875–1915.
    Well, in Anthology of Mexican poets, p. 109.

Barrera, Carlos, 1888–
    Longing, in Anthology of Mexican poets, p. 129.

Bolaños Cacho, Miguel, 1868–1928.
    In absence, tr. by A. S. Blackwell, in Revista ilustrada,
    (El Paso, Texas), Nov.-Dic., 1922.

Bonner y Robinson, Leighton.
    An Aztec girl sings, in Mexican life, Nov., 1936, p.22.
    Spring in Coyoacan, idem, Jan., 1939, p. 12.
    Sonnet for the New Year, idem, XII, Jan., 1936, p. 28.
    Barra de Teco, idem. XV, April, 1939, p. 19.
    Requital, idem. IX, March, 1933, p. 12.
    Retrato, idem., Aug., 1933, p. 12.

Bosques, Gilberto.
    Country drink shop, tr. by Underwood, in Mexican life, IX,
        June, 1933, p. 18.

Bustillo, José M., 1866-1899.
    The Carpenter, in Anthology of Mexican poets, p.327.

Cabrera, Rafaél, 1884-
    Rafaél, in Blackwell, p. 136.
    Nihil, in Blackwell, p. 130; also tr. in Blackwell, in Las
        Novedades, March 18, 1918; also in Goldberg, Mexican
        poetry, p.62-64; also tr. by Blackwell, in Stratford
        journal, V, Aug., 1919, p.59-66.
    Sin palabras, (Without words), tr. in Blackwell, p. 134;
        also in Pan Amer. mag., XXVI, Sept., 1918, p.256; also
        in Stratford journal, V, Aug., 1919, p.59-66.
    Song of Rosalia, tr. by Blackwell, in Springfield Republi-
        can, Aug. 10, 1917; also in Stratford journal, V, Aug.,
        1919, p. 59-66.
    Evening light, in Stratford journal, V, Aug., 1919, p.59-66.
    In the forest, idem.
    To Gloria, idem.

Calderón, Fernando, 1809-1845.
    To a faded rose, in Anthology of Mex. poets, p.233.
    The soldier of liberty, tr. literally, in Green and
        Lowenfels, p. 222-251.
    The tyrant's dream, idem.
    A memory, idem.
    The hereafter, idem.
    To Hidalgo, idem.

Camarillo y Roa de Pereyra, María Enriqueta, 1875-
    The forgotten path, in Anthology of Mex. poets, p. 111.
    To a shadow, idem, p. 113.
    Hail, idem, p. 114.
    The scissors grinder, idem, p. 115.
    Landscape, idem, p. 112; also tr. by Jean R. Longland, in
        Hispanic poets, p. 235.
    Sad song, in Blackwell, p. 162; also, tr. by Isaac Goldberg,
        in Mexican poetry, p.61.

Campobello, Nellie, ("Francisca"), 1909-
    Yo, (I), tr. by Langston Hughes, in APLC, p.213.
    Detrás de ti, (After you), idem, p.215.
    Sobre arena (On sand), idem, p. 217.
    Ruta (Route), idem, p. 219.

Campos, Rubén M., 1876-1930.
　　Tropic nocturn, in Anthology of Mex. poets, p.105-06.

Carpio, Manuel, 1791-1860.
　　To the river Cosamaloapan, in Anthology of Mex. poets, p.
　　　　228; also in Green and Lowenfels, p. 180-220.
　　Mexico, tr. literally in Green and Lowenfels, p.180-220.
　　Mexico, in 1847; idem.
　　Mount Popocatépetl, idem.

Casasús, Joaquín Demetrio, 1858-1916.
　　To an unknown woman, in Anthology of Mex. poets, p.136.

Chávez, Ezequiel A., 1868-
　　Sor Juana de la Cruz, a prose miniature, in Anthology of
　　　　Mex. poets, p. 218.

Colín, Eduardo, 1880-.
　　After the rain, in Anthology of Mex. poets, p. 120.

Contreras, Felipe T., 1864-
　　The middle age, in Anthology of Mex. poets, p.321.

Cosmes, Francisco G., 1850-1907.
　　Remember, in Anthology of Mex. poets, p. 306.

Cruz, Juana Inés de la, see Juana Inés de la Cruz.

Cuenca, Agustín F., 1850-1884.
　　Prismatic lights, in Blackwell, p. 162-164; also in Gold-
　　　　berg, Mexican poetry, p. 17-18; also, tr. by Blackwell
　　　　in Springfield Republican, Mar. 10 and 21, 1809; also
　　　　in Pan Amer. mag., XVIII, Sept., 1914, p. 29.
　　On the banks of the Atroyac, in Anthology of Mex. poets,
　　　　p. 308.
　　To Ch——, tr. by A. B. Poor, in Pan Amer. poems.

Dávalos, Balbino, (1836-1870)
　　The poet, in Blackwell, p. 168.
　　My glory, tr. by Thomas Walsh, in Hispanic anthology, p.
　　　　635-636; also in Goldberg, Mexican poetry, p.54.
　　Then, in Anthology of Mex. poets, p. 326.

Delgado, Juan B., 1868-1929.
　　Old sea wolf, in Blackwell, p. 172.
　　La Cañada, in Anthology of Mex. poets, p.137.

Delgado, Rafaél, 1853-1914.
　　In the mountains, in Anthology of Mex. poets, p. 138.

Díaz Covarrubías, Juan, 1837-1859.
　　Selections, in Anthology of Mex. poets, p.260-261.

Díaz Mirón, Manuel, 1821-1894.
    Ill-omened gift, tr. by A. S. Blackwell, in Springfield
        Republican, Aug. 8, 1909.
    Orizaba, in Anthology of Mex. poets, p. 303.

Díaz Mirón, Salvador, 1853-1928.
    Copo de nieve (Snow-flake) in Blackwell, p.118; also in
        Mexican review, June, 1918; also in Pan Amer. mag.,
        vol. 31, 1920, p. 190; also in Goldberg, Studies in
        American lit., p. 64-71; also in Stratford journal,III,
        Aug., 1918. p.73; also in Mexican life, III, June, 1927,
        p. 95; also in Goldberg, Mexican poetry, p. 18.
    A Piedad (To pity), in Blackwell; also in Pan Amer. mag.,
        vol.27, Sept., 1918, p.60; also in Goldberg, Mexican
        poetry, p. 18-19.
    The cloud, in Blackwell, p. 119.
    Envy, in Blackwell, p. 122; also in Goldberg, Studies in
        Spanish American lit., p. 71.
    The vision, tr. by Alice Jane McVan, in Hispanic poets, p.
        222.
    Green eyes, in Anthology of Mex. poets, p.35.
    The deserter, idem., p.37.
    Men of genius, idem. p.38.
    The dead man, tr. by Muna Lee, in Poetry, XXVI, (1925), p.133.

Enriqueta, María, see Camarillo y Roa de Pereyra, María Enriqueta.

Esteva, Adalberto A., 1863-1914.
    The sea by Vera Cruz, in Anthology of Mex. poets, p.318.
    On the shore (Vera Cruz), idem.
    At the ball, idem. p. 319.
    Tropic night, idem. p. 317; also "Tropic night by Vera Cruz"
        in West Ind. rev., II, Oct., 1935, p. 57; also idem. v.
        VI, May, 1940, p. 28,

Estrada, Genaro, 1887-1937.
    The colonial city; Mexico, tr. in Pan Amer. Bull., v. 68, p. 219-
        221; also in Anthology of Mex. poets, p. 302.
    Back to the sea; in Anthology of Mex. poets, p. 141.
    The treasure, a prose miniature, idem. p.22.
    Cancioncilla en el aire (Song in the air), tr. by Donald
        Walsh, in APLC, p. 433,
    Queja del perdido amor (Lament for lost love), idem. p.435.
    Paráfrasis de Horacio, (Paraphrase of Horace), idem, p.437.

Fernández de Lizardi, José Joaquín, ca. 1774-1827.
    Epitaph to the liberty of America, in Anthology of Mex. Poets,
        p. 227.

Fernández Granados, Enrique, 1867-1920.
    Mirtos (Wine of Lesbos), in Anthology of Mex. poets, p.43.
    Remembrance, in Blackwell, p.128.
    To some violets, idem. p.126; also tr. by A. S. Blackwell,
        in Goldberg, Mexican poetry, p.32-33.

Flores, Manuel María, 1840-1885.
    My dream, in Blackwell, p. 136-40; also in Goldberg,
       Mexican poetry, p. 14-16.
    Jasmine, tr. by Edna Underwood, in Anthology of Mexican
       poets, p.272.
    Ode to the fatherland, idem, p.273.

"Francisca", see Campobello, Nellie.

Frías, José Dolores, 1891-
    Sonata of Beethoven, in Anthology of Mexican poets, p.143,
       from Versos escogidos, (Mexico, 1933).

Gómez Vergara, Joaquín, d. 1894.
    My mountains, in Blackwell, p.176-180; also in Christian
       science monitor, March 24, 1927.

González Guerrero, Francisco.
    Apparition, in Anthology of Mexican poets, p.145.
    Fountain, idem, p. 146.

González Martínez, Enrique, 1871-
    Like brother and sister, tr. by A. S. Blackwell, in Gold-
       berg, Studies in Spanish American lit., also in Goldberg,
       Mexican poetry, p. 55; also in Blackwell, p. 106.
    A hidden spring, tr. in Goldberg, Studies in Spanish Amer.
       lit.; also in Blackwell, p. 104.
    To a stone by the wayside; idem.
    The sower of stars; idem; also tr. by Blackwell, in Pan
       Amer. bull., March, 1927; also in Three poems by González
       Martínez; (Pan Amer. culture pamphlet, no.9, Pan Amer.
       Union, 1927).
    The castle, tr. in Goldberg, Studies in Spanish Amer. lit.
    Throttle the swan, tr. by Thomas Walsh, in Hispanic antho-
       logy, p. 640; also: "Tuércele el Cuello al Cisne" (Wring
       the neck of the swan), in Modernist trend; also tr. by
       Muna Lee in Poetry XXVI (1925), p. 134; also tr. by John
       Beale Bishop in APLC, p. IX; also in Torres Rioseco, p. 111.
    Y pienso que la vida (Life escapes me), in Modernist trend.
    Mañana los poetas (Tomorrow poets will sing), idem.
    La piedad que pasa (Pity that passes), idem.
    Esta tarde he salido al campo (Afternoon in the country),
       idem.
    Canción de las sirenas (Siren's song), tr. by Salomón de la
       Selva, in Pan Amer. mag., XXVII, (1918), p.36-39.
    En el lloro del agua (The weeping water), tr. by Hipólito
       Mattonel, idem.
    La plegaria de la roca estéril (Prayer of the barren rock),
       tr. by J. P. Rice, idem., also tr. in Blackwell, p. 102;
       also tr. in Christian Register, June 27, 1918; also tr.
       by Blackwell, in Pan Amer. bull., March, 1927.
    La hora (The hour), tr. by J. Crowhurst-Rand, in Pan Amer.
       mag., XXVII, (1918), p. 158.

González Martínez, Enrique, 1871- (continued)
    The grief of autumn, in Anthology of Mex. poets, p.46.
    The captive, idem.
    Homesick memory, idem, p.51.
    Change, idem, p.54.
    The ballad of mad fortune, idem, p.55.
    Noli me tangere, idem, p.56.
    House with two doors, idem, p.48; also in West Ind. rev.,
        V, Aug., 1939, p.30.
    Useless days, idem.
    My grief is a rosebush always in flower, idem.
    The voice of long ago, idem.
    Three birds, in Blackwell, p. 110.
    To the spirit of the tree, idem ; also in Mex. Rev.,
        June, 1918.
    Do you remember? in Blackwell, p. 114.
    To the traveller, idem, p. 116.
    The dead rebel, idem.
    In a stately garden; tr. by Elizabeth du Gué Trapier, in
        Hispanic poets, p. 233.
    For one unjustly slain, tr. by Blackwell, in Pan Amer. bull.,
        March, 1927.

González Rojo, Enrique, 1899-
    The midday sea, in Anthology of Mex. poets, p.98.
    Stones, idem, p.100.
    Mujer desnuda (The naked woman), idem, p. 99; also tr. by
        J. L. Grucci. in New Mexico quarterly, Aug., 1941.
    Elegías Romanas, tr. by Lloyd Mallan, in Amer. Pref., win-
        ter, 1941-2.

Gorostiza, José, 1901*-
    Seashore, in Anthology of Mex. poets, p.168.
    Autumn, idem, p. 170.
    Twilight, idem, p. 171.
    Acuario (The aquarium), idem, p. 167; also tr. by Donald
        Walsh, in APLC, p.23.
    Una pobre conciencia, (A poor little conscience), tr. by
        Donald Walsh, in APLC, p.25.
    Mujeres (Women), idem, p. 25.

Gutiérrez Nájera, Manuel, 1859-1895.
    Ondas muertas (Dead waves), tr. by Alice S. Blackwell, in
        Goldberg, Studies in Spanish Amer. lit.; also in New
        York Call, June, 29, 1914; also in Blackwell, p. 2; also
        in Mexican rev., June, 1918; also in Poet lore, XXX, 1919,
        p.82-93; also in Goldberg, Mexican poetry, p.24.
    Mariposas (Butterflies), tr. by Blackwell, in Goldberg, Stu-
        dies in Spanish American lit; also in Goldberg, Mexican
        poetry, p. 24-32; also in Las Novedades, Oct. 22, 1916;
        also tr. by Underwood in Anthology of Mex. poets, p.22;
        also in Poet lore, XXX, 1919, p.82-93; also in West Ind.
        rev., V, Sept., 1939, p. 25.

Gutiérrez Nájera, Manuel, 1859-1895. (continued)
　　In the depths of night, tr. by Thomas Walsh, in Catholic
　　　　anthology, p.326; also in Hispanic anthology, p.551-558.
　　Beyond the mountains; tr. by Blackwell in Las Novedades,
　　　　Oct. 29, 1916; also in Poet lore, XXX, 1919, p.82-93.
　　To Salvador Díaz Mirón, in Anthology of Mex. poets, p. 12.
　　Sometime, idem, p. 13.
　　Calicot, idem. p. 16.
　　Para el corpiño, idem, p. 20.
　　Sad night, idem, p.24.
　　For a menu, idem, p. 19; also in West Ind. rev., V, Sept.,
　　　　1939, p.25.
　　The dutchess' job, idem.
　　Non omnis moriar, idem.
　　Shubert's serenade, tr. by Wendell, in Hispanic poets, p.
　　　　223-224; also tr. by Underwood, in Anthology of Mex. poets,
　　　　p.7.
　　A wish, tr. by Blackwell, in Poet lore, XXX, 1919, p.82-93.
　　To an unknown goddess, idem ; also in Blackwell, p.16; also
　　　　in Stratford journal, III, Aug., 1918, p.73.
　　Pax Animae, in Blackwell, p. 24; also tr. by Blackwell, in
　　　　Las Novedades, June 21, 1917.
　　To the wife of the Corregidor; in Blackwell, p. 30; also
　　　　tr. by Blackwell, in Revista universal, Sept., 1918.
　　White, tr. by Blackwell, in Hispanic anthology, p.551-
　　　　558; also in Mexican rev., Sept.-Oct., 1918; also in
　　　　Goldberg, Mexican poetry, p.24-32.
　　Whiteness, tr. by Blackwell, in Poet lore, XXX, (1919) p.
　　　　82-93; also in Blackwell, p. 12.
　　Epherma, idem; also in Blackwell, in Las Novedades, April
　　　　30, 1913.
　　Souls and birds, tr. by Blackwell, p. 10.
　　Longing, idem. p. 22.
　　In the country, idem,; also in Las Novedades, Sept. 16,1915.
　　Out of doors, tr. by Thomas Walsh, in Hispanic anthology, p.
　　　　551-558.
　　When I die, tr. by Alice Jane McVan, in Hispanic poets, p.
　　　　223-224.
　　The resurrection, tr. by Blackwell, in Springfield Republi-
　　　　can, May, 7, 1916.
　　To Benjamín Boleros, tr. by Blackwell, in Poet lore, XXX,
　　　　(1919), p. 82-93.

Icaza, Francisco A. de, 1863-1925.
　　La canción del camino (Song of the way), in Blackwell, p.128;
　　　　also in Pan Amer. mag., XXXII, 1921, p.208.
　　Landscape colours, tr. by Alice Jane McVan, in Hispanic poets,
　　　　p.228.
　　Landscape of the sun, in Anthology of Mex. poets, p.89.
　　Eastern music, idem, p.90.
　　A village of Andalucia, idem, p.88; also in West Ind. rev.,
　　　　VI, May, 1940, p.28.
　　El pobrecito ciego (Poor blind man), in Anthology of Mex.
　　　　poets, p. 90; also Blind boy, tr. by Mary and C. V. Wicker,
　　　　in Modern verse, Oct. 1941.

Icaza, Francisco A. de, 1863–1925. (continued).
    Autumn, in Anthology of Mex. poets, p. 91; also tr. by Black-
       well, in Springfield Republican, Oct. 16, 1909.

Irujillo, Mariano (from Yucatán), d. 1841*.
    Oh, Holy virtue, tr. by W. H. Hurlburt, in North Amer. rev.,
       vol.68, 1849, p. 136.
    My desire, idem.

Izaguirre Rojo, Baltasar.
    An old Mexican cemetery, tr. by Underwood, in Mexican life,
       X, June, 1934, p. 28.

Joublanc Rivas, Luciano, 1896–
    Sadness, in Anthology of Mex. poets, p. 147.

Juana Inés de la Cruz, Sor, 1651–1695.
    Roundels, in Blackwell.
    Sonnet, idem.; also tr. by Beatrice Gilman Proske, in
       Hispanic poets, p. 220.
    The Mexican nun, in Library of world's best literature,
       XXV, p.9956.
    On the contrarities of love, idem.
    Learning and riches, idem.
    Death is youth, idem.
    The divine narcissus, idem; also tr. by Roderick Gill, in
       Catholic anthology.
    The lost love, tr. by Thomas Walsh, in Hispanic anthology,
       p. 357-359.
    Caprice, idem.
    Arraignment of man, idem, also tr. by Peter H. Goldsmith,
       in Goldberg, Mexican poetry, p. 11-12.
    To her portrait, tr. by Thomas Walsh, in Hispanic anthology;
       also tr. by Muna Lee, in Pan Amer. bull., Sept.,1926;
       also in Torres-Rioseco, p.38; also tr. by K. A. Porter,
       in Survey, LIII, 1924; p.182; also tr. by G. W. Umphrey,
       in Fantasy, XXVI, 1942, p.43-44.
    To the Vicereine, in Anthology of Mex. poets, p.221.
    Cupid, idem.
    Salutation, idem, p.222 (from a play).
    Phoenix, idem, p.223 (from a play).
    Sonnet: When Cecilia in the meadow, tr. by G. W. Umphrey, in
       Fantasy, XXVI, 1942, p.43-44.
    Sonnet: Oh Rose whose form, idem,
    Sonnet: This which you gaze on, tr. by E. C. Hills, in Co-
       lorado college publication, series 80, Language series
       II, no.30, 1915; also in Hill, Hispanic studies, (Stan-
       ford univ., 1929), p.110.
    The evening when I spoke, idem.
    Redondilla, excerpt, idem.
    Song from Los empeños de la casa, tr. by James C. Barden,
       in Pan Amer. Bull.,v.   76, (April, 1942), pp.195-8.
    Villancico, sung in honor of the Blessed Virgin in Mexico,
       1865, tr. by Thomas Walsh, in Commonweal, Oct. 16, 1942,
       p.605.

Larrañaga Portugal, Manuel, 1868–
    Sonnet, in Anthology of Mexican poets, p. 104.

León del Valle, José, 1866–1924.
    The last of the Aztecs, in Blackwell, p. 156.

Llorente Vázquez, Manuel.
    Sunset, tr. by Blackwell, in Springfield rev., May 2,
       1908.

López Velarde, Ramón, 1888–1921.
    Wet land, in Anthology of Mexican poets, p. 66.
    The spell of return, idem, p. 67.
    My heart, idem, p. 68.
    Anchor, tr. by H. R. Hays, in Poetry, v. 58, Oct. 1940,
       p. 16–17.
    Ascension and assumption, tr. by H. R. Hays, in Decision, I,
       May, 1941, p. 52.
    What delightful madness, tr. by H. R. Hays, in Poetry, v.
       LXII (May, 1943), p. 71.
    If you die unwed, idem.

López, Rafaél, 1875–
    Manuel de la Parra, in Anthology of Mexican poets, p.
       74.
    Maximiliano (Maximilian), tr. by James Crowhurst-Rand,
       in Pan Amer. mag., XXVII (1918), p. 46 (with Spanish
       on opposite page).
    Colonial Puebla, a prose poem, tr. by Underwood in West
       Ind. rev., VI, Aug., 1940, p. 35.

Lozano, Raphael, 1899–
    The Aztec flutist, in Anthology of Mexican poets, p. 166.

Luchichí, Ignacio M., (Claudio Frollo), 1850–
    Verses for an album, in Anthology of Mexican poets, p. 299.
    Bluettes, idem, p. 300.

Maples Arce, Manuel, 1898–
    Metrópolis (Metropolis), tr. by John Dos Passos (Privately
       printed, 1930).
    Paroxysm, tr. in Underwood, Anthology of Mexican poets,
       p. 159.
    Parting, idem, p. 161.
    80 H. P., idem, p. 162.
    Canción desde un Aeroplano (Song from an Airplane), tr.
       by Mary and C. V. Wicker, in Fantasy, XXVI, (Dec., 1941)
       pp. 67–68.

Mar, María del.
    Cántico del amor que perdura (Mexico: Díaz de León, 1939).
    Your name, tr. by Underwood, in Mexican life, IX, (May, 1933).
       p. 12.

María Enriqueta, see Camarillo de Pereyra, María Enriqueta.

Mariscal, Ignacio, 1829-1910.
    The tomb of Juárez, Anthology of Mex. poets, p.241; also
        tr. by A. S. Blackwell, in Woman's Journal (March 29,
        1909).

Martes de Oca, Ignacio, 1840-1924.
    Farewell, My native land, in Anthology of Mex. poets, p.271.

Martínez, Miguel Gerónimo, 1817-1870.
    The pruning season, in Anthology of Mex. poets, p.236; also
        in West Ind. rev., VI, (May 1940), p.27.

Martínez de Navarrete, Fray Fernando Manuel, 1768-1809.
    Gratitude, tr. literally in Green and Lowenfels, pp.392-393.
    Love, in Anthology of Mex. poets, p.225.

Médiz Bolio, Antonio, 1884-
    La tierra del faisán y del venado (Mexico: Cultura, 1934).
    (The land of the Pheasant and the Deer),tr.literally
        by E. E. Perkins, (Mexico: Cultura, 1935) (a folksong
        of the Mayas).
    The theatrical world, in Anthology of Mex. poets, p.132-4.

Méndez de Cuenca, Laura, 1853-
    The Magdaline, in Anthology of Mex. poets, p.316.
    Winter, tr. by A. S. Blackwell, in Springfield Republican,
        (Feb. 28, 1909).

Nandino, Elías.
    My Village, tr. by Underwood in Mexican life, IX, (July,
        1933), p.16.
    Dovecot, idem.

Nervo, Amado, 1870-1919.
    Sister Water, including: The water that flows underground,
        The water that flows above ground, The snow, The ice, The
        hail, The vapor, The sea mist, The voice of the water,
        and The water of many forms, in Blackwell; all these also
        tr. in Stratford journal, VI, Jan-March, 1920, p.13-29;
        also tr. in Goldberg, Mexican poetry, p.44-54; Hail also
        tr. by Jessie Read Wendell, in Hispanic poets, p.231-2.

    If a thorn wounds me, in Blackwell, p.50; also tr. by Black-
        well in Zion's Herald (Aug. 11, 1926); also in Pan Amer.
        bull.(Feb. 1928); also tr. by Peter Goldsmith in Inter-
        Amer. II, (1919) p.346; also in Books Abroad V, 1931, p.
        366.
    Evocation, in Blackwell p.50; also tr. by Blackwell in
        Goldberg, Studies in Spanish Amer. lit; also in Pan Amer.
        mag., XXVIII (1919) p.158. (With Spanish on opposite page).
    Limpidity, in Blackwell p.52; also tr. by Blackwell in Zion's
        Herald (Aug. 11,1926); also in Pan Amer. bull., (Sept.1926).
    I was born today, in Blackwell p.54; also tr. by Blackwell,
        in Zion's Herald (Aug. 11,1926).

Nervo, Amado, 1870-1919. (continued)

Grief Vanquished, idem.

Deity, idem.

Revenge, idem; also tr. by Blackwell in Pan Amer. bull., (Jan.,1926); also in Torres-Rioseco, p.102.

To the clouds, in Blackwell, p.58.

The Daisies, idem, p.54.

The dark galley, idem, p.62.

The Leonora, idem, p.56; also tr. by Blackwell in Goldberg, Studies in Spanish Amer. Lit.

Death, in Blackwell, p.58; also tr. by Blackwell in Zion's Herald (Aug. 11,1926); also in Pan Amer. mag., XXXV (Aug.1922), p.75, (With Spanish on opposite page).

The story of my life, tr. anon., in Inter-Amer., VI (1922), p.97-98.

Let us love, tr. by Muna Lee in World Tomorrow, VIII, (April 1925), p.100.

En las noches de Abril, (On April nights), tr. by Blackwell, in Scholastic, Vol.39 (Oct. 6, 1941), p.15.

The gift, in Blackwell p.64; also tr. by Peter Goldsmith in Inter-Amer. V (1922), p.200.

I am All, tr. by Peter Goldsmith, in Inter-Amer., II, (1919), p.346.

Rejoice, idem.

Diafanidad, (Translucency), tr. by E. F. Lucas, in Pan Amer. mag., XXVI (1917), p.334. (With Spanish on opposite page); also tr. by Thomas Walsh, in Hispanic Anthology, pp. 626-634.

Ecstasy, in Blackwell, p.66; also in Pan Amer. bull. LXII (1928); also in Good Neighbor tour, VI, p.38.

Souls and birds, tr. by Blackwell, in Las Novedades (July 19,1917); also tr. by Torres-Rioseco, p.101.

The airship, tr. by Blackwell, in Springfield Republican, (Feb. 16, 1926).

Cobardía (Cowardice), in Modernist trend.

El día que me quieras (When thou lov'st me), idem.

Tel que'en songe (As in a dream), idem; also in Torres-Rioseco, p.102.

Si tu me dices—Ven! (If thou say'st "Come!") idem.

No todos (Not all who die), idem; also tr. by H. E. Fish, in Hispanic poets.

Delicta Carnis, in Modernist trend.

En paz (At peace), idem.

Rose, tr. by Blackwell, in Zion's Herald (Aug. 11,1926).

What are you doing? idem.

An old refrain, idem; also in Anthology of Mex.poets; also in West Ind. rev., IV (April, 1938), p.28.

The cortege, tr. by Thomas Walsh in Hispanic Anthology, p. 626-634.

Allegro Vivace, idem.

Purity, tr. by Beatrice Gilman Proske, in Hispanic poets, p. 232.

Rondo Vago, in Anthology of Mex. poets; also tr. by Underwood in West Ind. rev., IV, (April,1938),p.28-29.

Nervo, Amado, 1870–1919. (continued).
   The Buddha of Basalt, idem.
   The mountain, idem; also in Modernist trend.
   Los Místicos (Mystical Poets), in Anthology of Mexican
      poets; also in Catholic Anthology p.370; also in West
      Ind. rev. IV, April (1938), p.28–29.
   Hidalgos y Morelos, tr. by Blackwell, in New York Call,
      (Oct.,27, 1909).
   Puebla: Prose Poem, tr. by Underwood in West Ind. rev.,
      IV, (April, 1938), p.28–29.
   Plenitude, tr. by William F. Rice (Los Angeles, 1928); also
      tr. by Alfonso Teja Zabra (México, 1938), by Alfonso
      Teja Zabra (México, 1938).
   Confessions of a Modern poet, tr. by Dorothy Kress, (Boston,
      1935).

Novelo, José Inés, 1867–
   My muse (To Duque Job), in Anthology of Mexican poets, p.331.

Novo, Salvador, 1904–
   Nuevo Amor, tr. by Underwood in Anthology of Mex. poets;
      also in West Ind. rev., I, (April, 1935), p.37.
   Absence, tr. by Underwood, idem, IV, (May, 1938), p.43.
   Shipwreck, in Anthology of Mex. poets. p. 195.
   Deluge, idem, p.195; also (Diluvio), tr. by Mary and C. V.
      Wicker in Fantasy, XXVI (Dec.,1942), p. 59.
   Brief romance in time of absence: I, II, III, IV, V, in
      Anthology of Mex. poets, pp.189–193; also in West Ind.
      rev., IV, (July, 1938), p.72.
   Early, tr. in Mex. Life IV, (July, 1928), p. 16.
   Viaje (Journey), tr. by Mary and C. V. Wicker in Amer. pref.
      (Winter, 1941–2); also tr. by H. R. Hays, in APLC, p.87.
   Un amigo ido (The departed friend), idem; tr. by Lloyd
      Mallan, in APLC, p.87.
   Elegía (Elegy), tr. by Mary and C. V. Wicker, in Amer. pref.
      (Winter, 1941–2).
   La poesía (Poetry), tr. by Donald Walsh, in APLC, p. 89.

Olaguibel, Francisco Manuel de, 1873*–
   Jesús, in Anthology of Mex. poets, p. 108.
   Provenzal, idem, p. 107.
   Esperanza (Hope), tr. in Green and Lowenfels, pp.62–63.

Ortíz, Luis G., 1835–1894.
   My fountain, in Blackwell, p. 176; also in Stratford Journal,
      III, (Aug., 1918), p.74.

Ortíz de Montellano, Bernardo, 1899–
   The five senses, in Anthology of Mex. poets, p. 164.
   Sketch, idem, p. 165.
   Segundo sueño (Second dream), tr. by Thelma Lamb de Ortíz
      de Montellano, Donald Walsh, and Dudley Fitts, in APLC,
      p. 327.

Othón, Manuel José, 1858*-1906.
  The bell, in Blackwell; also in Goldberg, Mex. poetry, p. 23.
  The river, _idem_; also tr. by Thomas Walsh in Hispanic anthology,
    p. 549.
  Sonnet sequence I, II, III, in Anthology of Mex. poets, pp.40-
    41; also in West Ind. rev.,VI (Oct.,1939), pp.28-29.
  The light, tr. by Blackwell in Christian Science Monitor, (May 22,1926).
  The stars, tr. by Blackwell in Stratford Journal, III, (Aug.1918), p.74.

Owen, Gilberto, 1904-
  Interior, in Anthology of Mex. poets, p. 211.
  Poem in which the word love is often used, _idem_, p. 212.

Pagaza, Joaquín Arcadio, 1839-1918.
  Evensong, tr. by Ada Marshall Johnson, in Hispanic poets, p.221.
  In the night, in Walsh, Hispanic Anthology; also tr. by Blackwell in
    Woman's journal (June 25,1910).
  Twilight, in Hispanic anthology; also tr. by Blackwell in Catholic
    anthology; also in Las novedades, March 11,1915; also in Pan
    Amer. mag., XXXI, (1920), p.190.
  Evening prayer, in Anthology of Mex. poets; also in West Ind. rev.,
    VI, (May, 1940), p. 28.
  Night in Zempoala, _idem_.

Parra, Manuel de la, 1878-
  A fable by Grimm, in Anthology of Mex. poets, p. 95.
  The cistern, _idem_, p. 97.

Pellicer, Carlos, 1897*-
  To José Manuel Puig Cassauranc, in Anthology of Mex. poets, p. 150.
  Sorrow of the Andes, _idem_, p. 151.
  Uxmal, _idem_, p. 152.
  Study, _idem_, p. 155.
  Dawn, _idem_, p. 156; also tr. by Mary and C. V. Wicker, in Three
    Spanish Amer. poets.
  Rhetoric of the landscape, in Mex. life, VII, (April 1931), p. 15.
  Island of Curaçao, in West Ind. rev., II, (Oct.1935), p. 56.
  Tres estudios (Three etudes), tr. by Mary and C. V. Wicker, in
    Three Spanish Amer. poets; No. I (Etude) tr. by H. R. Hays, in
    APLC, p. 317.
  Sonetos de otoño (Autumn sonnets), in Three Spanish Amer. poets.
  A Eduardo Villaseñor, _idem_.
  Sonetos de los arc angeles, _idem_.
  Grupos de palomas (Groups of doves), _idem_.
  Esquemas para una oda tropical (Sketches for a tropical ode), _idem_.
  Nocturno X, _idem_.
  Tercera vez, (Third time), _idem_; also tr. by Dudley Fitts, in APLC,
    p. 319.
  Domingo (Sunday), _idem_; also tr. by Dudley Fitts, in APLC, p. 317.
  El recuerdo (Remembrance), _idem_.
  Horas de Junio (June hours), _idem_.

Pellicer, Carlos, 1897*- (continued)
Segador (Harvester),idem; also Reaper,in Anthology of Mex.poets,p.157.
Deseos (Desires), idem.

Peón del Valle, José, 1866-1924.
Omnia Pulvis! in Anthology of Mex.poets, p. 281.
No volvió! idem, p. 282.
Cuauhtemoc, last of the Aztecs, tr. by Blackwell, in Spring-
field Republican, (March 1,1908).

Peón y Contreras, José, 1843-1907.
Canticles, in Anthology of Mex.poets, p. 280.

Pérez Piña, Pedro I.
Dawn in Yucatán; a prose miniature, in Anthology of Mex. poets,p.286.

Peza, Juan de Dios, 1852-1910.
Meditation, tr. by Blackwell, in Las novedades (Feb.25,1917).
Mexico and Spain, tr. literally in Green and Lowenfels, p. 252-258.

Pino Suárez, José María, 1869-1913.
Love's language, in Blackwell, p. 174.
Rhyme, tr. by Blackwell, in Mexican rev.,(Sept.-Oct.,1918); also
in Goldberg, Mexican poetry.

Prieto, Guillermo, 1818-1897.
An old man's love, in Anthology of Mex. poets, p.237.

Puig Pérez, José, 1845-1897.
Nunca (Never), tr. in Green and Lowenfels, pp.64-65.

Quintanilla, Luis (Kyn Taniya, pseud.), 1900-
Storm, in Mexican life, IV, (Jan.,1928), p.16.
4861, idem., p. 20. (about a train).

Ramírez, Ignacio, 1818-1879.
My portrait, in Anthology of Mex. poets, p. 239.

Rebolledo, Efrén, 1877-1929.
Voto, in Anthology of Mex. poets, p. 93.
Imsomnio, idem, p. 94.
Hail, Lindbergh, tr. by Blackwell, in Springfield Republican,
(Jan.17, 1928).

Requena Legarreta, Pedro, 1893-1918.
Idyl, tr. by Thomas Walsh, in Hispanic anthology, p. 763-766.
I would enfold your death and mine, idem. p. 766.

Reyes, Alfonso, 1887*-
La Amenaza de la flor, in Anthology of Mex. poets, p. 76.
Glosa de mi tierra, idem.
A, idem.
I, idem.
Silencio Reglamentario (Regulative silence), tr. anon., in Pan
Amer. mag., XXXII (1928), p. 208.
West Indian dusk, in West Ind. rev., I, (Dec.1934), p.49.
Golfo de México, tr. by Dudley Fitts, in APLC, p. 45.

Riva Palacio, Vicente, ("Rosa Espina"), 1832-1896.
    Midday on the Coast of Mexico, in Anthology of Mex. poets,
        p.243.
    Evening in the Valley of Mexico, idem, p.245.
    Night on the Mountains of Mexico, idem, p.247.
    Two Swallows, idem, p.249.

Rivas, José Pablo, 1865-1919.
    Festival of love, in Anthology of Mex. poets, p.324.

Roa Bárcena, José María, 1827-1908.
    Founding of Mexico City, in Anthology of Mex. poets, p.240.
    Combates en el aire (Combats in the Air), in Starr, p.262.

Rosado Vega, Luis, 1876 -
    Nocturn of the Rain, in Anthology of Mex. poets, p.118.
    To the unknown Goddess. tr. by Muna Lee, in Poetry, XXVI
        (1925), pp.132-133.

Rosas Moreno, José, 1838-1883.
    The spider's web, in Hispanic anthology, p. 513.
    The Eagle and the Serpent, idem, p.514.
    The caterpillar and the butterfly, idem.
    The zentzontle, in Anthology of Mex. poets, p.264.
    The woodman and the sandel tree, tr. by W. C. Bryant, in
        Laurel leaves (Boston, 1876).
    The cost of pleasure, idem.
    Elm and the vine, tr. by W. C. Bryant, in Goldberg, Mexican
        poetry, p. 13.

Ruiz de Alarcón, Juan, 1580?-1639.
    To Vesuvius, in Anthology of Mex. poets, p.217; also in
        West. Ind. rev., VI, (May 1940), p.27.

Ruiz Esparza, Juan Manuel, ("Polifemo de Coastillac").
    U, in Anthology of Mex. poets, p.200.
    I, idem, p. 201.
    C, idem, p. 202.
    E, idem, p. 203.

Saénz Azcorra, Franz.
    November in Yucatan, in Anthology of Mex. poets, p.205.
    The path, idem, p.206.
    By the dead cities of Yucatan, idem, p.207.
    March in Yucatan, idem, p.331.

Sierra, Justo, 1848-1912.
    To Christopher Columbus, in Blackwell, p. 142; also tr.
        by Blackwell, in Woman's Journal, (Oct. 12, 1912).
    A poet who killed himself (Manuel Acuña), in Anthology of
        Mexican poets, p. 288.
    A song of the shore, tr. by Blackwell, in Springfield Re-
        publican, (June 20, 1909).

Solís, José María.
    Clear water, in Blackwell, p.170.
    The water, tr. anon., in Unity, (Oct.,23, 1924).

Sosa, Francisco, 1848-1925.
    Romance, in Blackwell, p. 166; also in Springfield Republican,
        (April 23, 1916).

Soto, Jesús S.
    An old mexican print, tr. by Underwood, in Mexican life,
        X, (April, 1934), p.16.

Tablada, José Juan, 1871-
    Pre-Raphaelitism, in Hispanic anthology; also in Goldberg,
        Mexican poetry, pp.59-61.
    Alternating Nocturne, in Anthology of Mex. poets, p.77.
    Á la Watteau, idem, p. 78.
    Heron, idem, p.82.
    Ballad of the Eyes. idem, p. 79; also in West Ind. rev.,
        VI, (Dec., 1939), p.15.
    Onyx, idem.
    Lawn Tennis, from Poesías en Nueva York, Lawn Tennis, tr. by
        J. Glenton, in Pan Amer. mag., XXVII, (1918), p.332.
    Six poems, tr. by Warren P. Carrier, in Entre Nosotros, IV,
        (Feb. 1942), p.14.

Téllez, Joaquín, 1823-
    Beside the sea by Vera Cruz, in Anthology of Mex. poets, p.
        135.

Terrazas, Francisco de, (16th Century).
    Sonnet, in Anthology of Mex. poets, p.215; also in West
        Ind. rev., VI, (May, 1940), p.27.

Torres Bodet, Jaime, 1902-
    Song, tr. by Beatrice Gilman Proske, in Hispanic poets,
        p. 236.
    Voyage, idem. p. 238; also in Mexican life, VII (July, 1931),
        p. 13.
    The well, in Blackwell, p. 166.
    The house, idem, p. 164.
    The cypress, idem, p. 166.
    Music, in Anthology of Mex. poets, p.173.
    Dream, idem, p.176.
    Romance, idem. p. 175; also in Mexican life, III (June,
        1927), p. 20.
    The shadow, in Anthology of Mex. poets, p. 174; also tr. by
        Mary and C. V. Wicker, in Amer. Pref., VII (Winter, 1941-
        2), p. 166.
    The sea, in Mexican life, III (Sept., 1927), p. 30.
    Chopin, idem, VII (May, 1931), p. 19.
    Ciudad (City), tr. by Rolfe Humphries, in APLC, p. 93.
    Mediodía (Noon), idem., p.95.
    Danza, idem, p.97; also in Mexican life, VII (Aug., 1931),
        p.28.

Torres Bodet, Jaime, 1902- (continued).
  Hueso (Core), tr. by Muna Lee, in APLC, p. 9 9
  Amor (Love), idem., p. 99.
  Abril (April), tr. by Blanca López Castellón, in APLC.p.101.

Torri, Julio, 1899-.
  Essays and Poems, tr. by Dorothy M. Kress (Publications of
    the Institute of French Studies, New York, 1938)   33.p.

Tovar, Pantaleón, 1828-1876.
  To a girl weeping for flowers, in Anthology of Mex. poets,
    p. 242; also in West Ind. rev., VI, (May,1940),p.27.

Unavez, Nicolás (Pen name of a physician turned Estridentista poet)
  Foreshortened Gaze, tr. by Rolfe Humphries, in Fantasy,
    XXVI (1942), p. 65.

Urbina, Luis Gonzaga, 1868-1934.
  Ascension, in Blackwell, p. 70.
  To a friend far away, idem. p. 98.
  Witchcraft, idem, p. 68; also tr. by Blackwell, in Strat-
    ford journal, I, (Autumn 1916) p. 63-76.
  Triumph of the blue, idem.
  Sunny morning, idem; also in Boston Record, (Sept.25,1915).
  The last sunset, idem.
  Birds, idem; also in Las Novedades, (Feb.4,1915); also in
    Mexican Rev., (June, 1918).
  On the lake, in Blackwell, p.68; also in Springfield Repub-
    lican; also in Stratford Journal I (Autumn, 1916) pp.63-
    76.
  Spare the nests, in Blackwell, p.74; also in Las Novedades,
    (Aug. 1916); also in Stratford Journal, III, (Aug. 1918),
    p.75.
  The mass at dawn, in Blackwell, p. 76; also in Goldberg,
    Mexican Poetry, pp.33-44; also in Stratford Journal, I,
    (Autumn, 1916) p. 63-76.
  To a dead composer (Ricardo Castro), in Blackwell, p.96;
    also in Springfield Republican, (May 10, 1908).
  The moonbeam, tr. by Blackwell in Hispanic Anthology; also
    in Spring. field Republican, (May 20, 1909); also in Strat-
    ford Journal, I, (Autumn, 1916), pp.63-76.
  Noche clara (Clear night), in Anthology of Mex. poets, p.
    83; also tr. by Muna Lee, in Pan Amer. bull., (July, 1925),
    also tr. by Muna Lee in Poetry, XXVI (1925), pp.132.
  Eventide, tr. by Blackwell, in Springfield Republican, (March
    25, 1909).
  First romantic interlude, in Anthology of Mex. poets, p.84.
  Alone, idem, p.85.
  Ballad, idem, p. 87.
  Beloved eyes, tr. by Blackwell, in Springfield Republican,
    (Aug. 9, 1915).
  A Spanish song, tr. by Blackwell, in Young People, (Phila)
    (April 20, 1918).
  March toward the ideal, tr. by Blackwell, in Stratford
    Journal I (Autumn, 1916) p.63-76.

Urbina, Luis Gonzaga, 1868-1934. (continued)
    School teachers, _idem_.
    Sunset, _idem_.
    Evening hour, idem.
    M. Gutiérrez Najera, tr. anon. in Inter-Amer. V. (1922),
        pp.285-297.
    Pobre galleguito, tr. by Lawrence Greenough, in Pan Amer.
        mag., XXVII (1918); p.105.

Usigli, Rudolfo, 1905-
    Nocturn, in Anthology of Mex. poets, p.198.

Valenzuela, Jesús E., 1856-1911.
    A song of hands, in Blackwell, p. 122; also in New York
        evening post, (May 27, 1915); also in Stratford jour-
        nal, III, (Aug., 1918) p.76; also in Goldberg Me-
        xican poetry, p. 21.
    To Duque Job, in Anthology of Mex. poets, p. 102.
    Don Quixote, tr. by Blackwell, in Goldberg, Mexican
        poetry, p. 22.

Valle, Juan, 1838-1865
    Romance, in Anthology of Mex. poets, p. 262.

Vidaurreta, Valentín.
    From decay, in Mexican life, XII (Feb., 1936), p. 13,
    The white cloud, _idem_, p. 16.
    Black shadow, _idem_, XI (Oct., 1935), p. 15.
    Goats, _idem_, XI Nov., 1935) p. 11.

Vilaire, Etzer, 1872-
    Soir triste, tr. by Underwood, in Mexican life,
        (Aug., 1934), p. 30.

Villaurrutia, Xavier, 1903⁼
    Air, in Anthology of Mex. poets, p. 180.
    Picture, _idem_, p. 184.
    Insomnia, _idem_, p. 185.
    Amplifications, _idem_, p. 181; also in Mexican life,
        VlI (Dec., 1931), p. 30.
    Pueblo (Village), in Anthology of Mex. poets, p. 182;
        also in Mexican life, VIII (Oct., 1931), p. 20,
    Phonographs, in Anthology of Mex. poets, p. 183; also
        Fonógrafos, tr. by J. L. Grucci, in Modern verse
        (Oct., 1941).
    North Carolina blues, tr. by J. L. Grucci, in Amer.
        pref., VII (Winter 1942). pp.164-165.
    Nocturno en que habla la muerte (Nocturne in which
        Death speaks), tr. by Dudley Fitts, in APLC, p.365.
    Nocturno de los ángeles (Angel -Nocturne), _idem_, p.367.

Zaragoza, Antonio, 1855-1910.
    Harmonies, tr. by Blackwell, in Las Novedades (Nov.18,
        1915).

Zayas Enríquez, Rafaél de, 1848-1932.
    Spring song, in Anthology of Mex. poets, p. 283.

POETRY -- NICARAGUA

Argüello, Lino, 1890-1935.
    Día de campo, tr. by Donald Walsh, in APLC, p. 463.

Argüello Barreto, Santiago, 1842*-
    The eagle and the dry leaf, in Blackwell, pp.202-204;
       also in Boston herald, (July 22, 1917).

Baca, Félix María.
    El idilio vulgar, (Vulgar idyll), tr. by J. Gleaton,
      in Pan Amer. mag., XXVII, (1918) p.154.

Darío, Rubén, 1867-1916.
    Era un aire suave, tr. anon. in Inter-Amer., I, (1917),
      pp.1-11.
    Por el influjo de la primavera, idem.
    Dezir, idem; also other excerpts.
    The grandmother's clavichord, tr. by Alice Jane McVan,
      in Hispanic poets, p. 241.
    Autumnal sonnet to the Marquis of Bradomín, idem. p.240.
    Leda, idem, p. 244.
    To Margarita Debayle, idem, p.247.
    Sinfonía en gris mayor (Symphony in grey major), idem,
      p. 245; also in Modernist trend, p.49; also in
      Goldberg, Studies in Spanish Amer. lit.
    Stories of the Cid, in Blackwell, p. 182; also tr. by
      Blackwell, in New York evening post,(April 5, 1915).
    Song of the pines, idem; also in New York evening post,
      (March 11, 1915); also in Pan Amer. mag., XXVII
      (1918), p. 254; also three stanzas reprinted in Pan
      Amer. mag., vol. 42 (1929), p. 168; also in Studies
      in Spanish Amer. lit.
    Sonnet to Cervantes, in Blackwell, p. 188; also tr.
      by Blackwell, in Boston herald (Jan. 16, 1916);
      also tr. Eleven poems; also in Books abroad, vol.
      V, (1931), p. 366.
    Slings, in Blackwell, p. 188; also tr. by Blackwell, in
      Las Novedades, (Jan. 31, 1918); also in Boston herald,
      (April 5, 1918); also tr. by Goldberg in Goldberg,
      Studies in Spanish Amer. lit.
    Caracol (A Shell), in Blackwell, p. 190; also in Pan
      Amer. mag., XXXV (July, 1922), p. 33, (with Spanish).
    The princess and the star, in Blackwell, p.192.
    The white page, idem, p. 198.
    The song of hope, idem, p. 200; also in Eleven poems
      of Rubén Darío; also tr. by Blackwell, in Goldberg,
      Studies in Spanish Amer. lit.; also tr. by Blackwell,
      in Las Novedades, (Oct. 21, 1915).

Darío, Rubén, 1867-1916. (continued)
    Sonatina, tr. by J. P. Rice, in Hispanic Anthology,
        pp. 598-613; also tr. by A. B. Poor, in Pan Amer.
        poems; also tr. by G. W. Umphrey and L. Forsberg
        in Poet lore, vol. 45, no.3-4 (1939), pp.353-354.
    Night fall in the tropics, in Hispanic Anthology pp.
        598-613.
    Song of Autumn in Spring, idem; also in Modernist
        trend; also in Eleven poems.
    Yo soy aquel (Portico), in Hispanic Anthology, p.606;
        also in Catholic Anthology, pp.347-351; also in
        Eleven poems; also (I am the man), in Modernist
        trend, p. 39.
    Philosophy, tr. anon. in Golden book mag., V (1927),
        p.640.
    To Roosevelt, tr. anon. in Literary digest, XCIII
        (May 21, 1927); also tr. by Isaac Goldberg in Pan
        Amer. mag., XXX (Feb., 1915), p.20; also tr. by E. C.
        Hills, in Colorado College publication language series
        II, No. 30; also tr. by E. C. Hills in Hispanic studies
        (Stanford Univ. 1929); also in Modernist trend; also in Studies
        in Spanish American lit.
    Letanía para nuestro Señor don Quixote (Litany of our Lord,
        Don Quixote), tr. by Muna Lee, in Pan Amer. mag., Vol.
        41 (1928), p. 25, (with Spanish on opposite page);
        also in Poetry, XXVI (1925), p. 135-137; also in Torres-
        Rioseco, p. 107.
    God save the Queen, tr. by Goldberg, in Goldberg, Studies
        in Spanish Amer. lit.
    Marcha triunfal, tr. Sylvester Baxter, idem.
    A votive urn, tr. by Blackwell, in Las Novedades, (Dec.
        3, 1916).
    To Del Casal, 4 stanzas tr. by Underwood, in West Ind. rev.,
        II (July, 1936), p. 24.
    The murmur from the stable, tr. by A. B. Poor in Pan Amer.
        poems; also in Catholic Anthology pp. 347-351.
    El cisne (The swan), in Modernist trend, p. 45.
    Blasón (Blazon), idem; also in Torres-Rioseco, p. 108.
    Friso (Frieze), idem.
    Mía (Mine), idem.
    Para una cubana (For a Cuban lady), idem.
    Margarita, idem.
    Salutación del optimista (The optimist's salutation), idem.
    Salutación al águila (Salutation to the eagle), idem; also
        in Pan Amer., p.42.
    Los tres reyes magos (Three wise kings), idem; also in
        Eleven poems.
    Primaveral (Primaveral), tr. in Eleven poems; also in Torres-
        Rioseco, p. 108.
    Autumnal (Autumnal), in Eleven poems.
    Torres de Dios! Poetas! (Poets! Towers of God!) idem.
    Oración por Antonio Machado, idem.
    Gaita Galaica (Bagpipes of Spain), idem.

Maldonado, Pedro, 1704-48.
    Simón el Cireneo (Simon the Cyrenean), tr. by Oswald
       Tenney in Pan Amer. Mag., XXVII (1918), p. 156.

Mayorga Rivas, Ramón, 1862-
    The mocking bird and I, in Blackwell, p. 484.

Méndez, Francisco, 1908-
    Sangre en una piedra (Blood on a stone), tr. by Donald
       Walsh, in APLC, p.173.

Selva, Salomón de la, 1893-
    Elegía (Elegy), tr. by Donald Walsh, in APLC, p. 527.

POETRY – PANAMA

Alain Acuña, Elías, 1893-
    Thus am I, tr. by Underwood, in West Ind. rev., III,
       (Aug., 1937), p. 33.

Arce, Napoleón, 1885-
    Outline of Panama, tr. by Underwood, in West Ind. rev.,
       III, (Aug., 1937), p.34.

Arjona Q., Julio, 1877*-
    Far away, tr. by Underwood in West Ind. rev., III,
       (Aug., 1937), p. 33.

Callejas, Félix ("Billiken"), 1878-
    To Don Quixote, tr. by Underwood, in West Ind. rev., III,
       (Aug., 1937), p. 33.

Castillo, Félix R., see Ricaurte Castillo, F.

Escobar, Federico, 1861-1912
    The carpenter, tr. by Underwood, in West Ind. rev., III,
       (March, 1937), p. 36.

Fabrega, Demetrio, 1888-
    The idyl of the mountain, in Blackwell, p. 524.
    Toledo, tr. by Underwood, in West Ind. rev., III, (Aug.,
       1937), p. 34.

Facio, Justo A., 1859-1931.
    Odio (Hatred), tr. by Salomón de la Selva, in Pan Amer.
       mag., XXVII (1918), p. 162.

Geenzier, 1887-
    Open sea, tr. by Underwood in West Ind., rev., III, (June,
       1937), p. 33.
    Black pearls, parts II and IV, idem.
    Once on a time there was an old joy, idem.

González Rodríguez, J.
    To one who is shy, tr. by Underwood, in West Ind. rev.,
       III, (Aug., 1937), p. 33.

Hernández Gaspar, Octavio, 1893-1918.
 Bell tower of gold, tr. by Underwood, in West Ind. rev.,
  III, (July, 1937), p. 34.
 Aria of gratitude, idem, p. 35.
 Head of Vasco, idem, p. 35.
 Tree by the side of the road, idem, p. 35.

Herrera, Darío, 1887-1914.
 Of the past, tr. by Underwood, in West Ind., rev., III,
  (June 1937), p. 34.
 On the Atlantic, idem.

Herrera S., Demetrio, 1902-
 En plena orgía, tr. by Underwood, in West Ind. rev., III,
  (Mar., 1937), p. 37.
 Entrenamiento (Training), tr. by Dudley Fitts, in APLC,
  p. 107.

Korsi, Demetrio, 1899*-
 Héroe Antiguo, tr. by Underwood, in West Ind. rev., IV,
  (Jan., 1938), p. 20.
 Palms, idem.
 Song of the prison bells, idem.

Llorent, José.
 Discussed in "Negro poets of Panama", by Underwood, in
  West Ind. rev., III, (Sept. 1937), pp.35-37.

Miró, Ricardo, 1883-1940.
 The captive herons, tr. by Underwood, in West Ind. rev.,
  III, (June, 1937), pp.34-35.
 The nightingale, idem.
 Panamá, idem.

Obaldía, María Olimpia de, 1891*-
 Alas sobre Europa (Wings over Europe), tr. by M. B. Davis
  in APLC, p. 549-555.

Palma, Benigno, 1882-
 To the Panama Canal, in Blackwell, p. 526.

Ricaurte Castillo, Félix.
 Sentimental landscape, tr. by Underwood, in West Ind. rev.,
  III, (Aug., 1937), p. 33.

Urriola, José Dolores ("El Mulato"), 1834-1883.
 Sonnet, tr. by Underwood, in West Ind. rev., III, (March,
  1937), p. 36.

Valdés Jr., Ignacio de J.
 Prayer, tr. by Underwood, in West Ind. rev., III, (Aug.,
  1937), p. 34.

Vásquez M., J. M.
 Give me your hands, tr. by Underwood, in West Ind. rev.,
  III, (Mar., 1937), p. 36.

Vilar, Ricardo Arturo.
    Statue of Christopher Columbus, tr. by Underwood, in West
        Ind. rev., III, (Aug., 1937), p. 34.

Villalaz, Carlos E.
    Evening bells, tr. by Underwood, in West Ind. rev., III,
        (Aug., 1937), p. 34.

POETRY - PARAGUAY

Folksongs.
    Tr. by Muna Lee, in Poetry, XXVI (1925), p. 138.

Guanes, Alejandro.
    Your soul, in Blackwell, p. 468.

Pane, Ignacio A., d. 1919.
    The Paraguayan woman, in Blackwell, pp.470—472.

Sánchez Quell, Horacio, 1907–
    Elogio de la Calle Saccarello (Praise of Saccarello St.),
        tr. by Dudley Fitts, in APLC, p. 149.

POETRY - PERU

"Quechua Poems from Peru", tr. by Anita Brenner, in
    Nation, vol. 192, (Nov. 27, 1929), p. 629. They in-
    clude: "The Foreigner","The Fountain" and "The Land
    Owner".

Abril de Vivero, Xavier, 1903–
    Elegía a la mujer inventada (Elegy to a woman) tr. by
        Underwood, in West Ind. rev., IV (Oct. 1937), p.26;
        also tr. by Muna Lee, in APLC, p. 337.
    Silence of the jasmine, in West Ind. rev., IV (Oct.,
        1937), p. 26.
    Elegy of memories under a sky threatening and dim, idem.
    Shot at Dawn: to García Lorca, idem, (Dec.,1937), p.18.
    Sentiment of the land and the furrow, tr. by H. R. Hays,
        in Decision, I, (May, 1941), p. 52.
    Nocturno, tr. by H. R. Hays, in APLC, p. 373.
    Exaltación de las materias elementales (Exaltation of
        Elementary material), idem, p. 379.
    Amanecer (Dawn), tr. by Muna Lee, in APLC, p. 373.
    Elegía a lo perdido (Elegy to the lost and already blurred
        by time), tr. by Blanca López Castellón, in APLC, pp.
        375–7.

"Adán, Martín", see La Fuente Benavides, Rafaél de.

Bustamante y Ballivián, Enrique, 1884*1937* .
    El poste (Telegraph pole), tr. by Muna Lee, in APLC, p.
        125.
    A Estados Unidos (To the United States), tr. by Willis
        Knapp Jones, in Fantasy XI, No.28, (1943).

Chocano, José Santos, 1875-1934.
>Spirit of the Andes, tr. by Underwood (Portland, Me.: Mosher
>>Press, 1935) 43 p.
>Horses of the conquerors, tr. by Jessie Read Wendell, in
>>Hispanic poets, p. 252; also tr. by Muna Lee, in Poetry,
>>XXVI (1925), pp.139-42; also in Torres-Rioseco, p. 115.
>Blasón (Blazon), tr. in Modernist trend, p. 131.
>Las punas (The frozen heights), idem.
>Cuacthemoc, idem.
>Tres notas de nuestra alma indígena (Three notes of our
>>indigenous spirit), including: Quién sabe? (Who knows),
>>Así será (So let it be), Ahí, no mas (Why, there, just
>>over there), idem; also tr. by Torres-Rioseco, in Books
>>Abroad, IX, (1935), p. 252.
>Los Andes (The Andes), idem; also in New York evening
>>post, (Oct.7,1916); also in Blackwell, p. 210.
>The magnolia, in New York evening post, (Oct.7,1916);
>>also tr. by J. P. Rice, in Poetry, XI (1918) pp.229-
>>236; also tr. by Underwood, in West Ind. rev., I,
>>(July 1935), p.21; also in Blackwell, p.208; also in
>>Goldberg, Studies in Spanish Amer. Lit.; also tr. by
>>Blackwell, in Boston record, (May 16,1916).
>Forest love, in New York evening post, (Oct.7,1916),
>The Rivers, idem.
>Archaeology, idem; also in Blackwell, p.206; also in
>>Goldberg, Studies in Spanish Amer. lit.; also tr. by
>>Blackwell, in Advocate of peace, (Aug.1916); also in
>>Books abroad, V (1931), p.365-6.
>Lightening, in New York evening post, (Oct.7,1916); also
>>in Blackwell, p.226.
>The Volcanoes, idem, p.216.
>A Queen's breast, idem, p.220; also tr. by Blackwell, in
>>Las Novedades, (March 11,1917).
>The Wind mills, tr. by Goldberg, in Goldberg, Studies in
>>Spanish Amer. lit; also in Blackwell, p. 222; also Los
>>molinos, in Pan Amer. mag. XXVIII (1919), p. 156.
>Mouths of the Orinoco, tr. by Goldberg, in Goldberg, Studies
>>in Spanish Amer. lit.; also in Blackwell, p. 218.
>Straits of Magellan, idem.
>The Orchids, idem.
>Arboles viejos, tr. by Goldberg, in Goldberg, Studies in
>>Spanish Amer. lit.
>Sun and moon, in Blackwell, p. 206; also tr. by Blackwell,
>>in Pan Amer. mag., XXXIV, (April 1922), p. 23 (with
>>Spanish on opposite page); also in Books abroad, V,
>>(1931), p.365.
>La alondra (The lark), in Blackwell, p. 224; also in Las
>>Novedades, (July 19,1917); also in Goldberg, Studies
>>in Spanish Amer. lit.
>Horn of plenty, in Blackwell, p. 208.
>The Boa-constrictor's dream, idem, p. 212.
>The Alligator's dream, idem, p.212.
>The Condor's dream, idem, p. 214.
>The Quena, idem, p. 216.
>Eagles and sparrows, idem, p. 224; also tr. by Blackwell,
>>in The Public, (May 12,1916).

Chocano, José Santos, 1875-1934. (continued)
    A Protest, in Blackwell, p.224; also tr. by Blackwell,
       in Boston herald, (Nov.9,1917).
    The spirit primeval, tr. by Isabel S. Sharpe, in Pan Amer.
       bull., (Oct. 1925).
    The plowers of the sea, tr. by J. McDonald, in Pan Amer.
       mag., XXVII (1918), p. 42.
    America to Spain, tr. by Blackwell, in Las novedades (Oct.
       29,1916); also in Boston herald, (April 15,1926).
    Oda salvaje, in Hispanic anthology, pp.672-678.
    A Song of the road, idem, pp.680-682; also tr. by J. P. Rice,
       in Poetry XI (1918), pp.229-236.
    El Charro, tr. by J. P. Rice, in Poetry, XI (1918), pp.229-236.
    The Pineapple legend, tr. by Blackwell, in Christian science
       monitor, (Sept.14, 1927).
    Epic of the Pacific, a four line excerpt tr. by Isaac Goldberg,
       in Pan Amer. mag., XX, (Feb.1915) p. 21.
    Excerpts in Santos Chocano, poet of America, by Torres-Rioseco,
       in Mexican life, XI, (Sept.,1935), p. 31.

Eguren, José María, 1882-1942.
    The abbey, in Catholic Antology, p. 438.
    La niña de la lámpara azul, tr. by Donald Walsh, in APLC,
       p. 453.
    Marginal, idem, p.453.
    Lied V, idem, p. 457.

González Prada, Manuel, 1844-1918.
    Triolet, tr. by Alice Jane McVan, in Hispanic poets, p.251.

La Fuente Benavides, Rafaél de, ("Martín Adán"), 1908-
    Navidad, tr. by Muna Lee, in APLC, p. 477.

Masías y Calle, D.
    The three epochs, tr. by A. B. Poor, in Pan Amer. poems.

Méndez Dorich, Rafaél, (born Argentina), 1903-
    Llevaba la lámpara (She was carrying the lamp), tr. by
       Donald Walsh, in APLC, p. 393.
    Porcelana del norte (Porcelain of the North), idem, p.393.
    Los gatos blancos de la duquesa (The duchess's white cats),
       idem, p. 395.
    El telegrafista muerto (The dead telegrapher), idem, p.397.

Moreno Jimeno, Manuel, 1913-
    Los malditos (The damned), tr. by H. R. Hays, in APLC, p.
       291-5.

Moro, César (César Quíspez Asín), 1906-
    Vienes en la noche con el humo fabuloso de tu cabellera,
       (You come in the night with the fabulous smoke of your
       hair), tr. by H. R. Hays, in APLC, p. 381.
    Visión de pianos apolillados cayendo en ruinas (Vision of
       moth-eaten pianos falling to pieces), tr. by Muna Lee,
       idem, p. 383.
    El mundo ilustrado (The illustrated world), idem, p. 385.

Oquendo de Amat, Carlos, 1909-1936.
    Poema del manicomio (Madhouse poem), tr. by H. R. Hays,
       in APLC, p. 323.
    Poema surrealista de elefante i del canto (Surrealist
       poem of the elephant and the song), idem, p.323.
    El angel i la rosa (Angel and the rose), idem, p. 325.
    Madre (Mother), idem, p. 325.

Palma, Ricardo, 1833-1919.
    Sun and dust, in Blackwell, p. 228; also in Hispanic antho-
       logy, p. 469; also tr. by Blackwell, in Boston herald,
       (June 15, 1917).
    Woman, tr. by Blackwell, in Pan Amer. bull., LXII (1938),
       pp.1214-1219; also in Good neighbor tour, VI, p.39.

Peña Barrenechea, Enrique, 1904-
    Elegía a Becquer (Elegy for Becquer), tr. by M. B. Davis,
       in APLC, p. 531.
    Poetas muertos (Dead poets), idem, p. 533.
    Camino del hombre (Man's road), tr. by Muna Lee, idem, p.531.

Peña Barrenechea, Ricardo.
    Romance of the desert, tr. by Underwood, in West Ind. rev.,
       VI, (Jan., 1940), p. 15.
    Love song to my mother in heaven, idem.
    Garden's jackass, idem.
    Romance of Quipachacha, idem.

Peralta, Alejandro, 1899-
    Travesia andinista (Andean crossing), tr. by Muna Lee, in
       APLC, p. 153.

Salaverry, Carlos Augusto, 1831-1890.
    Before the looking glass, in Blackwell, p. 230.

Vallejo, César, 1893*-1937*.
    Black Heralds, tr. by Underwood, in West Ind. rev., V,
       (July,1939), p. 28.
    Summer, idem, p. 28.
    Nerve, idem.
    Anguish, idem.
    Absent, idem.
    Prophecy, idem.
    Las personas mayores, (The grown-ups), tr. by Donald Walsh,
       in APLC, p. 405.
    Dobla el dos de noviembre (The Second of November Tolls),
       idem, p. 407.
    Si lloviera esta noche (If it rained tonight), idem, p. 409.
    La araña, (The spider), idem, p. 409.
    España, aparta de mi esta cáliz (Spain, take from me this
       cup), idem, p. 413.
    Heces (Dregs), tr. by Muna Lee, idem, p. 411.
    Himno a los voluntarios de la republica (Hymn to the Volunteers
       of the republic), tr. by H. R. Hays, Donald Walsh, J. P. Bishop
       and Dudley Fitts, idem. pp.417-27.

Varallanos, José, 1905-
    Tropel de montañas (Mob of mountains), tr. by Muna Lee,
      in APLC, p. 151.

Vásquez, Emilio, 1903-
    Imilla (Indian girl), tr. by Blanca López Castellón, in
      APLC, p. 467.

Vivero, Domingo de.
    To Edison, tr. by A. B. Poor, in Pan Amer. poems.

Westphalen, Emilio Adolfo, von, 1910-
    Andando el tiempo (As time goes on), tr. by H. R. Hays
      in APLC, p. 389.

Xammar, Luis Fabio, 1911-
    El puquial (The spring), tr. by Muna Lee, in APLC, p. 469.

Zegarra Ballón, Edilberto, 1880-
    Sighs, tr. by A. B. Poor, in Pan American poems.
    Excerpts from Vibraciones, tr. by Isaac Goldberg, in Pan
      Amer. mag., XX, (Feb. 1915), p. 22.

POETRY – PUERTO RICO

Benítez de Gautier, Alejandrina, 1819-1879.
    To my lamp, in West Ind. rev., IV, (Aug., 1938), p. 27.
    The cabin, excerpt, idem.

Blanco, Antonio Nicolás.
    Intimate prayer, tr. by Muna Lee, in Pan Amer. bull.,
      (July, 1925); also in Poetry, XXVI (1925), p. 143-4.

Cadilla, Carmen Alicia, 1908-
    Responsos (Responsories), tr. by Dudley Fitts, in APLC,
      p. 503.
    Aire triste, (Sad air), idem, p. 503.
    Angelus, idem, p. 505.
    The boy who sells sweet oranges, tr. by H. R. Hays, in
      Poetry, v. LXII (May, 1943), p. 65.

Dávila, Virgilio, 1880-
    Holy week, tr. by Thomas Walsh, in Hispanic anthology,
      p. 704.

Diego, José de, 1866-1918.
    The setting sun, tr. by A. B. Poor, in Pan American poems.

Gautier Benítez, José, 1850-1880.
    Puerto Rico, in Blackwell, p. 516-520; also tr. by Blackwell,
      in Christian science monitor, (July 22, 1927); also tr. by
      Underwood, in West Ind. rev., IV (Aug. 1938), p. 28.

Labarthe, Pedro Juan, 1906-
    The broken urn, tr. by Marshall Nunn, in West Ind. rev.,
        VI (July, 1940), p. 37.

Lee de Muñóz Marín, Muna, 1895-
    Symphony in white, in Hispanic anthology, pp. 769-771.

Llorens Torres, Luis, 1875-
    Bolívar, tr. by Muna Lee, in Poetry, XXVI, (1925), p.
        146.
    Psalms, tr. by Ulah Haynes (Gloria Grey), in West Ind.
        rev., IV (Nov., 1937), p. 35.
    High seas, idem, IV (March, 1938), p. 20.
    Drama of the forgotten, idem, (Apr., 1938), p. 30.

Meléndez, Concha, 1904-
    The mountains know, in Blackwell, p. 520; also tr. by
        Blackwell, in Christian science monitor, (Aug.,7, 1926).

Mercado, José, (Momo), 1863-1911.
    The speech of Spain, tr. by Underwood, in West Ind. rev.,
        V. (Sept.,1938), p. 30.

Muñóz Marín, Luis, 1898-
    Proletarios (Proletarians), tr. by Muna Lee, in APLC,
        p. 207.
    Panfleta (Pamphlet), idem, p. 207

Muñóz Marín, Muna Lee, see Lee de Muñóz Marín, Muna.

Padilla, José Gualberto, ("El Carib"), 1829-1896.
    The funeral dirge for Gautier Benítez, tr. by Underwood,
        in West Ind. rev., IV (Aug.,1938), p. 29.

Palés Matos, Luis, 1898*-
    San Sabas, tr. by Muna Lee, in Catholic anthology; also
        in Poetry, XXVI (1925), pp. 145-6.
    El pozo (The well), tr. by Donald Walsh, in APLC, p. 185.
    Claro de luna (Claire de lune), idem, p. 185.
    Elegía del Duque de la Mermelada (Duke of Marmalade),
        idem, p. 187.
    Lagarto verde (Look out for the snake), idem, p. 189.
    Nánigo al cielo (Nañigo to heaven), tr. by Dudley Fitts,
        in APLC, pp. 191-7.
    Danza Negra, tr. by Underwood, in West Ind. rev., VI,
        (April, 1940), p. 39; also tr. by Torres-Rioseco, in
        Torres-Rioseco, p. 131.
    Prelude in Boricua, tr. by William Carlos Williams, in Amer.
        Pref., VII (Winter, 1941-2), pp. 155-156.
    Lament, tr. by H. R. Hays, in Poetry, v. LXII (May, 1943,
        p. 79.

Pérez-Pierret, Antonio, 1883-
    My Pegasus, in Hispanic anthology, pp. 727-728.

Ramírez de Arellano, Clemente, 188—?
    Poetry, tr. by Underwood, in West Ind. rev., V, (Sept,,
        1938), p. 31.

Muñoz Rivera, Luis, 1865-1916.
    To her, in Hispanic anthology, pp.589-590.

Rodríguez Cabrero, Luis, 186?-1900.
    Don Quixote in Sierra Morena: A fantastic sonnet, tr. by
        Underwood, in West Ind. rev., V (Sept.1938), p.30.

Rodríguez de Tío, Lola, 1859*-1924.
    Mist, in Hispanic anthology, pp.559-561.
    My absent husband, tr. by Underwood, in West Ind. rev.,
        III (Sept., 1936), p. 38.

Vidarte, Santiago, 1827-1848.
    Insomnia, tr. by Underwood, in West Ind. rev., V (Sept.,
        1938), p. 29.

POETRY — URUGUAY

Acuña de Figueroa, F., 1790-1862.
    The African mother, tr. by A. B. Poor, in Pan Amer. poems.

Figueira, Gastón, 1905-
    Song of occupation, in Three songs of Gaston Figueira,
        tr. by Blackwell, (privately printed, Montevideo,1940).
    Night song, idem.
    Song of the sailor, idem.
    Enchantment of Rio de Janeiro: St. Francis' Park, tr. by
        Underwood in West Ind. rev., IV, (Aug.,1938), p.29.
    Rain over Rio, idem.
    St. Francis park, tr. by Underwood, in West Ind. rev.,
        VI, (March, 1940), p. 36.
    Old Pernambuco, idem.
    Angra dos reis, idem.
    Mulata hermosa, idem.
    On the banks of the Beberibe, idem.
    Coffee, idem.
    Olinda, idem.
    Shore of Amalina (Bahía), idem.
    Bridges of Recife, idem.
    Image, tr. by Madaline W. Nichols, in Two songs of Gaston
        Figueira (Montevideo: privately printed, 1942).
    The potter's song, idem.
    Ballad of life, tr. by Willis Knapp Jones, in Poet lore,
        vol. 47, (Spring,1941), pp.65-75.
    Pineapple, idem.
    Voice of Recife, idem.
    Prayer to moon of tropics, idem.
    Streets, idem.
    Song to maid of Baía, idem.
    Maracatú, idem.
    I believe in you, Pan America, tr. by Dorothy M. Ter-
        cero, in Pan American bull,, (Apr.,1943), p.196.

Figueira, Gastón, 1905 (continued)
    Little ballad of a sailor, tr. by Lloyd Mallan, in
        Poetry, vol. LXII (May, 1943), p. 83.

Herrera y Reissig, Julio, 1875-1910.
    Alba triste, (Mournful dawn), in Modernist trend.
    La sombra dolorosa (Doleful shadow), idem.
    La gota amarga (Anguish and love), idem.
    La cena, idem; also in Torres-Rioseco, p.112.
    Sonnet: exotic idealization, tr. by H. R. Hays, in De-
        cision, I, (May, 1941), p. 46.
    The house on the mountain, in Blackwell, p. 444.
    The cura, in Hispanic anthology, pp.683-6.
    The carts, idem.
    The parish church, idem ; also in Catholic anthology, p.
        396.
    Four sonnets, tr. by Muna Lee, in Poetry, XXVI (1925),
        pp.145-150.

Ibañez, Roberto, 1907-
    Elegía por los ahogados que retornan (Elegy for the
        drowned men who return), tr. by Lloyd Mallan and Do-
        nald Walsh, in APLC, p. 541.

Ibarbourou, Juana de, 1895-
    The smith, tr. by Beatrice Gilman Proske, in Hispanic poets,
        p. 261.

    The Shepherdess, idem, p. 262.
    Fleeting restlessness, tr. by Elizabeth de Gué Trapier,
        idem, p. 263.
    Noche de lluvia (Rainy night), tr. by Rolfe Humphries, in
        APLC, p. 479.
    Bond, tr. by Muna Lee, in Poetry, XXVI (1925), pp.151-2;
        also in Pan Amer. bull., (July, 1925); also in Torres-
        Rioseco, p. 122.
    The sweet miracle, tr. in Blackwell, p. 448; also in Pan
        Amer. bull., (Feb. 1928); also in Good neighbor tour,
        VI, p. 43.
    Como la primavera (Like the springtime), in Inter-Amer.,
        V, (1921), p. 107.

Luisi, Luisa, 1897-1940.
    I am a tree, in Blackwell, p. 450.

Magariños Cervantes, Alejandro, 1825-1893.
    Glory, tr. literally, in Green and Lowenfels, pp.314-323.

Oribe, Emilio, 1893-
    Music, tr. by Jessie Read Wendell, in Hispanic poets, p.
        259.

Pacheco y Obes, Melchor, 1809*-1851.
    Cemetery of Alegrete, tr. literally, in Green and Lowenfels,
        pp.334-341.

Pereda Valdés, Ildefonso, 1899-
    Canción de cuna para dormir a un negrito (Cradle song to
        put a negro baby to sleep), tr. by Muna Lee, in APLC,
        p. 471.

Rodó, José Enrique, 1872-1917.
    Bolívar, tr. anon, in Pan Amer. bull, LXIV (1930), pp.1390-
        1406.

Silva Valdés, Fernán, 1887-
    Ballad of the white colt, tr. by Helen Eldridge Fish, in
        Hispanic Poets, p. 256.
    Hymn to the man of the future, in Pan Amer. bull, LXVIII.
        From Intemperie (Montevideo, 1930).
    The Indian, tr. by Willis Knapp Jones, in Poet lore,
        XLVII, No.4 (Winter 1941).
    The gaucho troubadour, idem, including: Evocation, North,
        Sowing, Like the birds, The guitar, Singing, and Man.
    Romance de la tardecita, tr. by Warren Carrier, in Poet
        lore, XLVII, No. 4, (Winter, 1941).

Vasseur Alvaro, Armando ("Americo Llano"), 1878-
    The corsair, tr. by Underwood, in Mexican life, X,
        (Jan., 1934), p. 12.

Zorrilla de San Martín, Juan, 1857-1931.
    Tabaré, (1886) (Tabare), tr. by R. W. Huntington (Buenos
        Aires: 1934). 174 pp.
    The mother's farewell, in Blackwell, p. 444; also in
        Pan Amer. bull. (Jan., 1926); also in Good Neighbor
        tour, VI. p. 40.
    Thou and I, tr. by A. B. Poor, in Pan American poems.
    Does she not feel?, idem.

POETRY - VENEZUELA

Arraiz, Antonio, 1903-
    The mariner, tr. by Underwood, in West Ind. rev., V,
        (April, 1939), p. 29.

Baralt, Rafaél María, 1810-1860.
    To Christopher Columbus, tr. literally in Green and Lo-
        wenfels, pp.386-387.

Barrios Cruz, Luis, 1898-
    The lost footprint, tr. by Underwood, in West Ind. rev.,
        V, (April, 1939), p. 31.

Bello, Andrés, 1781-1865.
    To the Bío-Bío, in Blackwell, pp.438-440.
    The agriculture of the torrid zone, in Hispanic anthology,
        pp.390-394.
    Dialogue, idem, pp.389-390.

Blanco Fombona, Rufino, 1874-
   The horse on the shield, tr. by Jean Rogers Longland, in
      Hispanic poets, p. 265.
   Within the heart, in Blackwell, p. 428.
   The flight of Psyche, idem, p. 434.
   A little messenger dove, idem.
   Invitation to love, idem, p. 436.
   The inevitable, idem.
   Escape, tr. by Muna Lee, in Pan Amer. bull., (July, 1925);
      also in Poetry XXVI (1925), pp. 153-4.
   Eugenio M. de Hostos, tr. anon. in Inter-Amer., VII
      (1924), pp. 534-539.
   By the sea, tr. by Muna Lee in Poetry, XXVI (1925), p.
      154.
   Romancillo de la intrusa, tr. by J. Crowhurst-Rand in Pan
      Amer. mag., XXVII (1918), p. 108, (With Spanish on
      opposite page).
   La casa triste, idem.
   Por qué, señor? Idem.

Calcaño, José A., 1827-1897.
   The cypress, in Blackwell, p. 442.

Castro, Luis Luvera, 1909-1933.
   As the wind, tr. by Underwood, in West Ind. rev., V,
      (April, 1939), p. 30.

Ferrer, José Miguel, 1903*-
   Nocturno del pecado y su delación (Nocturne of sin and
      its accusation), tr. by Richard O'Connell, in APLC,
      p. 361.

Fombona-Pacheco, Jacinto, 1901-
   Muerte en el aire, tr. by J. L. Grucci, in Fantasy,
      XXVI (1924), pp. 69-70. From Las torres desprevenidas.
   Anuncio del Reino de la Estrella (Announcement of the
      reign of the stars), tr. by J. L. Grucci, in Amer.
      Pref. VII (Winter, 1941-1942), p. 151. From Virajes
      (Caracas: Elite, 1932).
   Nocturn, tr. by Underwood, in West Ind. rev., V, (April,
      1939), p. 31.
   Un alerta para Abraham Lincoln (A warning for Abraham
      Lincoln), tr. by Angel Flores, in APLC, p. 269.
   Muerte en el aire (Death over the air), idem, p. 271.
   Mientras yo decía mi canto (While I sang my song), idem,
      p. 275.

Gerbasi, Vicente, 1913-
   Look and music of my sweetheart, tr. by Underwood, in
      West Ind. rev., V (April, 1939), p. 30.

Heredia, José Ramón, 1900-
   Mi poema a los niños muertos en la guerra de España
      (My poem to the children killed in the war of Spain),
      tr. by Dudley Fitts, in APLC, p. 515.

Lozano, D. A., 1823-1866.
    A remembrance of Puerto Cabello, tr. by A. B. Poor, in
        Pan American Poems.
    The mangle, idem.
    America, tr. literally in Green and Lowenfels, pp. 342-349.

Mata, Andrés A. ("Adán Marset"), 1870-1931.
    Alma y paisaje (Soul and landscape), tr. by Muna Lee in
        Poetry, XXVI, (1925), p. 154; also in Pan American mag.,
        XLI (1928), p. 154.

Olivares Figueroa, R., 1892-
    Number XX, tr. by Underwood, in West Ind. rev., V (April,
        1929), p. 29.
    Sembrador, (The sower), tr. by Dudley Fitts, in APLC, p. 143.

Otero Silva, Miguel, 1908-
    Drill, tr. by Rolfe Humphries, in Nation, v. 153 (Dec. 27,1941),
        p. 671.
    Seed time, tr. by Underwood, in West Ind. rev., V (April,1939)
        p. 31.
    Music sleeping in America's branches, tr. by Rolfe Humphries,
        in Fantasy XXVI (1942), p. 54.
    Siembra (Sowing), tr. by Donald Walsh, in APLC, p. 283.
    Encrucijada (Crossroads), idem, p. 285.

Paz Castillo, Fernando, 1895-
    Autumn, tr. by Underwood, in West Ind. rev., V, (April, 1939),
        p. 30.

Pimentel Coronel, Ramón, 1872-1909.
    Jesus, tr. by Joseph I. C. Clarke, in Hispanic anthology,
        pp. 648-651; also in Catholic anthology, p. 377.

Queremel, Angel Miguel, 1899-1939.
    Romance de amor y de sangre (Ballad of love and blood),
        tr. by Donald Walsh, in APLC, p. 263.
    Manifiesto del soldado que volvió a la guerra (Manifesto
        to the soldier who went back to war), idem, p. 265.

Sola, Otto d', 1912-
    Plenitud (Plenitude), tr. by Angel Flores, in APLC, p. 297.
    Antes de llegar los aviones que incendian las ciudades,
        (Before the coming of the planes that burned the city),
        idem, p. 299.
    Canto final a una muchacha de puerto (Last song to a girl
        of the waterfront), idem, p. 299.

Sotillo, Pedro, 1902-
    Poema, tr. by Underwood, in West Ind. rev., V (April 1939,
        p. 30.

Spinetti Dini, Antonio (Born in Italy), 1900-1941.
    Romance of a soul, tr. by Underwood, in West Ind. rev.,
        V (April, 1939), p. 31.
    Parábola de la generosidad (Parable of generosity), APLC, 501.

Venegas Filardo, Pascual, 1911–
    Journey unto the endless night, tr. by Underwood, in West
        Ind. rev., V (April, 1939), p. 29.

POETRY – COUNTRY UNCERTAIN

Ancona Horruytiner, Ignacio (Country uncertain), –1912.
    Virtue, tr. by Blackwell, in Boston Record, (Oct. 11,1909).

POETRY – ANONYMOUS

Aztec Poetry:
    I the singer, tr. by J. H. Cornyn, in Mexican life,
        IX (Aug., 1933), p. 19.
    I am Huitzilopochtli, idem.

Coplas:
    Coplas of Spain and Latin America, tr. by Beryl Gray,
        in Pan Amer. mag., XLI (1931), pp.298-303.
    Others from Mexican arrieros, in Beal, C., Mexican
        Muleteers, idem, p. 388.

Folk Songs:
    Folk song of the Brazilian Gypsies, tr. by A. B. Poor,
        in Pan Amer. poems.
    Folk song of North Peruvian Indians, tr. in Pan Amer.,
        mag., XXVII (1918), pp.44.
    Folk songs of the Pampas, tr. by Muna Lee, in Pan Amer.
        bull., (July, 1925); also in Poetry, XXVI (1925), p.
        138.

Song of Quetzalcoatl, tr. by J. H. Cornyn (Antioch Press,1931)
    207 pp.
    Also the song of Quetzalcoatl, tr. by J. H. Cornyn in
        Mexican Folkways, IV No. 2. (April-June, 1928), p.
        78. (With Spanish.) Also El Canto de Quetzalcoatl, tr.
        by José de la Barrera, excerpts in Pan Amer. mag.,
        vol. 49 (1930), pp. 124-131.

D R A M A

ARGENTINA

Bayón Herrera, Luis.
Santos Vega (3 acts and epilog) tr. by J. S. Fassett,
in Bierstadt, pp.21-76.

Herrero Ducloux, Enrique, 1877—
The straight line (one act), tr. anon. in Inter-Amer.,
IV (1920), pp.57-68.

Manco, Silverio.
Juan Moreira (2 acts, 6 scenes) tr. by J. S. Fassett, in
Bierstadt, pp.1-20.

Leguizamón, Martiniano, 1858-1935.
Calandria (3 acts, 1898). Calandria, tr. by Orosi, in
H N M, (1932).

Méndez Calzada, Enrique,
Criminals, (one act), tr. anon, in Inter-Amer., VII
(1923), pp. 115-125.

Payró, Roberto, 1867-1928.
Canción trágica (one act, 1900,) The tragic song, tr.
by Willis Knapp Jones and Carlos Escudero, in Poet
lore, v. 49 (1943).

Pico, Pedro E.
No hay burlas con el amor (one act, 1907). You can't
fool with love, tr. by Willis Knapp Jones and Carlos
Escudero, in Poet lore, v. 49 (Summer, 1943).

Rojas, Ricardo, 1882—
Ollantay (Tragedy, 4 acts, 1940). Excerpts tr. by Angel
Flores, in Pan Amer. bull.,March 1940; also some tr.
by E. J. R. Isaacs, in Theatre Arts, XXIV (April,
1940), pp. 252-6.

Sánchez Gardel, Julio, 1879-1936.
La montaña de brujas (tragedy, 3 acts, 1914)The witches'
mountain, tr. by J. S. Fassett, Jr., in Bierstadt, pp.
77-130.

DRAMA - BRAZIL

Alencar, José Martiniano de, 1829-1877.
O jesuita (4 acts, 1875). The Jesuit, tr. by E. R. de
Britto, in Poet lore, XXX (1919), pp.475-547.

DRAMA - BOLIVIA

More, Federico, 1889 —
Interlude (one act), tr. by Audrey Alden, in Shay, p. 39.

DRAMA — CHILE

Barrios, Eduardo, 1884-
Papá y mamá (one act), 1916. Papa and Mama, tr. by Willis Knapp Jones, in Poet lore, v. 33 (Summer, 1922), pp.286-90.

Marín, Juan, 1897-
Orestes y yo (Three acts, Tokio, 1940) Orestes and I, tr. by R. P. Butrick, in Asia America, 1940.

Moock, Armando, 1894-
Cancionero del Niño Jesús (one act, 1920?) tr. by Willis Knapp Jones, in Poet lore, XLV (Winter, 1939), pp.23-53.
Las amigas de don Juan (one act, 1931), tr. by Willis Knapp Jones, in Poet lore, XLVI (Spring, 1940), pp. 47-75.

DRAMA — CUBA

Avellaneda, Gertrudis, see Gómez de Avellaneda, Gertrudis.

Gómez de Avellaneda y Arteaga, Gertrudis, 1814-1873.
Baltasar (Madrid; Rodríguez, 1858). Belshazzar (4 acts), tr. by W. E. Burbank (London: B. F. Stevens and Brown, 1914, and San Francisco: Robertson, 1914) 64pp; also summarized and with excerpts tr. by F. M. Noa, in Poet lore, XVII (Summer, 1906) pp.118-38.

Ramos, José Antonio, 1885-
When love dies (one act), tr. by Isaac Goldberg, in Shay, Twenty-five short plays, international, pp. 125-146.

DRAMA — MEXICO

Las pasiones (Passion play at Tzintzuntzan), tr. by Frances Toor, in Mexican Folkways, I (June-Nov., 1925) pp.21 ff.

Los pastores. Edited and tr. by M. R. Cole, in American Folklore Society, IX, also separately (1907) 234 pp.; also descriptions and excerpts, tr. by Marcus Bach, in Theatre arts, XXIV (April, 1940), pp.283-88.

Los Tastoanes. The Tastoanes, tr. by Frederick Starr, in Journal of American Folklore, XV (1902), pp.73-83.

Chavero, Alfredo, 1841-1906.
Xóchitl (3 acts, 1878). Selections from Xóchitl, in Starr, p. 63.

Farias de Issasi, Teresa, 1878-
  The sentence of death, (One act), tr. by Lilian Saun-
    ders, in Shay, Twenty-five short plays, pp.273-81.

Jiménez Rueda, Julio, 1896-
  The unforeseen (3 act play of Old Mexico), tr. by Gino
    V. M. di Solenni, in Poet lore, XXXV (1924), pp.1-24.

Juana Inés de la Cruz, Sor, 1651-1695.
  Los empeños de la casa. A song from it, tr. by J. C.
    Barden, in Pan Amer. bull., v. 76 (Apr., 1942), pp.
    195-8.
  Salutations (from a play), in Anthology of Mex. poets,
    p. 222.
  Phoenix (from a play), idem, p. 223.

Orozco R., Profesor Efrén.
  El mensajero del sol (editions in English and Spanish).
    Mexico: Secretaría de Gobernación, Dirección general
    de población, 1941) 64 pp. illus.

Peón y Contreras, José, 1843-1907.
  Hasta el cielo! (3 act, 1876). Excerpts in Starr, p.245.

Saavedra y Bessey, Rafael M.,
  La chinita (2 scene panorama of Uruapan), tr. by Lilian
    Saunders, in Poet lore, XXXVII (1926), pp.107-119.

Villaseñor Angeles, Eduardo.
  Café chino (one act). Chinese coffee shop, tr. by Howard
    S. Phillips, in Mexican life, III (Sept., 1927), pp.
    23-24.

DRAMA -- NEW MEXICO

Canto del niño perdido (300-year-old Penitentes folk
  play, annually performed during Lent), tr. by Mary
  R. Van Stone and E. R. Sims, with Spanish and English
  in parallel columns, in Spur of the Cock, v.   XI
  (1933) pp.44-89.

Coloquios de los pastores (Colloquies of the shepherds),
  tr. by Aurora Lucero-White (Santa Fe, N. M.: Santa
  Fe Press, 1940). 51 pp. illustrations; music by Alejandro Flores.

DRAMA -- PERU

Ollantay. Ollanta, an ancient Inca drama, tr. by Clement
  R. Markham (London, 1871); also in Markham, The Incas
  of Peru (Dutton, 1910); summary and excerpts tr. by
  L. E. Elliott, in Pan Amer. Mag., XXXIII (1921), pp.
  281-90; also excerpts tr. by E. C. Hills, in Hills
  Hispanic Studies, 48 pp.

DRAMA — PHILIPPINES

Reyes, Severino, 1861-
> Walang Sugat (Manila: M. Reyes, 1898). Not wounded, tr.
> by M. M. Reyes and J. A. D. Gush, Music by F. Tolen-
> tino (Manila, 1898).
> The martyrs of the country: Blooy (sic) pages of Philip-
> pine history, translated (sic) by J. Gálvez (Manila,
> 19—). Really a summary of the play, including the
> execution of the rebels and the finale in which De-
> vils carry off the friars responsible for the death
> of Paco and other revolutionists.
> Minda, tr. by P. Reyes, Revised by William Barrett (Ma-
> nila, 19—).

Rizal y Alonso, José, 1861-1896
> Noli me tangere. Famous Philippine novel dramatized by
> A. Vidal, "Meeting in the town hall", and "Souls in
> Torment", in Edades, J. Short plays from the Philip-
> pines (Manila, 1940).

DRAMA — URUGUAY

Pérez Petit, Víctor, 1871-
> Claro de Luna (One act, 1906). Moonlight sonata, tr. by
> Willis Knapp Jones and Carlos Escudero, in Poet lore,
> vol. 49 (1943).

F I C T I O N

SHORT STORY AND NOVEL

ARGENTINA

Alvarez, José S. (Fray Mocho), 1858-1903.
  Caza del cóndor (Hunting the condor)(S. S.), tr. anon. in
    Andean Monthly, III, (July, 1940), pp.241-3 (with Span-
    ish text).

Burgos, Fausto, 1888-
  Una mujer y un promsesante (A woman and a pilgrim), (S.S.),
    tr. anon., in Andean monthly, II, (Jan., 1940), pp.
    44-6 (with Spanish text).

Cerretani, Fausti, 1888-
  El infame señor Batet (The infamous señor Batet), (S.S.),
    tr. by Mary and C. V. Wicker, in Amer. pref., VII (Win-
    ter, 1941-2), pp. 175-83.

Dávalos, Juan Carlos, 1887-
  El viento blanco (The white wind), (S.S.), tr. by Angel
    Flores, in Flores and Poore, pp.421-34; also in Ju-
    nior Red cross journal (Jan., 1943), pp.131-5.

Eandi, Héctor I.
  Hombres capaces (Dangerous men), (S.S.), tr. by Alis de
    Sola, in Flores and Poore, pp.368-83.

Echeverría, Esteban, 1805-1851.
  El matadero (1840) (The slaughter house) (S.S.), tr. by
    Angel Flores in The New Mexico quarterly rev., Nov.,
    1942. (This is usually considered Argentina's first
    short story).

"Fray Mocho", pseud., see Alvarez, José S.

Gálvez, Manuel, 1882-
  Luna de miel y otras narraciones (María del Rosario),
    (S. S.), tr. anon, in Inter-Amer., IV (1921), pp.
    372-82.
  Miércoles santo (1930) (Holy Wednesday) (N.), tr. by
    W. B. Wells, (New York: Appleton, London: Lane, 1934),
    169 pp.
  Nacha Regules (1919) (Nacha Regules) (N.), tr. by L.
    Ongley, (New York: Dutton, London: Dent, 1923), 304 pp.

Güiraldes, Ricardo, 1886-1927.
  Don Segundo Sombra (1926) (Shadows on the pampas), (N.),
    tr. by Harriet de Onis, (Farrar and Rinehart, 1935),
    270 pp.
Rosaura (S.S.), tr. by Anita Brenner, in Tales from the Argen-
    tine, pp. 179-235.

Larreta, Enrique Rodríguez See Rodríguez Larreta, Enrique.

López, Lucio Vicente, 1848-1894.
La gran aldea (1882) (Holiday in Buenos Aires) (S.S.),
tr. by Anita Brenner, in Tales from the Argentine,
pp.103-124.

Lugones, Leopoldo, 1874-1938.
A good cheese (S.S.), tr. anon., in Inter-Amer., III
(1920), pp. 160-2.
La guerra gaucha (Death of a gaucho) (S.S.), tr. by
Anita Brenner, in Tales from the Argentine, pp.79-102.
Shepherd boy and shepherd girl (S.S.), tr. anon., in
Inter-Amer., III (1920), pp.157-60.

Mallea, Eduardo, 1903-
Bahía de silencio (Bay of silence) (N.), tr. by Stephen
Grummon, (Knopf, 1943).
La ciudad junto al río immovil (Conversation) (S.S.), tr.
by Hugo Manning, in Fantasy, no.26 (1942), p.61-5.
Fiesta en noviembre (Fiesta in November) (S.S.), tr. by
Alis de Sola, in Flores and Poore, pp.11-119.
Rapsodía del alegre malhechor (The gay goodfellow) (S.S.),
tr. by Lloyd Mallan, in Amer. pref., VII, (Winter,
1941-2), pp.106-24.

Mancilla de García, Eduarda ("Daniel")
Lucía Miranda (N.). An Argentine edition says that this
lady's novel, Daniel, was translated into English and
that C. Cushing translated in the United States the
romantic novel about Lucía Miranda. Publisher?

Mármol, José, 1818-1881.
Amalia (1850) (Amalia) (N.), tr. by Mary J. Serrano,
(Dutton, 1919), 419 pp.

Martínez Zuviría, Gustavo A. ("Hugo Wast"), 1883-
Desierto de Piedra (1925) Stone Desert) (N), tr. by Louis
Imbert and Jacques Le Clercq, (New York: Longmans, 1928)
302 pp.
Valle Negro (Black Valley) (N), tr. by Herman and Miriam
Hespelt (Longmans, 1929) 302 pp.
Flor de Durazno (1911) Peach Blossom (N), tr. by Herman
and Miriam Hespelt (Longmans, 1929) 300 pp.
Lucía Miranda (1909) The Strength of Lovers (N), tr. by
Louis Imbert and Jacques Le Clercq. (Longmans, 1930)
315 pp.
Casa de los Cuervos (1916) The house of the Ravens (N),
tr. by Leonard Matters (London: Williams and Norgate,
1924) 319 pp.
The Thatched Roof (S.S.), tr. anon. In Inter-Amer., IX
(1926), pp. 416-434.
The Missing Hand (S.S.), tr. anon, in Inter-Amer., VII
(1925), pp. 540-561.

Martorello, Noé S.
    Pedro (S.S.), tr. anon. in Inter-Amer., VIII, (April,
        1925), pp. 323-328. From Nosotros (B. A., Nov., 1924).

Morales, Ernesto, 1890-
    The Mburucuyá or Passion-flower (S.S.), tr. anon., in
        Inter-Amer., VII (1924), pp. 468-470.

Oliveira Cezar, Filiberto de.
    Supay-Chaca: A Quechua Legend (S.S.), in Inter-Amer.,
        IV (1921), pp. 256-7.

Palacios Mendoza, Alfredo.
    A Wedding in the Quechua Great World (S.S.), in Inter-
        Amer., IV (1920), p. 34. From El Hogar (B. A., June
        1920).

Payró, Roberto Jorge, 1867-1928.
    Casamiento de Laucha (Laucha's Marriage) (S.S.), tr. by
        Anita Brenner in Tales from the Argentine, pp. 1-76.
    Pago Chico (Barcelona: Mitre, 1908) The Devil in Pago
        Chico (S.S.), tr. by Anita Brenner, in Tales from the
        Argentine, pp. 153-178.

Pita Martínez, Lola.
    Argentine children of the past (S.S.), from Mundo Uru-
        guayo, in Amigos, I, (March, 1942), pp. 35-42.

Rodriguez Larreta, Enrique, 1875-
    La gloria de Don Ramiro (1908) (The glory of Don Ramiro)
        (N), tr. by L. B. Walton, (Dutton, 1924). 307 pp.

Sarmiento, Domingo Faustino, 1811-1888.
    Vida de Facundo Quiroga (1845) (Facundo: Life in the Ar-
        gentine republic in the days of the tyrants) (N), tr.
        by Mrs. Horace Mann (Hurd and Houghton, 1868) 400 pp.
    Excerpts, The private life of Facundo, tr. by Anita Bren-
        ner, in Tales from the Argentine, pp. 125-153.

Tenreiro, R. M.
    The moonlight piano player (S.S.), tr. in Amigos, I,
        (March, 1942), pp. 27-30.

Ugarte, Manuel, 1878-
    Tiger of Macuza (S.S.), tr. by H. C. Schweikert, in
        Stratford monthly, VII, (April, 1924), pp. 71-76.
    The gringo, in Tales from the ... Spanish, vol. 8.

"Wast, Hugo" see Martínez Zuviria, Gustavo A.

FICTION -- BOLIVIA

Céspedes, Augusto.
    El pozo, from Sangre de mestizos, (Santiago de Chile:
        Nascimento, 1936). (The Well)(S.S.), tr. by Mary and
        C. V. Wicker, in American pref. (Winter, 1941-2), pp. 125-39.

Costa du Rels, Adolfo, 1891–
    La misqui simi (S.S.), tr. by Elizabeth Wallace, in
    Flores and Poore, pp. 458–65.

Pereyra, Diómedes de, 1897–
    El valle del sol (The land of the golden scarab) (N),
        tr. by the author, (Indianapolis: Bobbs Merrill,1928).
    Caucho (Santiago de Chile: Nascimento, 1938) (Caucho: Rub-
        ber) (N), tr. by author, (Butterick, 1939).
    La trama de oro (Golden web) (N), tr. by Pereyra (Butter-
        ick Pub. Co., 1938).
    The land of mystery (S.S.), in Golden book, Feb–Mar.1928.
    Sun gold (N), in Golden book magazine, July–Sept.,1928.

FICTION – BRAZIL

Alencar, José Martiniano de, 1829–1877.
    Iracema (Rio Vianna, 1865) (Iracema the honey lips)
        tr. by Sir Richard and Isabel Burton. (London: Biclers,
        1886); also tr. by N. Biddell (Rio: Imprenza ingleza,nd).

Amado, Jorge, 1912–
    Mar morto, (Sea of the dead) (S.S.), tr. by Donald Walsh,
        in Flores and Poore, pp. 384–97.

Andrade, Mario de, 1893–
    Amar, verbo intranzitivo (1932) (Fraulein) (N), tr. by
        Margaret Richardson Hollingsworth. (Macaulay, 1933),
        252 pp.

Aranha, Graça, see Graça Aranha.

Azevedo, Aluízio de, 1858–1913.
    O Cortiço (1890), (A Brazilian tenement) (N), tr. by
        Harry W. Brown (McBride, 1926) 320 pp.

Barreto, Paulo, 1878–.
    An episode in a hotel, (S.S.), tr. anon., in Inter-
        American, I, (1917), pp. 350–354.

Barroso, Gustavo, 1888–
    Mapirunga (N), tr. with explanatory preface by R. B.
        Cunninghame Graham (London: Heinemann, 1942).

Carneiro, Cecilio J., 1911–
    A foguerira (1941) (The bonfire) (N), tr. by Dudley Poore
        (Farrar and Rinehart, 1942) (Honorable mention in In-
        ter–Amer. contest).

Coelho Netto, see Netto, Coelho.

Cunha, Euclydes da, 1866–1909.
    Os Sertões (N), announced by University of Chicago Press,
        1943.

"Dolores, Carmen", see Moncorvo, Emilia.

Duarte, Margarita Estrela Bandeira.
Lenda de carnaubeird (1939)(Legend of the palm tree)
(Grosset and Dunlap, 1940).

Escragnolle Taunay, Alfredo, see Taunay, Alfredo.

Ferreira de Castro, José María.
A selva (Jungle, a tale of Amazon Rubber trappers (N),
tr. by Charles Duff, (London: Dickson, 1934, and New
York: Viking Press, 1935), 340 pp.

Freyre, Gilberto, 1900-
Casa grande y senzala (N), tr. by Vera Kelsey, announced
by Yale University Press, 1942.

Graça Aranha, José Pereira da, 1868-1931.
Marta: Legend of the celestial voice (S.S.), in Inter-
Amer., IV (1920), pp.95-96.
Chanaan (1902) Canaan) (N.), tr, by Mariano Joaquin
Lorente (Boston: The four seas, 1920), 321 pp.

Jardim, Luis, 1901-
The armadillo and the monkey (S.S.), tr. by María Cimino
(Coward-McCann, 1942), 46 pp.

Lobato, José Benito Monteiro, 1883-
The balm—cricket and the ant (S.S.), tr. anon. in Inter-
Amer., VI (1922), pp.47-48.
Modern torture (S.S.), in Brazilian short stories; also
in Stratford monthly, VII, (April 1924), pp.77-85.
Penitent wag, (S.S.), in Brazilian short stories.
The plantation buyer (S.S.), in Brazilian short stories.
The farm magnate, in Clark and Lieber, pp.926-36.

Machado de Assis, Joaquim María, 1839-1908.
The attendant's confession (S.S.), tr. by Isaac Goldberg,
in Clark and Lieber, pp.903-911; also in Stratford
journal, I, (Sept. 1917), p. 31.
Life (S.S.), tr. by Isaac Goldberg, in Stratford journal,
V, (Sept. 1919), pp. 119-129; also in Goldberg, Bra-
zilian tales.
The fortune teller (S.S.), in Goldberg, Brazilian tales.

Medeiros e Albuquerque, José, 1867-1934.
The vengeance of Feliz (S.S.), tr. by Isaac Goldberg, in
Brazilian tales.

Moncorvo Bandeira de Mello, Emilia, 1852-1910.
Aunt Zeze's tears (S.S.), in Goldberg, Brazilian tales.

Netto, Henrique Coelho, 1864-1934.
The pigeons, (S.S.), tr. by Isaac Goldberg, in Stratford
journal, I, (Sept. 1917), pp.23-31; also in Brazilian
tales.

Setubal, Paulo de Oliveira, 1893-1937.
    A Marquesa de Santos (1924). Domitila (N), tr. by Mar-
        garet Richardson (New York: Coward-McCann, 1930)
        324 pp.

Taunay, Alfredo Escrognolle ("Sylvio Dinarte") 1843-99.
    Innocencia (1872) (Innocencia, a story of the Prairie
        Region of Brazil) (N), (London: Chapman and Hall,
        1889) 312 pp.

Verissimo, Erico, 1905-
    Caminhos cruzados (1935). Crossroads (N.), tr. by L. C.
        Kaplan (Macmillan, 1943), 373 pp.

FICTION – CHILE

Acevedo Hernández, Antonio, 1886-
    El velorio (S.S.), in Andean Monthly, II, (Nov. 1939),
        p. 31, (With Spanish.)

Arriaza, Armando ("Hermes Nahuel").
    La manda (Pilgrimage) (S.S.), in Flores and Poore, pp.
        480-7.

Barrios, Eduardo,1884-
    El hermano asno (1926). Brother Ass, (N.), tr. by R.
        Selden Rose and Francisco Aguilera, in Flores and
        Poore, pp.488-608.

Blest Gana, Alberto, 1831-1920.
    Martín Rivas (1862) Martin Rivas (N.), tr. by Mrs.
        Charles Whitham. (London: Chapman, 1916,also New
        York: Knopf, 1918).

Castro Z., Oscar, 1910-
    Huellas en la tierra (Zigzag, 1940) Lucero (S.S.), tr.
        by J. L. Grucci, in Amer. pref. VII, (Winter, 1941-2),
        pp. 167-174.

Danke, Jacobo, 1905-
    Agitador. (The agitator), (S.S.), in Andean Monthly,III,
        (May, 1940), p. 147, (With Spanish).

Díaz Garcés, Joaquín ("Angel Pino"), 1878-1921.
    A christening (S.S.), in Inter-Amer., I, (1918), pp.
        179-185.
    Parisian bargain day in Chile (S.S.), idem, pp. 35-38.
    Un bautismo (A baptismal feast in Chile) (S.S.), in
        Andean Monthly; reprinted in Amigos, I, (Jan. 1942),
        pp. 11-12.

Durand Durand, Luis, 1894-
    El alicanto (S.S.), tr. by Bradley Premers, in Andean
        Monthly, IV, (Feb-Mar., 1941), pp. 103-112.

Edward Vives, Alberto, 1872-1932.
    Trail of D. Antonio Pérez: A tale of Roman Calvo, the
        Chilean Sherlock Holmes, in Inter-Amer., I (1918),
        pp.85-93.
    Aventuras de Román Calvo (Adventures of Román Calvo: The
        lost sweetheart), in Andean Monthly, II (June, 1939),
        p. 35.

Fuenzalida, Miguel de, see Edwards, Alberto.

Gana y Gana, Federico, 1868-1926.
    A tale of a winter morning (S.S.), from Cuentos completos
        (Santiago: Nascimento, 1926), in Tales from the ...
        Spanish, vol. 8.

Garrido Merino, Edgardo, 1895-
    El sombrero de nadie (The hat that belonged to no one),
        (S.S.), in Andean Monthly, I, (Dec. 1938), p. 38
        (With Spanish).

Godoy Alcayaga, Lucila ("Gabriela Mistral"), 1889-
    El caleuche de Chile [An American myth: El caleuche (Pi-
        rate Boat) de Chile] (S.S.), in Andean Monthly, II,
        (Oct. 1939), p. 43.

Goeminne Thomson, Augusto ("D'Halmar, Augusto"), 1882-
    Navidad en el mar, from Nirvana (Ercilla, 1935).
        (Christmas At Sea) (S.S.), in Andean Monthly, II,
        (Dec., 1939), p. 40. (With the Spanish).

Guzmán, Nicodemes, 1914-
    La sangre y la esperanza (1914) (N.) Part of Chap I
        (Mapocho district), tr. by George Garvin, in An-
        dean monthly, IV (July, 1941), pp. 198-203 (with
        the Spanish).

Huidobro, Vicente, 1893-
    Cagliostro (Mirror of a mage) (N.), tr. by W. B. Wells,
        (Houghton Mifflin, 1931).
    Mío Cid campeador (Portrait of a paladin),(N.), tr. by
        W. B. Wells (Liveright, 1932), 316 pp.
    El moro anónimo (Nameless Moor) (S.S.), tr. by H. A.
        Holmes, in Vicente Huidobro and creationism. (Co-
        lumbia Univ. Press, 1934).
    Temblor del cielo (Skyquake), (S.S.), idem.

Latorre, Mariano, 1870*-
    El secreto (The secret of the Pine Cone), (S.S.), in
        Andean Monthly, II, (April, 1939), p. 46. (With the
        Spanish).
    The buried jar, from Mundo Uruguayo, in Amigos, I,
        (Feb. 1942), pp. 18-30.

Lazo Baeza, Olegario, 1878-
    Limosna (Alms) (S.S.), in Andean Monthly, III, (Aug.
        1930), p. 303. (With the Spanish).

Maluenda Labarca, Rafaél, 1885-
    La fuerza de lo verosímil (The strength of Evidence),
        (S.S.), in Andean Monthly, III, (March, 1940), p.
        45 (With the Spanish); also in Amigos, I, (March
        1942), pp. 11-16.
    Si Dios quiere (When God desires it) (S.S.), in Andean
        Monthly, I, (June, 1939), p. 24.
    Perseguido (Escape), (S.S.), tr. by Alis de Sola, in Flo-
        res and Poore, p. 473-9.
    A Man of erudition (S.S.), tr. anon, in Inter-Amer., IV,
        (Oct., 1920), p. 17.

"Mistral, Gabriela", see Godoy Alcayaga, Lucila.

Montenegro, Ernesto, 1885-
    Por una docena de huevos duros (For a dozen of hard eggs)
        (S.S.), tr. by Bradley Premers, in Andean Monthly, III,
        (June, 1940), p. 187, (With Spanish).
    Los pájaros juegan a la chueca (Birds play hockey), (S.S.),
        in Andean Monthly, I, (Feb. 1939), p. 42-44.

Orrego Luco, Luis, 1886-1918.
    A poor devil, (S.S.), in Inter-Amer. I (1918), pp.357-62.

Pablete, Egidio ("Rònquillo"), 1869-?
    The out-come of a wager, (S.S.), tr. anon, in Inter-
        Amer., VI (1923), pp. 279-288.

Petit Marfán, Magdalena.
    Tormenta (Storm) (S.S.), in Andean Monthly, II, (April,
        1940), p. 89. (With the Spanish.)
    La quintrala (1932) (La quintrala) (N.), tr. by Lulú
        Vargas Vila (Macmillan, 1942) 190 pp.

Pombal, María Luisa.
    La mujer de la mortaja (The woman in the shroud) (N.),
        announced for 1943 by Knopf.

Prado, Pedro, 1886-
    The cloister, (S.S.), in Inter-Amer,, I (1918), p.227.

Prieto, Jenaro, 1889-,
    El socio (1928) (Partner), (N.), tr. by Blanca de Roig
        and Guy Dowler. (London: Butterworth, 1931) 255 pp.

Reyes, Salvador, 1899-
    Nochebuena de los vagabundos (Vagabunds' Christmas Eve)
        (S.S.), in Andean Monthly, III, (Dec. 1940), p. 509
        (With the Spanish); also tr. by Alis de Sola, in Flo-
        res and Poore, pp. 466-72.

Rojas, Manuel, 1896-
    Bandidos en los caminos (Bandits of the highway) (S.S.),
        in Andean Monthly, II, (Aug. 1939), p.39.
    A glass of milk, (S.S.), tr. by J. L. Grucci, in Amer.Pref.
        VII, (Winter, 1941-42), p. 184-192.

Santibáñez Puig, Fernando ("Santivan"), 1886-
    La hechizada (1916), (N.), Won first prize in Ateneo
    contest and is considered one of Chile's ten great-
    est novels. One chapter "An Episode of Rustic Sport
    in Chile", tr. in Andean Monthly, IV, (Jan., 1941),
    pp. 43-50.

Silva Vidósola, Carlos, 1870-1931.
    El señor Malvoa (Senor Malvoa), (S.S.), tr. by E. F.
    Thackwell, in Andean Monthly, II, (Feb. 1940), p.
    42. (With the Spanish).

Subercaseaux, Benjamín, 1902-
    From west to east, tr. by J. G. Underhill (Putnam, 1940),
    215 pp.
    Four stories contained in West are: Green Owl, Captain
    Louise, The Salt Sea and The little blue book, and
    are taken from: Y al oeste límite con el Mar (1937).
    East: Rahab taken from Rahab Chile o una loca geo-
    grafía (Chile, a geographic extravaganza) (N.). tr.
    by Angel Flores (Macmillan, 1943).

Varas. Calvo, José Miguel, 1807-1833.
    The legend of the crucifix. Andean Monthly II (July, 1939);
    also in Tales from the Spanish, vol. 8.

Vattier, Carlos.
    Los héroes ya estaban casados. (When man is already married)
    (S.S.), in Andean Monthly II (May, 1939), p.29, with
    the Spanish.

Vega, Daniel de la, 1892-.
    Las vacaciones escolares (Abolition of vacations) (S.S.),
    in Andean Monthly, II (July, 1939), p.45, with the
    Spanish.

Yankas, Lautharo.
    El cuco, in La Nación (The bogey-man) (S.S.), in Amigos,
    I (April, 1942), pp. 10-18.

FICTION -- COLOMBIA

Isaacs, Jorge, 1837-1895.
    María (1867) (María, a South American romance) (N.), tr.
    by R. Ogden, (Harpers, 1890, also 1918) 302 pp.;
    also excerpts (The jaguar hunt) in Universal anthology,
    vol. XXXII, p. 174; also (A jaguar hunt in the Cauca)
    in Tales from the ... Spanish, vol. 8.

Marroquín, Lorenzo, 1856-1918.
    Pax (1907) (Peace) (N.), tr. by Isaac Goldberg and W. V.
    Schierbrand, (Brentano, 1920), 480 pp.

Pardo Farelo, Enrique, ("Tablanca, Luis") 1883-
  Muchacha campera (Country girl) (S.S.), tr. by Alida
  Malkus, in Flores and Poore, pp. 265-82.

Rivera, José Eustasio, 1889-1928.
  La vorágine (1924) (The vortex) (N.), tr. by E. K.
  James (Putman, 1935), 320 pp.

Samper Ortega, Daniel, 1895-1943.
  Zoraya (1931) (N.) Excerpt: Storm in the jungle (S.S.),
  in Pan-Amer. Bull, Vol. 68 (1933).

"Tablanca, Luis", see Pardo Farelo, Enrique.

FICTION — COSTA RICA

Calderón Ramírez, Salvador, 1869-
  That donkey that wanted gold (S.S.), tr. by L. E. El-
  liott in Pan Amer. mag., XLI (1929), pp. 382-383.
  Cuentos para mi Carmencita, (New York, 1915) (Stories
  for Carmencita),(Book of S. S.),tr. by A. C. Gahan
  (Brooklyn: Darby Eagle Press, 1914).

Fernández García, Rafaél, 1898-
  Chivalry (S.S.), in Clark and Lieber, p. 897-902.

Fernández Guardia, Ricardo,1867-
  A Central American Arcadia (S.S.), tr. by Gray Case-
  ment, in Cuentos ticos; also in Inter Amer. mag., V
  (1921), p. 25.
  El estreno (The debut) (S.S.), tr. by Gray Casement in
  idem; also in Pan- Amer. mag., IX (1910), pp.200-232.
  Un héroe (A hero) (S.S.), tr. by Gray Casement in idem.
  Un santo milagroso (A miraculous saint) (S.S.), tr. by
  Gray Casement in idem; also in Costa Rican tales.
  La politica (Politics) (S.S.), tr. by Gray Casement in
  idem; also in Costa Rican tales.
  Un espadachín (A real swordsman) (S.S.), tr. by Gray
  Casement in idem; also in Tales from the ... Spanish,
  vol. 8.
  El ahorcado (The hanged man), (S.S.), tr. by Gray Case-
  ment in idem; also in Pan-Amer. mag., XVI (1916), pp.
  59-62.
  Los gatos endemoniados (Bewitched cat) (S.S.), tr. by
  Gray Casement in idem.
  El clavel, idem.
  Hidalguía (Chivalry), tr. by Gray Casement in idem; also
  in Pan Amer. mag., IX (1910), pp. 361-364; also in
  Costa Rican tales.
  La botija (Buried treasure), tr. by Gray Casement in
  idem; also in Pan Amer. Mag., IX (1910), pp.458-463.
  The magic duck, tr. by L. E. Elliott in Pan Amer. mag.,
  XXV (1917), pp. 23-27.
  Number 13013 tr. anon. in Inter-Amer. VIII (1924), pp.
  39-42.

García, R. F., see Fernández García, Rafaél.

FICTION - CUBA

Castellanos, Jesús, 1879-1912.
    An idyl in a minor key (S.S.), in Tales from the ...
    Spanish, vol. 8.

Hernández Catá, A. 1885-1940.
    Beneath the revolting light, (S.S.), tr. Anon, in Inter-
      Amer. VII (1924), pp. 277-297.
    Death in the light house (S.S.), in Mexican life, X
      (1934), p. 15; also in Alhambra, June 1929, p. 10.

Martínez Moles, Manuel.
    A roof-thatching party in Cuba (S.S.), tr. in Amigos,
      I (March, 1942), pp. 17-21.

Villaverde, Cirilo, (Simón de la Paz), 1812-1894.
    Cecilia Valdés o la loma del ángel, (1882) The quad-
      roon or Cecilia Valdés (N.), tr. by Mariano J. Lo-
      rente, (Boston, 1935) 339 pp.

FICTION - DOMINICAN REPUBLIC

Bosch, Juan, 1909 -
    Camino real (The great highway) (S.S.), tr. by Under-
      wood, in West Ind. rev., VI (June, 1940), p. 18.

Fíallo, Fabio, 1865 —
    The rivals, in Inter-Amer., IX, (1926), p. 481-487.

Fresneau, Mme. Armand.
    Theresa at Santo Domingo: A tale of negro insurrection
      (N.), tr. by E. G. Magrath, (Chicago: A. C. McClurg,
      1889), 213 pp.

FICTION - ECUADOR

Aguilera Malta, Demetrio, 1909-
    Don Goyo (1931) (Don Goyo) (N.), tr. by Enid Eder Per-
      kins, in Flores and Poore, pp. 120-228.

Campos, José Antonio, ("Jack the Ripper"), 1868-
    The unifying father, (S.S.), in Inter-Amer. I (1918),
      pp. 276-277.
    The enchanted cock, (S.S.), in Inter-Amer. II (April
      1919), pp. 223-226.
    Visits of condolence, idem.
    The three crows, in Inter-Amer. IV (Dec. 1921), pp.
      94-95.
    Guaranteed timepieces, in Inter-Amer. III (Oct. 1919),
      pp. 43-46; also Guaranteed watches, in Andean Month-
      ly I, (Jan. 1939), p. 38, (with the Spanish).

Campos, José Antonio, ("Jack the Ripper"), 1868- (continued).
    The fire-proof house -- the mistake of the Creator, in Inter-
       Amer. VII (1924).
    Rayos catódicos y fuegos fatuos, etc., (Guayaquil: Impta.
       de la Reforma, (1911), Ecuatorian sketches:
    Lights and shadows, in Inter-Amer. VI (1923), pp. 361-373.
    Postal Cards, idem.
    The original and the copy, idem.
    The terrible breakfast, idem.
    Hawk Lard, idem.
    The greased pig, idem.
    How to unmarry, idem.
    The Odyssey of an alderman, idem.
    The silver cannon, idem, pp. 324.
    House signs, idem, p. 326.
    The monk and the rustic, idem, p. 328.
    Popular Festival of San Pedro and San Pablo in Guayaquil,
       in Inter-Amer. III, (Oct. 1919), p. 43-46.
    King of swimmers, in Inter-Amer. (April 1920), pp. 235-240.
    Momerto's mother-in-law, idem.
    The cura's hat, idem.
    At the civil registry, idem. (1919), p. 387.

Gallegos, Luis Gerardo, 1905 -
    An old pirate print of Haiti, (S.S.), tr. by Underwood, in West
       Ind. rev., (March, 1939), p. 29, from Niños de America en
       Cuba.
    The Mountains of Trinidad, in Amigos, I (March, 1942), pp.
       43-48.

Gil Gilberto, Enrique, 1912-
    Nuestro pan, (1942) (Our bread), (N), tr. by Dudley
       Poore, (Farrar and Rinehart, 1942) (Honorable Mention in
       Inter-Amer. novel contest).

Icaza, Jorge, 1902-
    Huasipungo (1934) (Huasipungo) (N.), in International Lit-
       erature, (Moscow, Feb. 1936).

"Jack the Ripper", see Campos, José Antonio.

FICTION - EL SALVADOR

Arévalo, Adrián M. 1870-
    The earrings, (S.S.), in Inter-Amer. I (1918), p. 76-7.

Gavidia, Francisco.
    The return of the hero, (S.S.), in Amigos, I, (April, 1942)
       pp. 56-61.

Ramírez Peña, Abraham.
    The sad reality, (S.S.), in Inter-Amer., IV (1921), pp. 383-4.

FICTION — GUATEMALA

Arévalo Martínez, Rafaél, 1884–
    Nuestra señora de los locos, (Our lady of the afflicted),
        (S.S.), tr. by Victor S. Clark, in Living Age, vol.
        321 (1924), pp.800-806.
    Las fieras del trópico, (The panther man) (S.S.), idem,
        pp. 1005-11 and 1046-52.

Wyld Ospina, Carlos, 1881–
    The woman Tona, (S.S.), tr. by Underwood, in West Ind.
        rev., VI (Feb–Mar.1940), p.27.

FICTION — MARTINIQUE

Herpen, Thérèse.
    Christmas in the French West Indies, tr. by Underwood,
        in West Ind. rev., V (Dec. 1938), pp.20-22.

Maran, René.
    Batoula (N), Paragraphs tr. by Underwood, in West Ind.
        rev., II (Oct. 1935), p.36-7.

FICTION — MEXICO

Altolaguirre, Manuel.
    My brother Luis, tr. by Stephen Spender, in Mexican life,
        XIII (Dec. 1937), p. 18.

"Atl, Dr." see Murillo, Gerardo.

Azuela, Mariano, 1873–
    Los de Abajo (1915) The underdogs, (N), tr. by Enrique
        Munguía, Jr. (Brentano's, 1929), also (S.S.), in
        Mexican life, III (April, 1936); First chap. tr. by
        E. Munguía, Jr., in Alhambra, August, 1929, p. 28.
    Mala Yerba (1909) Marcela (N), tr. by Anita Brenner (Fa-
        rrar and Rinehart, 1932).

Blanco, Jorge J.
    Morning of a dictator, (S.S.), in Mexican life, XI
        (July, 1935), p. 31.

Cabada, Juan de la.
    A sailor in Campeche (S.S.), tr. by Abel Plenn, in
        Mexican life, X (April, 1934), p.15.

Campo, Enrique del.
    True love is stronger than false teeth, (S.S.), in Mexican
        life, X (Feb. 1934), p. 21.
    I pull Tiburcio out of a hole, (S.S.), in Mexican life,
        X (Dec. 1934), p. 22.
    Sucklehoney magic, in Mexican life, XI, (Nov. 1935), p.
        23.
    Reducing business, in Mexican life, VI (May,1930), p.19.

Campo, Enrique del. (continued).
Kakahuates Limited, in Mexican life, III (June, 1927),
pp. 108.
Tranquilino's wholesale teeth, in Mexican life, IV,
(Dec. 1928), p. 29.
Pedro becomes vindictive, idem, (July, 1928), p. 25.
The goatery club: Transplanting a 100 [per cent]
American idea, idem, (June, 1928), p. 23.
My illustrated ancestor, in Mexican life, VII (March,
1931), p. 27.

Chas de Chruiz, Israel (Grismer calls him "Argentine.")
El asesino de si mismo y otros cuentos (B.A.: Tomalis y
Sella, 1929). (The Job), (S.S.), tr. by Anita Brenner,
in Menorah Journal, Vol: 18 (Feb.1930), pp.159-163.

Delgado, Rafaél, 1853-1914.
Calandria (N), Excerpts in Starr, p. 395.
El desertor (The deserter) (S.S.), tr. by H. C. Schweikert,
in Golden Book, III (1927), pp. 689-92.

Durán y Casahonda, J. M.
The general's promise: A revolutionary episode. (S.S.),
in Mexican life, IV (April, 1928), p. 19.

Elizondo, José F. 1880 -
The man who craved to be everything, (S.S.), tr. anon.,
in Mexican life, X (Aug. 1934), p.17.
The portera, (S.S.), in Mexican life, X (May, 1934),p.17.
Poor Jeremías, (S.S.), in Mexican life, X (June, 1934),p.21.

Fernández de Lizardi, José Joaquín, ca. 1774-1827.
El periquillo sarniento (1816) (The itching parrot), (N),
tr. by K. A. Porter (Doubleday Doran, 1942) 290 pp.

Ferretis, Jorge.
The man who dreamed of pigs, (S.S.), in Mexican life,
XIII, (Dec. 1937), p. 13.

Frías y Soto, Heriberto, 1870-1925.
Flower of victory; a Mixtecan legend, (S.S.), tr. anon.,
in Mexican life, VI (April, 1930), p.17.
Cult of the sun: a Texcocan legend, idem, (May, 1930), p.21.
Cosijolza: a Zapotec legend, idem, (July, 1930), p.20.
Bird of love and beast of hate: a Mije legend, idem, (Aug.
1930), p. 16.
Warriors' paradise: an Aztec legend, idem, (Oct.1930), p.
15.
Conqueror of the sun: Aztec legend, idem, (Dec.1930),p.31.

Gamboa, Federico, 1864-1939.
Suprema Ley (Paris: Bouret, 1896) (N), Excerpts in Starr,
p. 408.

Gorostiza, Celestino.
    The yap, (S.S.). in Mexican life, VI (May, 1930), p.13.

Guzmán, Martín Luis, 1887-
    El águila y la serpiente (1928) (The eagle and the ser-
        pent), (N), tr. by Harriet de Onis (Knopf, 1930)
        359 pp.
    The death of David Berlanga: a dramatic revolutionary
        episode, (S.S.), in Mexican life, III (Sept.1927),p.19.
    The sleep of compadre Urbina: A dramatic episode from the
        life of Francisco Villa, (S.S.), in Mexican life,
        (Nov.-Dec. 1927), p. 23.
    The gaucho's last job: revolutionary episode from life
        of Francisco Villa, (S.S.), in Mexican life, IV,
        (July, 1928), p. 15.

Hoffman, F. C. ("R.H. Torres"), 1911-
    The brothers Jiménez, (S.S.), in Mexican life, (Mar,
        1937), p. 15.

López-Portillo y Rojas, José, 1850-1923.
    The colonel's arm, (S.S.), in Inter-Amer.,II (1919),
        p. 365; also in Tales from the ... Spanish, vol.8.
    Amalie's jewels, (S.S.), idem, p. 365-7.
    La Parcela (N), Excerpts in Starr, p. 314.

López y Fuentes, Gregorio, 1895-
    En indio (1935) (El indio or they that reap) (N), tr. by
        Anita Brenner, (Bobbs Merrill, 1937) 256 pp.
    Fear (S.S.), tr. anon., in Mexican life, (Jan, 1943),
        pp. 11-12 and 58-60.

Magdaleno, Mauricio.
    El resplandor (1937) (N), reported tr. by Ilse P. Loas,
        (publisher?).

Martínez, Conchita.
    Pig sausage, in Mexican life (Jan.1936).
    A remedy for rheumatism, idem, (April,1936).
    The street of Juan de Dios, idem, X, (Nov.1934), p.11.
    La pasadita, idem, (Dec. 1934), p. 15.
    Fifty cents for the leave of it, idem, XI (Jan.1935), p.14,
    The hat, idem, (Dec. 1935), p. 29.

Médiz Bolio, Antonio, 1884-
    La tierra del faisán y del venado, (1934) (The land of
        the pheasant and the deer) (N), tr. by Enid E. Per-
        kins, (Mexico: Cultura, 1935). (Children's book of
        legends.)

Menéndez, Miguel Angel, 1905-
    Nayar (1940) (Nayar) (N). tr. by Angel Flores, (Farrar
        & Rinehart, 1941), 277 pp. (2nd prize Inter Amer. con-
        test.)

Molina Solís, Juan Francisco, 1850-
    El conde de Peñalva, (Mérida: Caballero, 1896) (N).
        Excerpt, (The horrors of 1648 in Yucatán) in Starr,
        p. 108.

Montenegro, Carlos, 1900-
    The disciple, (S.S.), in Mexican life. (Feb. 1931).

Monterde, Francisco, 1894-
    Road to Taxco, (S.S.), tr. by Underwood, in West Ind.
        rev. VI, (Sept. 1940), p. 35, also in Anthology of
        Mexican poets, p. 131. (Prose-poem).

Munagorri, J. F. de.
    Patharra's recuperation (S.S.), tr. anon., in Mexican
        life, VII, (May, 1931), p. 11.

Muñoz, Rafaél F.
    Revolutionary tales from Vamos con Pancho Villa, (Ma-
        drid: Espasa Calpe, 1930).
    Villa Ahumada, (S.S.), in Mexican life VI (Jan. 1930),
        p. 11.
    The baby, (S.S.) idem (Feb. 1930), p. 21.
    The wedding march, (S.S.) idem (Sept. 1930), p. 15.
    The bonfire, (S.S.), idem, VII (Oct. 1931), p. 11.
    Hell dogs, (S.S.), in Liberty mag., (Oct. 28, Nov.4-25,
        1933).

Murillo Gerardo, ("Dr. Atl"), 1875-
    Cuentos de todos colores, (1933) The cantinero (S.S.)
        in Mexican life, IX, (Nov. 1933), p. 10.
    The wake, (S.S.), idem, (Dec. 1933), p. 13.

Nava, Pepe, see Elizondo, José F.

Nervo, Amado, 1870-1919.
    Leah and Rachel, (S.S.), in Inter-Amer. II (Aug. 1919),
        pp. 343-345; also tr. by W. K. Jones, in Stratford
        Journal, VI, (Jan-Mar. 1919), pp.7-12.

Noriega Hope, Carlos, 1896.
    The bewitched goat: a revolutionary episode, (S.S.), tr.
        by V. M. Cuzado in Mexican life, IV, (Sept. 1928), p.19.

Parra, Porfirio, 1856-1912.
    Pacotillas (N), Excerpts in Starr, p. 361.

Piña, Roberto
    Close-up of Gallardo, (S.S.), in Mexican life, IX,
        (Aug. 1933), p. 13.

Rabasa, Emilio ("Sancho Polo"), 1856-1930 .
    Sancho Polo, (N), Excerpts in Starr, p. 375.

Riva Palacio, Vicente, ("Rosa Espina"), 1832-1896.
His Excellency rules, (N), tr. by M. A. de Vitis.
(Doubleday, Doran, 1934).

Rojas González, Francisco.
Sed, (pequeñas novelas) (Mexico: Juventudes de iz-
quierda, 1837?).
Guadalupe's gold tooth (S.S.), in Mexican life, (June,1938).
Lancaster kid (S.S.), in idem, p. 11.
Watch out for me (S.S.), idem, (Nov.1937).
The mysterious alkaloid (S.S.), in Inter-Amer.,II
(1918), pp. 288-301.

Romero, José Rubén, 1890-
La vida inútil de Pito Pérez (1938)(The futile life of
Pito Perez, (N), tr. by Jane Coyne, in Flores and
Poore, pp. 303-67.

Sáenz Azcorra, Franz.
The mestiza, (S.S.), in West Ind. rev., I, (April,1935),
pp. 35-36.
The prostitute, (S.S.), idem.
The path, (S.S.), idem, II, (Oct. 1936), p.57.

Salazar Mallén, Rubén.
Foam, (S.S.), in Mexican life, VI, (Aug.1930), p. 11.

Sánchez Mármol, Manuél, 1839-1912.
Antón Pérez, (N), Excerpts in Starr, p. 336.

Sierra, Justo, 1848-1912.
Cuentos románticos (Story of Starei), (S.S.), in Starr,
pp. 276.

Taracena, Alfonso, 1899-
Extravagant characters, (S.S.) in Mexican life, VI,
(Oct. 1930), p. 11.
The volcano goblin, (S.S.) idem, (Nov. 1930), p. 10.

Torres Bodet, Jaime, 1902 -
Margarita de Niebla (Mexico: Cultura, 1927). (Margaret).
(N), tr. by Abel Plenn, in Mexican life, VI, (Jan.-
April, 1930).
A close-up of Mr.Lehar, (S.S.), in Mexican life, VI,
(Dec. 1930), p. 17.
Death of Proserpina, (N), tr. by Abel Plenn, in Mexican
life, VII (Jan.-April, 1931)

Torres, R. H., see Hoffman, B. C.

Turrent Rozas, Lorenzo.
Vida de "El Perro", (S.S.), tr. by Lloyd Mallan, in
Amer. Pref., (Winter, 1941-2).

"Verduguillo".
>The fifth bull was the greatest, (S.S.), in Mexican life,
>>(Jan. 1937), p. 21.
>Six good bulls, (S.S.), tr. by D. H. Hart, idem, XI,
>>(April, 1935), p. 19.

Zayas Enrique, Rafaél de, 1848-1932.
>When is a coward not a coward? (S.S.), in Tales from
>>the ..... Spanish, vol. 8.

FICTION -- NICARAGUA

Darío, Rubén, 1867-1916.
>The deaf satyr, (S.S.), in Clark and Lieber.
>The litany of our lord Don Quixote, (S.S.), tr. by
>>Muna Lee in Pan Amer. bull, (Aug. 1928).
>El cuento a Margarita, (S.S.), tr. by Margaret Ros-
>>coe, in Mexican life, (Aug. 1936).
>El viaje a Nicaragua (Madrid, 1919) My visit to Ni-
>>caragua, (S.S.), in Pan Amer. bull, Vol. 68, p.222.
>Death of empress of China, (S.S.), in C. B. McMichael,
>>Short stories from the Spanish.
>Veil of Queen Mab, (S.S.), idem.
>The box, (S.S.), idem.
>Impressions of Santiago, (S.S.), in Andean Monthly, IV,
>>(Feb.-Mar. 1941), pp.84-8.
>Seascope, (S.S.), tr. by G. W. Umphrey, in Fantasy, No.
>>26, (1942), p. 44.

FICTION -- PANAMA

Andreve, Guillermo, ("Mario Marín Mirones"), 1879-
>Mountain idyl, (S.S.), tr. by Evelyn Moore, in Sancocho,
>>Stories and Sketches of Panama (Panama: Pan American
>>Pub. Co., 1938).
>Adventures of a Chamba, (S.S.), idem.
>Manolo's little drinks, (S.S.), idem.

Arjona, Julio, 1877-
>Costumbres de mi tierra, La junta, (S.S.), in San-
>>cocho pp. 126-129.

Bárcena, Lucas, 1906-
>The will of Don Julian, (S.S.), in Sancocho, pp.
>>152-157.
>Chola Facunda, idem.

Carrasco, M. Francisco, 1899-
>Voices, (S.S.), in Sancocho, pp. 130-137.

Castillo, Moisés, 1899-
>Bajo el cielo del istmo (Counterpoint) (S.S.), in San-
>>cocho, pp. 138-151.
>The witch's wake, (S.S.), idem.

Castillero R., E. J.
    The technique of the tamborito, (S.S.), in Sancocho,
        pp.81-86.

Crespo, Elida L. C. de.
    Village siesta, (S.S.), in Sancocho, pp.102-125.
    Maruja, (S. S.), idem.
    Seña Paula, (S. S.), idem.

Herrera, Darío, 1887-1914.
    Violets, (S.S.), tr. by Underwood, in West Ind. rev.,
        III, (June, 1937), p. 21.

Huerta, José, 1900-
    Alma campesina (The little lap dog of Yvonne) (S.S.), in
        Sancocho, pp. 61-80.
    A well-planned insult, (S.S.), idem.
    Dead of a toothache, (S.S.), idem.
    Tamborito in Pesé, (S.S.), idem.

Lewis, Samuel, 1871-
    The legend of La Campana (S.S.), in Sancocho, pp.
        27-44.
    Crossing the Isthmus in 1853 (S.S.), idem.
    The ransomed Indian Maid (S.S.), idem.

McKay, Santiago, ("Fray Rodrigo"), 1898-
    Sal-si-Puedes, (S.S.), in Sancocho, pp.45-55.
    The cross of the Escortines, (S.S.), idem.
    Piruli and Longolon, (S.S.), idem.

Méndez Pereira, Octavio, 1887-
    Christmas eve in Aguadulce (S.S.), in Sancocho, pp.
        87-89.

Ponce Aguilera, Salomón, 1868-
    De la Gleba (The recruit)(S.S.), in Sancocho, pp.56-60.

Rojas Sucre, Graciela, 1904-
    Terruñadas de lo chico (On account of the piñata), (S.S.),
        in Sancocho, pp. 90-101.

Sinán, Rogelio.
    A la orilla de las estatuas maduras (They came to a
        river) (S.S.), tr. by Jane Coyne, in Flores and Poore,
        pp. 409-20.

Valdés, Nacho, 1902
    Cuentos panameños and Tradicción nativa (Carnival in
        Santiago) (S.S.), in Sancocho, pp. 158-190.
    A country wedding (S.S.), idem.
    Savage Litany, (S.S.), idem.
    The little deer of the Virgin (S.S.), idem.
    Justice (S.S.), idem.
    Evil eyes (S.S.), idem.
    Devil's peak (S.S.), idem.

FICTION — PARAGUAY

Lamas Carísimo, Teresa, 1889–
Paraguayan household traditions (S.S.), in Inter-Amer.
VI, (1922), p. 3–17.
Py-chay, in Inter-Amer., VIII (1925), pp.236-240.

Odena, E. León.
The death of Aná: a Guaraní legend, (S.S.), in Inter-
Amer., VI, (1922), pp.124-127.

FICTION — PERU

Alegría, Ciro, 1909-
El mundo es ancho y ajeno, (1941), (Broad and alien is
the world) (N), tr. by Harriet de Onís, (Farrar and
Rinehart, 1941).(1st prize, 1941 Pan American Com-
petition).
Serpiente de oro, (N), tr. by Harriet de Onís, (Farrar
and Rinehart, 1942).

Cavero Egusquiza, Ricardo.
From newsboy to painter (S.S.), in Amigos, I, (April,
1942), pp. 24-26.

Díaz Canseco, José.
Gaviota (El gaviota) (S.S.), tr. by Harriet de Onís, in
Flores and Poore, pp. 229-64.

García Calderón, Ventura, 1884–
La venganza del cóndor, (1924) (The white llama), (S.S.),
tr. by Richard Phibbs (London: Golden cockerel, 1939)
123 pp. (Contains 22 short stories).
Honeymoon (S.S.), in Living Age, (1924), p. 178.
Ancestral Sin (S.S.), idem, (1927), p.263.
The legend of Pygmalion (S.S.), in Clark and Lieber, pp.
912-917.

López Albújar, Enrique, 1872–
El blanco (The target) (S.S.), in Andean Monthly, III,
(Sept.–Nov., 1940), p. 354 (With the Spanish.).

Matto de Turner, Clorinda, 1854-1909 –
Aves sin nidos (Birds without nest) (N), tr. by J. G.
Hudson, (London: Thynne, 1904).

Palma, Ricardo, 1833-1919.
The knights of the cloak (S.S.), in Inter-Amer., III,
(1920), pp. 135–143.
The opening of the Peruvian academy (S.S.), idem, I,
(1918), pp. 280–284.
The Christ in agony, idem, II, (1918), p.88.
The first steamboat, idem, V, (1922), p. 251.
The 'Achirana' of the Inca, idem.
The two millions, idem.

Palma, Ricardo, 1833-1919, (continued)
A famous excommunication, idem, VI, (1923), pp. 295-302.
Three historical questions regarding Pizarro, idem.
The grotto of wonders, idem.
La camisa de Margarita, in Andean Monthly, I, (Nov.1938),
p. 34 (With the Spanish); also in Inter-Amer., VII, (1924)
pp.278-283.
One of Abascal's wiles, in Inter-Amer., VII, (1924), pp.278-283.
The scorpion of Father Gómez, in Tales from the Spanish, v.8.

Polar, Juan Manuel, 1863-
Don Quijote in Yankeeland, in Inter-Amer., III, (1920),
IV, and V, (to Oct.1921).

Valdelomar, Abraham, 1888-1919.
El caballero Carmelo, The good knight Carmelo (S.S.), tr.
by Angel Flores in Flores and Poore, pp.448-57.

Velarde, Héctor, 1899-
Peter the tourist (S.S.), in Amigos, I, (April, 1942),
pp.39-43. (S.S.).

FICTION – PHILIPPINES

Arguila, M. E.
How my brother León brought home a wife, and other stories,
(Manila: Philippine Book Guild, 1940); also contains:
The long vacation.
Caps and lower case.

Rizal y Alonso, José, 1861-1896.
Noli me tangere (The eagle flight) (N), McClure, Philips,
1900; also tr. and abridged by F. E. Gannett; also tr.
by F. Basa and C. M. Mellen, (Manila; Oriental commercial co., 1933); also Friars and Filipinos (New York:
St. John Press, 1900, and Lewis Scribner, 1902); also
The social cancer, tr. by C. Derbyshire, (Manila: Phi-
lippine education co., 1912).
Filibusterismo, (Barcelona, 3rd. ed. 1908) (The sign of God)
(N.), tr. by C. Derbyshire, (Manila: Philippine education
co., 1912).
Letter to the young women of Malolos, (Manila: Bureau of Printing,
1932), in Tagalog, Spanish and English.
Mariang Markeling, (N), tr. by C. Derbyshire, (Manila 1916); also
in Basa and Mellen, tr. of Noli me tangere.
A Filipino picnic, in Tales from the ... Spanish, v. 8.

FICTION – URUGUAY

Ibarbourou, Juana de, 1895-
Military police! in Amigos, I, (January, 1942), pp. 35-36,
from article in Mundo Uruguayo.

Nieto, Asdrúbal.
    Padre José, cowboy priest, (S.S.), in Amigos, I,
        (April, 1942), pp.19-22.

Quiroga, Carlos Buenaventura.
    Llastay's response (S.S.), in Inter-Amer., VIII, (1925),
        pp. 467-473.
    An Incan legend, (S.S.), idem.

Quiroga, Horacio, 1879-1937.
    The return of Anaconda (S.S.), tr. by Anita Brenner, in
        Tales from the Argentine, pp.237-268.
    Los fugitivos (The fugitives) (S.S.), tr. by Drake de Kay,
        in Flores and Poore, pp. 398-408.
    Cuentos de la selva, (1918) (South American jungle tales),
        tr. by A. Livingston, 1922 and 1940, containing:
    Story of two raccoon cubs.
    Parrot that lost its tail.
    Blind Dog.
    Alligator war.
    How the rays defended the ford.

Reyles, Carlos, 1868-1938.
    El embrujo de Sevilla, (1922) (Castanets) (N), tr. by
        Jacques LeClercq, (Longmans Green, 1929), 297 pp.

Rodó, José E., 1872-1917.
    Christ on horseback, tr. anon, in Alhambra, June, 1929,
        p. 12.

FICTION - VENEZUELA

Blanco-Fombona, Rufino, 1874-
    Hombre de Oro, (1916) The man of gold (N), tr. by Isaac
        Goldberg, (Brentano, 1920), 319 pp.
    Creole democracy, (S.S.), in Clark and Lieber, pp. 918-
        922; also in Goldberg, Studies in Span. Amer. lit.

Fabbiani Ruiz, José, 1911-
    Agua Salada (Guaritoto) (S.S.), tr. by Underwood, in West
        Ind. rev., VI, (April, 1940) pp.23-26.

Gallegos, Rómulo, 1882-
    Doña Barbara (1929) Doña Barbara (N), tr. by R. Malloy,
        (Cape and Smith, 1931), 440 pp.

Meneses, Guillermo, 1911-
    Tres cuentos venezolanos (Caracas: Elite, 1938) Moon (S.S.),
        tr. by Underwood, in West Ind. rev., V, (May-June,
        1939).
    La balandra Isabel llegó esta tarde. (The sloop Isabel),
        tr. by Angel Flores in Flores and Poore, pp. 283-302.

Parra Sanojo, Ana Teresa, ("Teresa de la Parra"), 1895-1936.
    Mama Blanca, in Pan Amer. bull., v. 68 (1934),

Uslar Pietri, Arturo, 1906-
    La lluvia (Rain), (S.S.), tr. by Dorothy Conzelman, in
    Flores and Poore, pp. 435-47.

FICTION – COUNTRY UNCERTAIN

Bernáldez, A.
    The voyages of Columbus, (N), tr. by Cecil Jane, (Lon-
    don: Argonaut Press, 1930).

Calpe, Adadus, see Pascual, Antonio Diodoro de.

Ferry, Gabriel.
    The winning of Sacramento (S.S.), in Tales from the...
    Spanish, vol. 8.

Fierro Blanco, Antonio.
    The journey of the flame (N), tr. by Walter de Steigner
    (Boston: Houghton, 1934).
    Ghosts (S.S.), in Mexican life, XII (May, 1936), p.11.
    Rico: bandit and dictator (N), (Houghton Mifflin, 1934).

Pascual, Antonio Diodoro de, 1822-1874*
    The two fathers (N), tr. by Adadus, Edgar, and Henry
    Calpe, (New York: Stringer and Townsend; n. d.)

FICTION – ANONYMOUS

Fable of the frog, (S.S.), tr. by J.H. Cornyn in
    Mexican life, IX (Aug. 1933), p. 20

Do pol vuh (Book of wisdom). Libro del Consejo (N)., ed. by
    Monterde.
    Excerpts tr. by A. Dewey Ammer, from"Section of 1939
    edition in Spanish", in Hispanic American Culture,
    (Granville, Ohio, 1942).

Peruvian tales related in one thousand and one hours by one
    of the virgins of Cusco to the Inca of Peru (N), tr. by
    Samuel Humphreys, 4th. ed. (London: 1764) 3 vol.

Quetzalcoatl (Song of Quetzalcoatl) (N), tr. by J. H. Cor-
    nyn (Antioch Press, 1930).

The Indians of La Guajira, tr. by Edward Huberman, from the
    Colombian Magazine Rin Rin, in Story Parade, April,
    1939, pp. 21-4.

A D D E N D A

ESSAYS

CHILE

Pereira Salas, Eugenio.
Notas para la historia del intercambio musical entre
las Américas (Chile: 1941) Notes on the history of
the musical exchange between the Americas before
1940, tr. by Josefina de Román, (Washington: Pan
American Music Division, 1943). 37 p.

ECUADOR

Carrera Andrade, Jorge, 1903-
The new American and his point of view toward poetry,
tr. by H. R. Hays, in Poetry, vol. LXII (May, 1934).
pp. 88-104.

MEXICO

Avila Camacho, Manuel.
Continental Solidarity (Speech of Dec. 1, 1940), in
Pan Amer., p. 212.

URUGUAY

Rodó, José Enrique, 1872-1917.
Ariel. Selections also appear in Van Doran, Anthology
of World prose (Reynal and Hitchcock, 1935), pp.
618-23.

HISTORY - ARGENTINA

Mitro, Bartolomé, 1821-1906.
See also History, Argentina.
Belgrano. Summarized in Chapman, C. E., Republican
Historic America (Macmillan, 1937) chaps. III-V.

CENTRAL AMERICA

Saavedra, David.
Bananas, gold and silver, (Tegucigalpa: Talleres ti-
pográficos nacionales, 1935), 436 pp dealing in both
Spanish and English with the economic resources of
Honduras.
Trails to and through El Salvador (Imprenta diario del
Salvador, 1934). 39 pp. in Spanish and English about
Salvador's resources.

PARAGUAY

Azara, Félix de.
Natural history of the quadrupeds of Paraguay and the
River La Plata, tr. by W. Percival Hunter (Edinburgh:
A. and C. Black, 1838) 2 vols. 340 and 310 pp. Tr.
from the Paris: Walekenaer, 1809 edition.

POETRY — ARGENTINA

Campo, Estanislao del ("Anastasio el pollo"),1834-80.
 Fausto (1870) Faust, tr. by Walter Owen (Buenos Aires:
  privately printed, 1943).

Anania, José, ("José Portogalo").
 Poem about a little girl who owned a city and a river,
  tr. by Lloyd Mallan, in Poetry, vol. LXII (May, 1943) p.77

LIST OF ABBREVIATED REFERENCES TO
BOOKS MENTIONED MORE THAN ONCE IN THIS BIBLIOGRAPHY

Anthology of Mex. Poets. Underwood, Edna W., Anthology of
    Mexican Poets from Earliest Times to the Present Day.
    (Portland, Me.: The Mosher Press, 1932) 332 pp. $5.00

APLC. Fitts, Dudley, Ed., Anthology of Contemporary Latin
    American Poetry, Antologia de la Poesia Americana Con-
    temporanea. (Norfolk, Conn.: New Directions, 1942) 608
    pp. $3.50. Containing translations from half a hundred
    modern Latin American poets.

Bierstadt, E. H. Bierstadt, Ed., Three Plays of the Argentine.
    (tr. by J. S. Fassett, Jr.) (New York: Duffield, 1920) pp.
    147. $1.75

Blackwell. Blackwell, Alice Stone, Some Spanish American Poets.
    (Philadelphia, Pa., University of Pennsylvania Press, 1937)
    559 pp. $1.50

Brazilian Short Stories. See Goldberg.

Brazilian Tales. See Goldberg.

Brenner, Anita, Tales from the Argentine, (New York: Farrar
    and Rinehart, 1930) 268 pp. $3.50

Casement, Gray, Cuentos Ticos: Short Stories of Costa Rica.
    (Cleveland: Burrows Bros., 1905 and 1925) 307 pp. $2.50.
    A dozen sketches from Fernández Guardia.

Catholic Anthology. Walsh, T. Ed., Catholic Anthology. (Macmi-
    llan, 1939) 584 pp. $1.69

Clark and Lieber. Clark, B. H. and Lieber, M., Great Short
    Stories of the World.(McBride, 1929, Garden City Pub. Co.,
    1938) pp. 1072. $1.79

Costa Rican Tales. See Goldberg.

Cox, E. G. Reference Guide to the Literature of Travel. (Seattle,
    Wash.: University of Washington Press, 1938) pp. 591, $4.25

Craig, G. Dundas. The Modernist Trend in Spanish American Poe-
    try. (Berkley: University of California Press, 1934)
    pp. 347. $4.00

Eleven Poems. Walsh, T. and Salomón de la Selva, Eds., Ele-
    ven Poems of Rubén Darío. (Putnam, 1916). With Spanish
    and English versions on opposite pages.

Flores and Poore. Flores, Angel and Poore, Dudley. Fiestas in
    November. (Houghton, Mifflin, 1942) pp. 608 $3.00. Con-
    taining short and long stories in translation by present –
    day Latin American authors.

Goldberg, Isaac. Brazilian Literature. (Knopf, 1922) 303 pp.
    Not indexed here because the translations are prose foot-
        notes to Brazilian poetry quoted.
    Brazilian Short Stories. (Girard, Kans. Haldeman-Julius,
    1925) Little Blue Book No. 733. 64 pp. 10¢
    Brazilian Tales. (Boston: Four Seas Co., 1921) $2.00
    Costa Rican Tales. (Girard, Kans.: Haldeman-Julius,
    1925) Little Blue Book No. 803. 64 pp. 10¢

Mexican Poetry. (Girard, Kans.: Haldeman-Julius, 1925) Little
    Blue Book No. 810. 64 pp. 10¢
    Studies in Spanish American Literature. (Brentano, 1920)
    377 pp. $2.50

González del Valle, Francisco. Poesías de Heredia traducidas
    a otros idiomas. (Havana: Molino, 1940).

Good Neighbor 'Tour": Documentary Material for the Good Neighbor
    Tour. (Washington, D. C.: Pan American Union, 1941 and 1942)
    Ten vols. mimeographed, of which vol. VI, pp. 38-43 con-
    tains translations. $2.00

Green and Lowenfels. Green, E. S. and Von Lowenfels, Miss.
    Mexican and South American Poems. (San Diego, Calif.:
    Dodge and Burbeck, 1892) Containing poetry literally
    translated into prose.

Hakluyt Society Publications. A series of semi-annual volumes
    about travels, published for members of the Society, in
    England, beginning in 1846.

Hammond, G. P. and Agapito Rey, Translators, History of 16th
    Century Exploration. (Los Angeles, Wetzel, 1928) pp. 351.
    $10.00

Hills, Elijah C. Odes of Bello, Olmedo, and Heredia. (Putnam's
    Sons, 1920) pp. 153. $1.50

Hills, Elijah C. Some Spanish American Poets. (Colorado College
    Publication, Series II, No. 30, 1915) Also in Hispanic
    Studies. (Stanford Univ. Press, 1929)

Hispanic Anthology. Thomas Walsh, Ed., Hispanic Anthology.
    (Putnam's Sons, 1920) pp. 779 $2.50

Hispanic Poets. Translations from Hispanic Poets. (New York:
    Hispanic Society of America, 1938) pp. 271 $1.00

Holmes, H. A. Vicente Huidobro and Creationism. (Institute of
    French Studies, Columbia Univ. Press, 1934) $1.00. Con-
    taining translations of other poets, also.

Joyas. See Vingut.

Library of the World's best Literature. C. D. Warner, Ed.,
    Library of the World's Best Literature. (New York: J. A.
    Hill, 1896-1902) 31 vols.

Livingston, A. See South American Jungle Tales.

McMichael, Chas. B. Prosas Profanas and Other Poems. (New
    York: Frank-Maurice, 1922) Translations from Rubén Darío.
    pp. 60 $1.20

McMichael, Chas. B. Short Stories from the Spanish. (Boni and
    Liveright, 1920) pp. 116 $1.50

Mexican Poetry. See Goldberg.

Modernist Trend. See Craig.

Moore, Evelyn. Sancocho, Stories and Sketches of Panama.
    (Panama: Pan American Publishing Co., 1938)

Pan-Amer. Paulmier, H. and Schauffler, R. H. Pan American Day.
    (Dodd, Mead, 1943) pp. 327

Pan American Poems. Poor, Agnes Blake, Pan American Poems.
    (Boston: Gorham, 1918) pp. 80. $1.00

Quivira Society Publications. Chiefly translations of Spanish
    works dealing with the United States Southwest, publi-
    shed in Los Angeles for members of the society since 1929.

Selections from the Best Spanish Poets. See Vingut.

Shay, Frank. 25 Short Plays, international (Appleton,1925)
    pp. 381 $4.00

Shay, Frank and Loving,Pierre. Fifty Contemporary One Act
    Plays. (Cincinnati, Stewart and Kidd, 1920, and New York:
    Appleton, 1925) pp.582. $5.00

South American Jungle Tales. Edited by A. Livingston, (Duffield,
    1922, and Dodd Mead, 1940) 166 pp. $1.75 (Tr. of Quiroga's
    Cuentos de la Selva)

Starr. Starr, Frederick. Reading from Modern Mexican Authors.
    (Chicago: Open Court Publishing Co., 1904) $1.25

Tales from the Argentine. Brenner, Anita, Ed., Tales from the
    Argentine. (Farrar and Rinehart, 1930 Containing seven
    translations from six authors. pp. 268 $3.50

Tales from the Italian and Spanish. (Review of Reviews,1920) The last
    part of Vol. 8 is devoted to Latin America.

Three Spanish-American Poets. Edited by Grucci, Mallan, and
    Wickers. (Albuquerque: Swallow and Critchlow, 1942) 73
    pp. 50¢. Translations from Carrera Andrade, Pellicer,
    and Reyes.

Torres-Rioseco, Arturo. The Epic of Latin American Literature.
    (Oxford University Press, 1942) 279 pp. $2.75

Walsh, T. See Hispanic Anthology.

Underwood. See Anthology of Mexican Poets.

Underwood, Edna, W., Poets of Haiti. (Portland, Me.: Mosher Press, 1934) pp. 159 $4.00

Universal Anthology. R. Garnett, L. Vallee and A. Brandl, Eds., Universal Anthology. in 33 vols. (New York: Merrill and Baker, 1898-1902.)

Vingut, F. J. and G. F. Joyas de la Poesía Española. (New York: Vingut Press, 1855)

Vingut, G. F. Selections from the Best Spanish Poets. (New York: Vingut Press, 1856) Largely a duplication of the above.

MAGAZINES CONTAINING TRANSLATIONS
MENTIONED IN THIS BIBLIOGRAPHY

Advocate of Peace (est. 1837: now World Affairs) Boston and Washington
    (monthly)

Alhambra (est. 1929) 1E. 42 St.., New York City (monthly)

Amer. Pref. American Prefaces (est.1935) Paul Engle and Wilber Schramm,
    Eds., University of Iowa, Iowa City, Ia. (quarterly)

Amigos: A South American Digest (est. 1941) P. J. Cooke, Ed. 1137 Loyola
    Ave., Chicago. (monthly)

Andean Monthly (est. 1938) E. F. Thackwell, Ed., Casilla 13076, Correo 11,
    Santiago de Chile (monthly)

Asia America (est. 1935 Tokio, Japan (monthly)

Birth Control Review (est. 1917) Miss L. K. Simon, Ed., 501 Madison Ave.,
    New York (monthly)

Bolivia (est. 1926) Jaime Gutiérrez Guerra, Ed., 10 Rockefeller Plaza,
    New York City (bi-monthly)

Books Abroad (est. 1927) R. T. House, Ed., University of Oklahoma, Norman,
    Okla. (quarterly)

Boston Herald (est. 1846) Boston, Mass. (daily)

Boston Record (est. 1813) Boston, Mass. (daily)

Boston Transcript (est. 1830) Boston, Mass. (daily)

Canadian Forum (est. 1920) Eleanor Godfrey, Ed., 28 Wellington St. W.,
    Toronto, Canada (monthly)

Chilean Gazette (est. 1942) 9 Rockefeller Plaza, New York (monthly)

Chile Pan-Am (1926-1933) New-York (monthly)

Christian Register (est. 1821) Boston, Mass.

Christian Science Monitor (est. 1908) Boston, Mass. (daily)

Commonweal (est. 1924) Philip Burnham, Ed., 386 Fourth Ave., New York
    (weekly)

Decision (est. 1941) Klaus Mann, Ed., 141 E. 29 St., New York (monthly)

Entre Nosotros (est. 1938) Sigma Delta Pi Headquarters, Miami University,
    Oxford, Ohio. (quarterly)

Fantasy (est. 1932) Stanley D. Meyer, Ed., 950 Heberton Ave., Pittsburgh,
    Penna. (quarterly)

Florida Historical Quarterly (est. 1908) Jacksonville and Deland, Fla.

Golden Book (est. 1925 ; now Fiction Parade) New York City (monthly)

Hispania (est. 1917) H. Grattan Doyle, Ed. George Washington University, Washington, D. C. (quarterly)

H. N. M. Hispanic Notes and Monographs (Publications of the Hispanic Society of America) New York City

Inter-America (1917-1926) Doubleday-Page, New York (bi-monthly)

Inter-American Monthly (est. 1942) J.I.B. McCulloch, Ed., 1200 National Press Bldg., Washington, D. C.

Journal of American Folklore (est. 1888) Boston, New York, and Lancester, Pa.

Journal of Education (est. 1875 ; now New England Journal of Education) Boston, Mass. (monthly)

Land of Sunshine (1894-1910) Los Angeles, Calif. (monthly)

Las Novedades (1876-1918) New York City (daily)

Latin American Digest (1933-1934) Salomón de la Selva, Ed., Supplement to Panamá Americana , Panama.

Liberty (est. 1924) New York City (weekly)

Liberty Bell (1905-1906 in New York. Since 1909, in Chicago.

Literary Digest (1890-1937) New York City (weekly)

Literary Review (of the New York Evening Post) (1920-1927) New York City

Living Age (est. 1844) Boston, Mass.

London Quarterly Review (est. 1853) London, Eng. (quarterly)

Menorah Journal (est. 1915) 63 Fifth Ave., New York (quarterly)

Mexican Folkways (est. 1925) Apartado postal 1994, Mexico, D. F., Mexico

Mexican Life (est. 1924) Howard S. Phillips, Ed., Calle Uruguay 3, Mexico, D. F. (monthly)

Mexican Review (1916-1920) Washington and Mexico

Modern Verse (est. 1940) Allan Swallow, Ed., Albuquerque, New Mexico.

Nation (est. 1865) Freda Kirchway, Ed., 55 Fifth Ave., New York City .

New Leader (est. 1922) London, Eng.

New Mexican Historical Review (est. 1926) Santa Fe. N. M.

New Mexican Quarterly Review (est. 1930) Dudley Wynn, Ed. University of New Mexico, Albuquerque, N. M.

New York Call (1908-1924)

New York Evening Post (est. 1801) New York City (daily)

North American Review (est. 1815) Boston, Mass. (monthly)

Others: A Magazine of the New Verse (1915-1916) Grantwood, N. J. (monthly)

Pan. Amer. Bul. Bulletin of the Pan American Union. (est. 1893) Washington, D. C. (monthly)

Pan Amer. Mag. Pan American Magazine (est. 1900) New Orleans and Washington, D. C. (monthly)

Poet Lore (est. 1889) Philadelphia and Boston (quarterly)

Poetry: A Magazine of Verse (est. 1912) 232 E. Erie St., Chicago, Ill. (monthly)

Public (1898-1919) Chicago (weekly)

Puerto Rico Bul. Puerto Rico Bulletin (est. 1932) Univ. of Puerto Rico

Republic (1882-1925) Boston, Mass. (weekly)

Revista Ilustrada (est.   ) El Paso, Texas. (monthly)

Scholastic (est. 1920) Scholastic Corp., Dayton, Ohio. (weekly)

Springfield Review (est. ——) Springfield, Mass.

Springfield Republican (est. 1844) Springfield Mass. (daily)

Spur of the Cock (est. 1922) Texas Folk Lore Society, Austin, Texas (bi-monthly)
Stratford Journal (1916-1920): Then Stratford Monthly (1926-1932) Henry Schnitkind and Isaac Goldberg, Eds., Boston, Mass. (monthly)

Theatre Arts (est. 1916) Edith J. R. Isaads, Ed., 40 E.59 St., New York (monthly)
United States Review and Literary Gazette (1826-1827) Boston and New York

Unity (est. 1878) Chicago, Ill. (monthly)

West Ind. Rev. West Indian Review (est. 1934) Edith Chapman, Ed., 71 Harbour St., Kingston, Jamaica

Woman's Journal (est. 1870) Boston and Chicago: (Since 1917 from New York) (weekly till 1929, then monthly)

World Affairs (formerly American Advocate of Peace, est. 1837) A. Curtis Wilgus, Ed., George Washington Univ. Washington, D. C. (monthly)

World Tomorrow (1918-1934) now Christian Century.   52 Vanderbilt
    Ave., New York.   (weekly)

Young People (est. 1880)   American Baptist Publications Society,
    Philadelphia, Pa.   (weekly)

Zion's Herald (est. 1823)   Boston, Mass.   (monthly)

I N D E X

Abril de Vivero, Xavier.........82
Acevedo Hernandez, Antonio......103
Achad, Marcel..................59
Acosta, Jose de................1
Acuna, Christobal de...........1
Acuna, Manuel.................59/60
Acuna de Figueroa, F. 88
Adan, Martin, see La Fuente Bena-
    vides...................82/84
Agueros, Victoriano............20
Aguilera Malta, Demetrio.......108
Alain Acuña, Elías.............80
Alarcón, Fernándo..............1
Alarcón, Juan Ruiz de, see Ruiz
    de Alarcón, Juan...........60
Alas, Claudio de, see Escobar
    Uribe, Jorge...............42
Alberdi, Juan Bautista.........14
Alborno, Pablo.................24
Alegría, Ciro.................117
Alencar, José M. de.........94/101
Alfaro, Ricardo Joaquín........24
Almafuerte, see Palacios, Pedro
    B..........................27
Almagro, Diego de..............12
Almeida, Guilherme de..........32
Almeida, Seabra B. H., see Sea-
    bra, Bruno.................32
Alpuche, Wenceslao.............60
Altamirano, Ignacio M.......20/60
Altolaguirre, Manuel........60/110
Alvarado, Pedro de.............1
Alvares Cabral, Pedro..........1
Alvarez, José Sixto.........14/98
Alvarez Henao, Enrique.........42
Alvarez Suárez, Agustín Enrique...9
Amado, Jorge..................101
Ambrogi, Arturo................19
Américo Llano, see Vasseur Alva-
    ro A......................90
Ananía, José..................122
Ancona Horruytiner, Ignacio......93
Andagoya, Pascual de...........1
Andrade, Carlos Drummond, see
    Drummond de Andrade, C.....33
Andrade, Mario de.............101
Andrade, Olegario Víctor........27
Andreve, Guillermo............115
Anguita, Eduardo............35/36
Anjos, Augusto dos.............32

Aranha, Graça, see Graça Aran-
    ha.......................101
Arce, Napoleón.................80
Arciniegas, Germán.............10
Arenales, Ricardo, see Osorio, Mi-
    guel Angel.................44
Arévalo Martínez, Rafaél.....57/110
Arévalo, Adrián...............109
Argilagos, R. G................18
Argüello, Lino.................78
Argüello Barreto, Santiago.......78
Argüello Bringas, Roberto.......60
Arguore y Arguere, Brígida.......46
Arguila, M. E................118
Arjona, Julio Q.............80/115
Arraíz, Antonio................90
Arriaza, Armando..............103
Arrieta, Rafaél Alberto........27
Arroyo, César E................19
Arrubla, Gerardo, see Henao,J.M..10
Asturias, Miguel Angel.........57
"Atl, Dr." see Murillo, Gerardo.110
Avellaneda, Gertrúdis Gómez de,
    see Gómez de Avellaneda, G...95
Avila Camacho, Manuel..........121
Azara, Félix de...............121
Azevedo, Aluizio de...........101
Aztec poetry..................93
Azuela, Mariano...............110

-B-

Baca, Félix María.............78
Ballagas, Emilio...............46
Banchs, Enrique................27
Bandeira, Manoel...............32
Baralt, Rafaél María...........90
Bárcena, Lucas................115
Barrera, Carlos................60
Barreto, Paulo................101
Barrios, Eduardo...........95/103
Barrios Cruz, Luis.............90
Barros Borgoña, Luis...........16
Barroso, Gustavo..............101
Bayón Herrera, Luis............94
Bazil, Oswaldo.................53
Belaúnde, Víctor Andrés........24
Bello, Andrés..................90
Benavides, Fray Alonso de........1
Benítez de Gautier,Alejandrina...86
Bermúdez, Federico.............53
Bernal, Emilia,.............18/46
Bernáldez, A.................120

Bietti, Oscar.....................27
Bilac, Olavo...................16/33
Blanco, Antonio Nicolás...........86
Blanco, Jorge J..................110
Blanco Fombona, Rufino........91/119
Blasio, José Luis.................11
Blest Gana, Alberto..............103
Blomberg, Héctor Pedro............27
Bobadilla, Emilio (Fray Candil)...46
Bolaños Cacho, Miguel.............60
Bolívar, Simón....................13
Bolivia, National anthem, see
    Sanjinés......................32
Bollo, L. Cincinato...............13
Bonner y Robinson, Leighton.......61
Book of Chilam Balam..............14
Borges, Jorge Luis................27
Borno, Louis......................57
Borja, Francisco..................55
Borrero de Luján, Dulce María.....46
Bosch, Juan......................108
Bosques, Gilberto.................61
Bravo, Mario......................27
Brenes Mesén, Roberto.............45
Brierre, John.....................57
Brouard, Carl.....................57
Brull, Mariano....................46
Bruno Seabra, see Seabra Bruno....33
Buesa, José Angel.................46
Bulhão Pato,Raymundo Antonio de...33
Burgos, Fausto....................98
Bustamante, R. J..................31
Bustamante y Ballivián,Enrique....82
Bustillo, José M..................61
Byrne, Bonifacio..................46

-C-

Cabada, Juan de la...............110
Cabeza de Vaca, Alvar Núñez........1
Cabrera, Raimundo.................18
Cabrera, Rafaél...................61
Cadilla, Carmen Alicia............86
Calcaña, José.....................91
Calderón, Fernando................61
Calderón Ramírez, Salvador.......107
Callejas, Félix...................80
Calojeras, João...................10
Calpe,Addadus,see Pascual,Antonio
    Diodoro de....................120
Camarillo y Roa de Pereyra,María
    Enriqueta...................61/69
Campo, Estanislao................122
Campo,Enrique del............110/111
Campobello, Nellie................61
Campos,José Antonio..............108
Campos, Rubén M...................62

Cané, Luis........................27
Canto del niño perdido............96
Carvajal, Gaspar de................1
Carbonell y Rivero,José Manuel...46
Cardoza y Aragón,Luis.............57
"Carib, El",see Padilla José.....87
Carneiro,Cecilio J...............101
Caro,José Eusebio.................42
Carpio, Manuel....................62
Carranza, Eduardo.................42
Carrasco M.,Francisco............115
Carrasquilla, Ricardo.............42
Carrera Andrade, Jorge....55/56/121
Carrión, Alejandro................56
Carvalho, Elysio..................16
Carvalho, J. R. de................16
Carvalho, Ronald de............16/33
Casal, Julián del..............46/47
Casas, Fray Bartolomé de las.......2
Casas, José Joaquín...............42
Cassasús, Joaquín Demetrio........62
Casseús, Mauricio..............57/58
Castañeda, Pedro de................2
Castellanos, Jesús............47/108
Castellanos, Joaquín..............28
Castillero R.,E. J...............116
Castillo, Félix R., see Ricaurte
    Castillo,F....................80
Castillo, Moisés.................115
Castillo de González,Amelia.......47
Castillo y Guevara,Francisca Jo-
    sefa de.......................42
Castro, Luis Luvera...............91
Castro Z., Oscar..............36/103
Cavero Egusquiza, Ricardo........117
Celiz,Fray Francisco...............2
Cerretani, Arturo.................98
Céspedes, Augusto................100
Chacón y Calvo,José María.........18
Chavero, Alfredo...............20/95
Chávez, Carlos....................20
Chávez, Ezequiel A................62
Chas de Chruiz, Israel...........111
Chilam Balam, see Book of.........14
Chocano, José Santos..........83/84
Cieza de León, Pedro de............2
Clavijero, Francisco...............2
Codex Peresianus..................14
Coelho-Netto, see Netto,Coelho...101
Colín, Eduardo....................62
Coll, Pedro Emilio................26
Collado,María,see García Collado,
    José María....................47
Coloquios de los Pastores.........96
Columbus, Christopher..............2
Conchalí,Inocencia,see Riquelme,

Daniel........................10
Constitution, see International
    Bureau......................5
Contardo, Luis Felipe.........36
Contreras, Felipe T...........62
Contreras, Francisco..........36
Conquest of Peru...............2
Coplas of Spain and Latin America.93
Cordero Romero, see Romero Cordero.56
Córdoba, Federico.............18
Cornejo, Mariano H............24
Coronado, see Vásquez de Coronado...8
Correia, Raymundo.............33
Cortés, Hernando..............2/3
Cortés, José Manuel...........31
Cosmes, Francisco de..........62
Costa Alvarez, A..............14
Costa du Rels, Adolfo........101
Costa, Luiz Eduardo da........10
Crespo, Elida L. C...........116
"Crisantema" see Sansores Prén R..52
Cruchaga Santa María, Angel.......36
Cruz, Juana Inés de la, see Juana
    Inés de la Cruz.............62
Cruz, Martinus de la..........20
Cruz Varela, Juan.............28
Cuenca, Agustín F.............62
Cunha, Euclydes de...........101

-D-

Danke, Jacobo................103
Darío, Rubén.........78/79/115
Dávalos, Balbino..........20/62
Dávalos, Juan Carlos..........98
Dávila, Virgilio..............86
D'Halmar, Augusto, see Goeminne, A.104
Delgado, Juan B...............62
Delgado, Rafael...........62/111
Del Picchia, Menotti..........33
Dessein Merlo, Justo G........28
Díaz Canseco, José...........117
Díaz Covarrubias, Juan........62
Díaz del Castillo, Bernal......3
Díaz Garcés, Joaquín.........103
Díaz Loyola, Carlos...........36
Díaz Mirón, Manuel............63
Díaz Mirón, Salvador..........63
Diego, José de................86
Discovery and conquest of Terra
    Florida......................3
Dodd, Walter Fairleigh.........3
Dolores, Carmen, see Moncorvo,
    Emilia.....................102
Dominguez, Luis L. 28
Donoso, Armando...............17

Do pol Vuh 120
Doreste, Arturo...............47
Dorta Duque, Manuel...........31
Drummond de Andrade, Carlos......33
D'Sola, Otto, see Sola, Otto d'.....92
Duarte, Margarita Estrela Bandeira
   102
Duble Urrutia, D..............36
Duque, Manuel, see Dorta Duque, M...31
Durán y Casahonda, J. M......111
Durand Durand, Luis..........103

-E-

Eandi, Héctor I...............98
Echeverria, Esteban.......28/98
Edwards, Agustín..............17
Edwards Vives, Alberto.......104
Eguren, José María............84
Eichelbaum, Samuel............14
Elizondo, José F.............111
Enriqueta, María, see Camarillo y
    Roa de Pereyra..............63
Enriquez de Guzmán, Alonso.........3
Ercilla y Zúñiga, Alonso de.......36
Escobar, Federico.............80
Escobar Uribe, Jorge..........42
Escragnolle Taunay, Alfredo see
    Taunay.....................102
Escudero, Gonzalo.............56
Escuti Orrego, Santiago.......36
Espejo, Antonio de...........3/4
Esténguer, Rafael.............45
Esteva, Adalberto A...........63
Estrada, Genaro...............63
Estrada, Rafael...............45

-F-

Fabbiani Ruiz, José..........119
Fable of the Frog............120
Fábrega, Demetrio.............80
Facio, Justo A................80
Fagundes Varela, Luiz Nicolau.....33
Falla, Salvador...............20
Farías de Issasi, Teresa......96
Fernández Artucio, Hugo.......13
Fernández de Lizardi, José Joaquín
    ....63/111
Fernández de Quirós, Pedro.........4
Fernández García, Rafael.......107
Fernández Granados, Enrique.......63
Fernández Guardia, Ricardo....11/107
Fernández Madrid, José........42
Fernández Montalvo, Ricardo......36
Fernández Moreno, Baldomero......28
Fernández y García, Eugenio.......25

Ferreira de Castro, José María...102
Ferreira de Lacerda, Bernarda.....33
Ferrer, José Miguel...............91
Ferretis, Jorge..................111
Ferry, Gabriel...................120
Fiallo, Fabio...........53/54/108
Fierro Blanco, Antonio de........120
Figueira, Gastón..................88
Flores, Manuel María..............64
Florez, Julio.....................42
Florida Exploration................4
Florit, Eugenio...................47
Fombona Pacheco, Jacinto..........91
Folksongs of Brazilian Gypsies....93
Folksongs of Paraguay.............82
Font, Pedro.......................11
Fornaris, José....................47
"Fray Mocho", see Alvarez,
    Jose S. 14/98
"Francisca", see Campobello,
    Nellie.................. 63/64
Francisca Josefa de la Concepción,
    see Castillo y Guevara........43
Franco, Luis L....................28
Fresnesu, Mme.Armand.............108
Freyre, Gilberto.................102
Frías, José Dolores...............64
Frías y Soto, Heriberto..........111
Fuenzálida, Miguel de, see Edwards,
    Alberto.......................104

-G-

Gahisto, Manuel...................16
Galdames, Luis....................10
Galíndez, Bartolomé...............28
Galindo y Villa,Jesús.............21
Gallegos, Luis Gerardo...........109
Gallegos, Rómulo.................119
Gallegos Lamerto, Hernán...........4
Gallinal,Gustavo..................25
Gálvez, José......................24
Gálvez, Manuel....................98
Gama, Basilio de..................33
Gamboa, Federico.................111
Gamio, Manuel.....................21
Gana y Gana, Federico............104
García, Rafael Fernández, see Fer-
    nández García, R..........108/107
Garcia Calderón,Francisco.........24
García Calderón,Ventura..........117
Garcia Collado, José María........47
Garcia Cubás, Antonio.............21
Garcia Icazbalceta,Joaquín........21
Garcia Gemes, Julia...............28
García Naranjo, Nemesis...........13

Garcia Tejada, Juan Manuel......43
Garcilaso de la Vega.........4/12
Garrido Merino, Edgardo........104
Gautier Benítez, José...........86
Gavidia, Francisco.............109
Geenzier.......................80
Gerbasi, Vicente...............91
Ghiraldo, Alberto..............28
Gil Gilberto, Enrique.........109
Gimenez Pastor, A. 28
Girondo, Oliverio..............28
Godoy, Alcayaga, Lucila..37/38/104
Godoy, Juan................28/29
Goeminne Thomson, Augusto.....104
Gómez, Jaime Alfredo...........43
Gómez Carrillo, Enrique........20
Gómez de Avellaneda,Gertrudis...48
Gómez Restrepo, Antonio......17/43
Gómez Vergara, Joaquín.........64
Gondavo, Pedro de Magalhães......4
Gonçalvez Dias, A.............33/34
González, Luis Felipe..........18
González Manrique, Mariano.....43
González, Pedro Antonio........38
González Arrili,Bernardo........9
González Bastias, Jorge........38
González de Mendoza,Fray Juan....4
González Guerrero,Francisco....64
González Martínez,Enrique....64/65
González Obregón, Luis.........21
González Peña, Carlos..........21
González Prada, Manuel.........84
González Rodríguez, J..........80
González Rojo,Enrique..........65
González Rucavado,Claudio......45
González y Contreras,Gilberto...57
González Zeledón,Manuel........18
Gorostiza,Celestino.........65/112
Gorostiza, Jose................65
Graça Aranha, José Pereira da 102
Guanes, Alejandro..............82
Guerreiro Ramos, A.............34
Guerrero, Julio................21
Guerrero, Miguel...............54
Guido y Spano, Carlos..........29
Guillén, Nicolás...............48
Guillén Zelaya, Alfonso........59
Guimarães, Luiz................34
Guimarães Villela, Iracema.....35
Güiraldes, Ricardo.............98
Gutierrez, Ricardo.............29
Gutierrez Nájera,Manuel.....65/66
Guzmán, Martin Luis...........112
Guzmán, Nicomedes.............104
Guzmán Cruchaga, Juan..........38

Halmar, Augusto d', see Goeminne..104
Haya de la Torre, Víctor Raúl.....24
Henao, Jesús María................10
Henríquez Ureña, Max..............54
Henríquez Ureña, Pedro...........19
Heredia, José Ramón...............91
Heredia y Campuzano, José María48/49
Hernández, José...................29
Hernández Catá, A................108
Hernández Gaspar,Octavio.........81
Hernández Miejares, Enrique......49
Herpen, Thérèse.................110
Herrera, Darío..............81/116
Herrera, Luis Bayón, see Bayón
   Herrera, L.....................94
Herrera, Manuel de J.............54
Herrera S., Demetrio.............81
Herrera y Reissig, Julio.........89
Herrera y Tordesilla,Antonio de...4
Herrera Ducloux,Enrique..........94
Herzon, G. B......................4
Hine, David......................45
Hippolyte, Domique...............58
Hoffman, F. C...................112
Hostos, Eugenio María de.........25
Hübner, Jorge....................38
Huerta, José....................116
Huidobro, Vicente.......38/39/104

-I-
Ibáñez, Roberto...................89
Ibarbourou, Juana de.......89/118
Ibérico y Rodríguez, Mariano.....24
Icaza, Francisco A., de......66/67
Icaza, Jorge....................109
Ill-fated expedition of Miranda...5
Indians of La Guajira...........120
Ingenieros, José.................14
International Bureau of American
   Republics......................5
Irisarri y Trucio, Hermógenes....39
Irrugillo, Mariano...............67
Isaacs, Jorge..........17/43/106
Issasi, Teresa Farias,see Farias 96
Ivanovitch, Dimitri..............43
Izaguirre Rojo, Baltazar.........67
-J-
"Jack the Ripper", see Campos,J.A.,
   ....108/109
Jardim, Luis....................102
Jaimes Freyre, Ricardo.....31/32
Jiménez Rueda, Julio.........22/96
Joublanc Rivas, Luciano..........67

Juan y Santacilia, Jorge..........5
Juana Inés de la Cruz,Sor.....67/96

-K-
Korsi, Demetrio..................81
"Kyn Taniya", see Quintanilla,L..73

-L-
Labarthe, Pedro Juan.............87
LaFuente Benavides,R. de.....82/84
Lamar Schweyer, A................18
Lamas Carísimo, Teresa..........117
Landa,Diego de (Bishop of Yuca-
   tán)...........................11
Lara, Jesús......................32
Larrañaga Portugal,Manuel........68
Larreta,Enrique, see Rodríguez
   Larreta........................99
Lars, Claudia....................57
Las Casas,Fray Bartolome de, see
   Casas...........................2
Lasso, Ignacio...................56
Lastra, Juan Julián..............29
Latorre, Mariano................104
Lazo Baeza, Olegario............104
Lee de Muñoz, Muna...............87
Le-Reve-Fort,Abdel Saadi.........58
Legendre, Georges................58
Leguizamón, Martiniano.......29/94
León, Miguel Angel...............56
León del Valle, José.............68
León Odena,E.see Odena León,E...117
Levene, R.........................9
Lewis, Samuel...................116
Leynaz y Muñoz,Dulce María.......49
Lillo, Samuel....................39
Lima, Jorge de...............16/34
Lles, Fernando...................50
Lles, Francisco..................50
Llorens Torres, Luis.............87
Llorent, José....................81
Llorente Vásquez, Manuel.........68
Lobato, José Monteiro...........102
Lombardo Toledano,Vicente........11
Longinos Martínez, José..........22
López, Lucio Vicente.............99
López, Rafael....................68
López, René......................50
López Albújar, Enrique..........117
López Contreras, Eleázar.........13
López de Briñas,Felipe de........50
López de Gómara,Francisco.........5
López Merino, Francisco..........29

López-Portillo y Rojas,José......112
López Velarde,Ramón.............68
López y Fuentes, Gregorio.......112
Lorente, Mariano Joaquín........14
Los pastores....................95
Los Toastones...................95
Lozano, D. A....................92
Lozano, Rafael Jr...............68
Luaces, Joaquín Lorenzo.........50
Luchichí, Ignacio M.............68
Lugones, Leopoldo........29/30/99
Luisi, Luisa....................89
Luján. Fernando.................45

-M-

Machado de Assis, Joaquin M. 16/102
Macías y Calle, see Masías......84
Madiedo, Manuel María...........44
Maestre y Arredondo, R..........18
Maeztu, Ramiro de...............14
Magalhães de Gondavo, Pedro......5
Magalhães, Fernão de.............5
Magallanes Moure, Manuel........39
Magariños Cervantes, Alejandro....89
Magdaleno, Mauricio............112
Magellan,Ferdinand,see Magalhaes,
   Fernao de......................5
Magloire-Fels, Clement..........58
Maisias y Calle, see Masías.....8 4
Maldonado, Pedro................80
Mallea, Eduardo.............14/99
Manco, Silverio.................94
Maluenda Labarca, Rafael.......105
Mansilla de García,Eduarda ("Da-
   niel")........................99
Maples Arce, Manuel.............68
Mar, María del..................68
Marán, René....................110
Marechal, Leopoldo..............30
María Enriqueta, see Camarillo de
   Pereyra.......................69
Marín, Juan.....................95
Marín de Solar, Mercedes........39
Mariño, José Julián.............50
Mariscal, Ignacio...............69
Markham, Sir Clements Robert.....5
Mármol, José.................30/99
Marroquín, Lorenzo.............106
Martes de Oca, Ignacio..........69
Martí, José Julián..............19
Martínez, Conchita.............112
Martínez, Miguel Gerónimo.......69
Martínez de Navarrete, Fernando Ma-
   nuel..........................69
Martínez Galindo, Arturo........59
Martínez Márques, G.............19

Martínez, Leónidas..............30
Martínez Moles, Manuel.........108
Martínez Villena, Rubén.........50
Martínez Zuviría,Gustavo A......99
Martorello, Noé S..............100
Masías y Calle, D...............84
Mata, Andrés A..................92
Matto de Turner, Clorinda......117
Maya, Rafael....................44
Mayan Codex....................14
Mayard, Pierre..................58
Mayorga Rivas, Ramón............80
McKay, Santiago................116
Medeiros e Albuquerque, José...102
Médiz Bolio, Antonio.......69/112
Mejía, Juan Tomás...............54
Meléndez, Concha................87
Membreño, Alberto...............59
Mendes, Murilo..................34
Méndez, Francisco...............80
Méndez, Santiago (and others)...22
Méndez Calzada, Enrique.........94
Méndez de Cuenca, Laura.........69
Méndez Dorich, Rafael...........84
Méndez Pereira, Octavio........116
Mendive, Rafael María de........50
Menéndez, Miguel Angel.........112
Meneses, Guillermo.............119
Menotti del Picchia, see Del Picchia
   P.............................33
Mercado, José...................87
Mezieres, Athanase de...........5
Milanés y Fuentes,José Jacinto....50
Miranda, Ignacio de.............22
Miró, Ricardo...................81
Mistral, Gabriela, see Godoy Alca-
   yaga, Lucila.............39/105
Mitre, Bartolomé...........9/30/121
Molina, Cristóbal...............12
Molina, Juan Ignacio............10
Molina, Juan Ramón..............59
Molina Solís, Juan Francisco...113
Moncorvo Bandeira de Mello,Emilia102
Mondaca, Carlos R...............39
Montagú y Vivero,Guillermo de...50
Montalvo, Juan..................19
Monteagudo Escámez, Antonio M...25
Monteiro Lobato, José, see Lobato...
  102
Montenegro, Carlos.............113
Montenegro, Ernesto........39/105
Monterde, Francisco............113
Montes de Oca y Obregón,Ignacio...22
Montesinos, Fernando............5
Montoya, Juan..................5/6
Moock, Armando..................95

Morales, Ernesto..................100
More, Federico....................94
Moreno, Gabriel René, see René Mo-
    reno, G.......................15
Moreno Jimeno, Manuél.............84
Moreyra, Alvaro...................34
Morfi, Pedro Juan Agustín......... 6
Morga, Antonio de.................11
Moro, César.......................84
Morpeau, Pierre Moraviah..........58
Moscoso, Gonzalo Escudero, see Es-
    cudero Gonzalo................56
Mota, Arturo de la................15
Mouchet, Enrique..................15
Munagorri, J. E. de..............113
Mulato, El, seeUrriola, José D....81
Muñoz, Rafaél F..................113
Muñoz Marín, Muna Lee, see Lee de
    Muñoz........................87
Muñoz Marín, Luis.................87
Muñoz Rivera, Luis................88
Murilo, Méndez, see Méndez.......34
Murillo, Gerardo................113

-N-
Nalé Roxlo, Conrado...............30
Nandino, Elías....................69
Naón, P. J........................30
Narrative of some things of New
    Spain......................... 6
Nava, Pepe, see Elizondo, José F.
    ....113/111
Navarrete, Fray Manuel, see Martí-
    nez de Navarrete.............69
Neruda, Pablo, see Reyes, Neftalí 40
Nervo, Amado.............69/71/113
Nery, Ismael......................34
Netto, Henrique Coelho...........102
Nieto, Astrúbal..................119
Niza, Fray Marcos de, see Niza,
    Marco de 6
Nizza, Fray Marco da, see Niza..... 6
Noé, Julio........................15
Nogales, Rafaél...................13
Noriega, Eduardo..................22
Noriega Hope, Carlos.............113
Novelo, José Inés.................71
Novo, Salvador....................71
Núñez Cabeza de Vaca, Alvaro....1/ 6

-O-
Obaldía, María Olimpia de.........81
Obligado, Rafaél..................30
Obregón, Baltasar de.............. 6
Octavio, Rodrigo..................34
Odena, E. León...................117

Olaguibel, Francisco Manuel de....71
Olivares Figueroa, R..............92
Oliveira, Alberto de..............35
d'Oliveira, Felippe...............35
Oliveira Cezar, F. de............100
Ollantay..........................96
Olmedo, José Joaquin..............56
Olvera, Augustín..................22
Opazo Maturana, Gustavo...........17
Oquendo de Amat, Carlos...........85
Orgallez, Manuél..................51
Oribe, Emilio.....................89
Orozco R., (Prof.) Efrén..........96
Orpen Dudgeon, Patrick............15
Orrego Luco, Luis................105
Ortíz, Luis G.....................71
Ortíz de Montellano,Bernardo......71
Ospina Rodríguez, Mariano.....17/18
Osorio, Miguel Angel..............44
Otero, J. Pacifico................15
Otero Reiche, Raúl................32
Otero Silva, Miguel...............92
Othon, Manuel José................72
Ovalle, Alonso de.................10
Ovando, Leonor de.................54
Owen, Gilberto....................72

-P-
Pablete, Egidio..................105
Pacheco y Obés, Melchor...........89
Padilla, José Gualberto...........87
Pagaza, Joaquín Arcadio...........72
Palacio, Pedro Bonifacio..........30
Palacios Mendoza, Alfredo........100
Palés Matos, Luis.................87
Palma, Benigno....................81
Palma, Martín.....................17
Palma, Ricardo.........85/117/118
Palma y Romay, Ramón de...........51
Pandía Calogeras, see Calogeras,
    João.........................10
Pané, Ignacio.....................82
Pardo Farelo, Enrique............107
Pardo García, Germán..............44
Parra, Manuel de la...............72
Parra, Porfirio..................113
Parra Pérez, C....................26
Parra Sanojo, Ana Teresa de la...119
Pascual,Antonio Diodoro de.......120
Pato Bulhão,see Bulhão Pato,Ray-
    mundo A. de..................35
Payro, Roberto Jorge.........94/100
Paz, Ireneo.......................22
Paz Castillo, Fernando............92
Pedroso, Regino...................51
Pellerano Castro, Arturo B........54

Pellicer, Carlos................72/73
Peña, Rafaél Angel de la.........22
Peña Barrenechea, Enrique........85
Peña Barrenechea, Ricardo........85
Peón del Valle, José.............73
Peón y Contreras, José........73/96
Peralta, Alejandro...............85
Perea, Estevan de.................7
Pereda Valdés, Ildefonso.........90
Péres y Péres,Ramón Domingo......51
Pereyra,Diomedes de.............101
Pérez, Felipe....................44
Pérez, José Joaquín..............54
Pérez de Luxán, Diego.............7
Pérez de Villagra, Gaspar.........7
Pérez Petit, Victor..............97
Pérez-Pierret, Antonio...........87
Pérez Piña, Pedro I..............73
Pérez Rosales, Vicente...........17
Peru discoveries.................12
Peruvian tales..................120
Petit Marfán, Magdalena.........105
Peza, Juan de Dios............22/73
Pezoa Véliz, Carlos..............40
Picchia, Menotti del, see Del
     Picchia Menotti, P. M. 35
Pichardo, Manuel Serafín.........51
Pico, Pedro......................94
Pierra de Poo....................51
Pimentel Coronel, Ramón..........92
Piña, Roberto...................113
Pino, Angel, see Díaz Garcés,J...103
Pino Suárez, José María..........73
Pinochet Lebrúm, Tancredo........17
Pita Martínez, Lola.............100
Pizarro, Pedro...................13
Plácido,see Valdés,Gabriel de la
     C...........................51
Poetry, note....................122
Polar, Juan Manuel..............118
Pombal, María Luisa.............105
Pombo, Rafaél....................44
Ponce Aguilera, Salomón.........116
Pons, José B.....................51
Poveda, José Manuel..............51
Prado, Pedro.................40/105
Preciado, Francisco...............7
Préndes Saldías, Carlos..........40
Prieto, Guillermo................73
Prieto, Jenaro..................105
Puig Pérez, José.................73

                    -Q-

Quechua poems from Perú..........82
Queremel, Angel Miguel...........92
Quetzalcoatl....................120

Quintanilla, Luis................73
Quiroga, Carlos Buenaventura...119
Quiroga, Horacio................119

                    -R-

Rabasa, Emilio..................113
Ramallo, Miguel (General).......32
Ramírez, Ignacio.................73
Ramírez de Arellano, Clemente...88
Ramírez Peña, Abraham...........109
Ramos, Arthur....................16
Ramos, José Antonio..............95
Rangel Baéz, Carlos..............26
Rebolledo, Efrén.................73
Relaciones, etc...................7
René-Moreno Gabriel.............15
Requena Legarreta, Pedro.........73
Reve-Fort,Abdel Saadi,see Le-Reve-
     Fort......................58/68
Revilla, Manuel Gustavo Antonio 22
Reyes, Alfonso................22/73
Reyes, María Francisca...........59
Reyes, Neftalí Ricardo........40/41
Reyes, Rafaél....................18
Reyes, Salvador.................105
Reyes, Severino..................97
Reyles, Carlos..................119
Ribeiro Couto, Ruy...............35
Ribero, Mariano Eduardo de.......24
Ricaurte Castillo,Félix..........81
Ried, Alberto....................41
Rinaldini, R.....................23
Riquelme, Daniel.................17
Riva Agüero, José de la..........25
Riva Palacio, Vicente....23/74/114
Rivas, José Pablo................74
Rivera, Agustín..................23
Rivera, Diego (and others)......23
Rivera, José Eustasio...........107
Rivera,Luis Muñoz, see Muñoz
     Rivera, Luis................88
Rivera Indarte, José.............30
Rizal y Alonso, José........97/118
Roa Bárcena, José María..........74
Rodó, José Enrique...25/90/119/121
Rodríguez, Agustín................7
Rodríguez Cabrero,Luis...........88
Rodríguez Cabrillo, Juan.........21
Rodríguez de Tío, Lola...........88
Rodríguez Embil, Luis............51
Rodríguez Larreta,Enrique.......100
Rohde, Jorge Max.................15
Rojas, Casto.....................16
Rojas, Manuel................41/105
Rojas, Ricardo...............9/15/94
Rojas González,Francisco........114

Rojas Sucre, Graciela 116
Rokha,Pablo de, see Díaz Loyola,
    Carlos......................36
Rokha, Winette de..............41
Romero, José Rubén.............114
Romero y Cordero, Remigio.......56
"Ronquillo", see Pablete, E. ... 105
"Rosa Espina", see Riva Palacio,
    Vicente............. 23/74/114
Rosado Vega, Luis............... 74
Rosas, Noel.................... 35
Rosas Moreno, Jose............. 74
"Rosa Te", see Trujillo A., R. .. 52
Roumain, Jacques............... 58
Roumer, Emile.................. 58
Ruiz de Alarcon, Juan.......... 74
Ruiz Esparza, Juan Manuel....... 74
Runkhen, Juan Enrique.......... 19

-S-

Saavedra, David...............121
Saavedra y Bessey,Rafaél M.......95
Sáenz, Carlos Luis..............45
Sáenz Azcorra, Franz.........74/114
Sahagún, Bernardino de..........11
Salado Alvarez, Victoriano.......23
Salas Aloma, Mariblanca..........51
Salaverri, Vicente A............25
Salaverry,Carlos Augusto.........85
Salazar Mallén, Rubén...........114
Salom, Diwaldo.................51
Samper Ortega, Daniel...........107
Samperio, Manuel J.............15
Sánchez, Luis Alberto...........25
Sánchez, Luis Aníbal............56
Sánchez Chamuscado,Francisco......7
Sánchez Gardel,Julio............94
Sánchez Mármol, Manuel..........114
Sánchez Quell, H...............82
Sancho, Pedro..................13
Sanderson, Luisa Anabalon, see
    Rokha, Winette de.......... 41
Sanin Cano, Baldomero.......... 18
Sanjines, Jenaro............... 32
Sansores Pren, Rosario......... 52
Santibanez Puig, Fernando 106
Santivan, see Santibañez P. 106
Santos Chocano, see Chocano... 83/84
Santos, Joaquín da Silveira......16
Sarmiento, Domingo Faustino.....100
Sarmiento de Gamboa, Pedro........7
Sarrett, Cecilio V.............52
Schmidel, Ulrich ..../
Schmidt,Augusto Frederico.........35
Schmidt,Ulrich,see Schmidel........7

Seabra,Bruno.................32/35
Seeber, Francisco...............9
Sellén, Antonio................52
Selva, Salomón de la............80
Setúbal, Paulo de Oliveira.....103
Sierra, Antonio M..............19
Sierra, Justo..............74/114
Sigüenza y Góngora, Carlos de...12
Silva, José Asunción........44/45
Silva, Medardo Angel...........57
Silva, Víctor Domingo..........41
Silva Valdés, Fernán...........90
Silva Vidósola, Carlos.........106
Silveira Santos, Joaquín, see
    Santos Silveira.............16
Simón, Pedro...................7
Sinán, Rogelio................116
Sola, Otto d'.................92
Solís, José María..............75
Song of Quetzalcoatl...........93
Sosa, Francisco.............23/75
Sotillo, Pedro.................92
Soto, Hernando de..............8
Soto, Jesús S.................75
Soto, Marco Aurelio............20
Spinetti Dini, Antonio..........92
Stade, Hans, see Staden,H........8
Staden, Hans..................8
Storni, Alfonsina...........30/31
Suárez, Marco Fidel............18
Suasnávar, Constantino.........59
Subercaseaux, Benjamin........106

-T-

Tablada, José Juan.............75
"Tablanca,Luis", see Pardo Fare-
    lo, Enrique.................107
Talero Núñez, Eduardo..........45
Tallet, José Zacarías..........52
"Taniya, Kyn" see Quintanilla,
    Luis........................73
Taracena, Alfonso.............114
Taraval, Segismundo............8
Taunay, A. E.................103
Tejeda, Juan García, see García
    Tejeda, J. M................43
Tejera, Diego Vicente..........52
Téllez, Joaquín...............75
Tenreiro, R. M................100
Terrazas, Francisco de.........75
Thaly, Daniel.................54
The natural history of the qua-
    drupeds of Paraguay, see Aza-
    ra, F. de...................121
Tiempo, César, see Zeitlin,I....31
Tolón, Miguel Teurbe...........52

Tondreau Valin, Narciso..........41
Torres Bodet, Jaime.....23/75/76/114
Torres, R. H.,see Hoffman, F.C.....
..........................114/112
Torres-Rioseco,Arturo..........17/41
Torri, Julio..;...................76
Tovar, Pantaleón...................76
Trujillo Arredondo, Rosa..........52
Turcios, Froilán..................59
Turrent Rozas, Lorenzo...........114

-U-
Ugarte, Manuel..............15/100
Uhrbach, Carlos Pío..............52
Uhrbach, Federico................52
Ulloa, Antonio de.................8
"Unavez, Nicolás"................76
Urbina, Luis G..............76/77
Ureña de Henríquez, Salomé.......54
Uribe, Diego.....................45
Urriola, José Dolores............81
Usigli, Rudolfo..................77
Uslar Pietri, Arturo.........26/120

-V-
Valdelomar, Abraham.............118
Valdés, Gabriel de la Concepción..
........................52/53
Valdés Jr.,Ignacio de J..........81
Valdés, Nacho...................116
Valdés Mendoza, Mercedes.........53
Valencia, Guillermo..............45
Valenzuela, Jesús E..............77
Valle, Rosamel de................41
Valle, Juan......................77
Valle, Margarita del.............53
Valle, Rafaél Heliodoro..........59
Vallejo, César...................85
Varallanos, José.................86
Varas Calvo, José Miguel.........106
Varela, Florencio................31
Varela, J. C.....................31
Varona, Enrique José.............19
Vasconcelos, José................23
Vásquez, Emilio..................86
Vásquez, M. J....................81
Vasseur, Alvaro Armando..........90
Vattier, Carlos.................106
Vaval, Durained..................58
Vázquez de Coronado,Francisco.....8
Vedia y Mitre, Mariano de........15
Vega, Daniel de la...........41/106
Velarde, Héctor.................118
Velásquez, Primo Feliciano.......23
Velásquez Chávez, Agustín........23
Velgas, Juan José................41

Veliz, Carlos Pezoa, see
    Pezoa Veliz, C. 40/41
Venegas, Miguel.................8/9
Venegas Filardo, Pascual........93
Verissimo, Erico...............103
Verissimo de Mattos, Jose......35
"Verduguillo"..................115
Vespucci, Americo...............9
Vidalita.......................27
Vidarte, Santiago..............88
Vidaurreta, Valentín...........77
Vieux, Dámocles................58
Vigil, José María..............23
Vignale, Pedro Juan............31
Vilar, Ricardo Arturo..........82
Vilaire, Etzer.................77
Villar Buceta, María...........53
Villalaz,
    Carlos E. 82
Villarronda, Guillermo.........53
Villaseñor Angeles,Eduardo...23/96
Villaseñor y Villaseñor,Alejan-
    dro........................23
Villaurrutia, Xavier...........77
Villaverde,Cirilo Simón de la
    Paz.......................108
Villela, Iracema...............35
Vivero, Domingo de.............86
Vizardi, Ligio.................55
Vizcarrondo Rojas,Fernando.....26
-W-
"Wast, Hugo",see Martínez Zuviría,
    G.........................100
Westphalen,Emilio Adolfo von....86
Wilde, Eduardo.................15
Winette,see Rohka,Winette......41
Wyld Ospina, Carlos...........110
-X-
Xammar, Luis Fabio.............86
-Y-
Yankas,Lautaro................106
-Z-
Zaldumbide,Gonzalo.............25
Zamora, Luis A.................42
Zañartu Bustos, Sady...........17
Zapiola, José..................17
Zaragoza,Antonio...............77
Zárate,Augustín de..............9
Zárate, Julio..................24
Zayas Enríquez,Rafaél de 24/78/115
Zegarra Ballón,Edilberto........86
Zeitlin,Israel.................31
Zenea, Juan Clemente...........53
Zepeda, Jorge Federico.........59
Zorrilla de San Martín,Juan....90
Zum Felde, A...................26